"... the reason for the repression of free speech at Berkeley, concurred in by the Governor and the Lieutenant Governor, is that the Berkeley campus has become like the coffee houses of pre-1956 Hungary, a major source of energy and leadership for one of the most powerful attempts to alter 'existing social relationships'—the civil rights movement."—*The liberal democrat* (Berkeley)

"Improbably as it may have seemed to outsiders, events at the Berkeley campus ... constituted a small-scale but genuine revolution. Through continuous violation of university regulations, sit-ins, almost daily mass demonstrations, and finally a strike by students and teaching assistants, the authority of both the administration and the faculty had become virtually nonexistent by December."—*The Reporter*

"The legitimate authority of the university is being challenged and attacked in a revolutionary way."—Chancellor Edward Strong

"We cannot compromise with revolution, whether at the University or any other place."—Governor Edmund G. Brown

"... this minority managed to inflame one of the largest collections of young brains in the U.S., caused a shutdown of classes, brought 500 cops to Sproul Hall to make 782 arrests, got nearly 10,000 signatures on a petition to the Regents and won an endorsement of its demands from a pretty big majority of the faculty. How did they do it?"—*Life*

Originally published in 2010 by Center for Socialist History

This edition published in 2020 by
Haymarket Books
P.O. Box 180165
Chicago, IL 60618
773-583-7884
www.haymarketbooks.org
info@haymarketbooks.org

ISBN: 978-1-64259-125-5

Distributed to the trade in the US through Consortium Book Sales and Distribution (www.cbsd.com) and internationally through Ingram Publisher Services International (www.ingramcontent.com).

This book was published with the generous support of Lannan Foundation and Wallace Action Fund.



ACKNOWLEDGMENTS: "An End to History" by Mario Savio, which originally appeared in *Humanity*, is reprinted by permission of the author. "The Free Speech Movement and Civil Rights" by Jack Weinberg copyright 1965 by Campus CORE is reprinted by permission of the author and Campus CORE. "On Mounting Political Action" by James Petras is printed by permission of the author. The following articles which appeared in the "FSM Newsletter" are reprinted by permission of the authors: "Catch-801" by Marvin Garson, "Freedom Is a Big Deal" by Barbara Garson, "How to Observe Law and Order" by Hal Draper. "The Regents" by Marvin Garson copyright 1965 by Marvin Garson is reprinted by permission of the author. "The Mind of Clark Kerr" by Hal Draper copyright 1965 by Hal Draper is reprinted by permission of the author. "The Campus and the Constitution" is reprinted by permission of the Berkeley-Albany chapter of the ACLU.

Cover design by Jamie Kerry.

Library of Congress Cataloging-in-Publication data is available.

10 9 8 7 6 5 4 3 2 1

# BERKELEY

## THE STUDENT REVOLT

**HAL DRAPER**

INTRODUCTION BY MARIO SAVIO

Haymarket Books
Chicago, Illinois

TO THE 800

The beginning is the most important
part of the work

## Contents

*Hal Draper, on the staff of the University of California Library since 1960, was a founder and editorial board member of the quarterly* New Politics, *and a former editor of the weekly* Labor Action *and the magazine* New International; *he was chairman of the Independent Socialist Committee, an educational enterprise. Mr. Draper has written a number of pamphlets and brochures in the field of socialist education.*

## *Introduction by Mario Savio*

There are many things that happened at Berkeley which will not be of interest to people elsewhere, and need not be; it is to be hoped that others will have their own problems to contend with, and will have interesting things of their own to do. Others should not have to get their experience second hand. But there are certain things that happened at Berkeley which it would be useful for people in other places to know about, as an aid in understanding themselves, as help to them in preparing revolts of their own.

There were some things which made the Berkeley revolt peculiarly Berkeley's, but other things made it a revolt among white middle-class youth that could happen at any state university. And it is the second set of factors which will probably be of most importance to people outside Berkeley.

Why did it happen in Berkeley? The important question to ask, rather, is: why did it happen in Berkeley first? Because there are several universities in the East and Midwest where, since last semester, little home-grown revolts have flared up.

Asking why it happened in Berkeley first is like asking why Negroes, and not Americans generally, are involved in securing access for all, to the good which America could provide for her people. This may seem strange to those who imagine America to be a virtual paradise except for certain groups, notably Negroes, who have been excluded. But this is a distortion. What oppresses the American Negro community is merely an exaggerated, grotesque version of what oppresses the rest of the country—and this is eminently true of the middle class, despite its affluence. In important ways the situation of students at Berkeley is an exaggerated representation of what is wrong with American higher education.

The forces influencing students at Berkeley—not merely those resulting from participation in the university itself, but also those deriving from student involvement in politics —these forces are likewise exaggerations of the forces to which society subjects other university students in other parts of the country. So probably the reason it could happen here first is this: while the same influences are present elsewhere, there is no university (none that I know of, at all events) where these influences are present in as extreme a form as here in Berkeley.

The influences upon students are of three main kinds: those deriving from personal history; "internal" problems resulting directly from being a student; and "external" problems deriving from after-class political activities. The external influences on students result primarily from involvement in the civil-rights movement, both in the Bay Area and in the South. The internal derive primarily from the style of the factory-like mass miseducation of which Clark Kerr is the leading ideologist. There are many impersonal universities in America; there is probably none more impersonal in its treatment of students than the University of California. There are students at many Northern universities deeply involved in the civil-rights movement; but there probably is no university outside the South where the effect of such involvement has been as great as it has been at Berkeley.

One factor which helps explain the importance of civil rights here is the political character of the Bay Area. This is one of the few places left in the United States where a personal history of involvement in radical politics is not a form of social leprosy. And, of course, there are geographical considerations. The Berkeley campus is very close to the urban problems of Oakland and San Francisco, but not right in either city. On campus it is virtually impossible for the thoughtful to banish social problems from active consideration. Many students here find it impossible not to be in some sense *engagé*. The shame of urban America (just south of campus or across the bay) forces itself upon the conscience of the community. At the same time it is possible to think about political questions by retreating from their immediate, physical, constant presence. Thus, at Columbia or CCNY it is difficult to tell where the city ends and the university begins, whereas at Berkeley there is a clearly demarcated university community, with places where students and faculty members can enjoy a certain sense of retreat and apartness. At Berkeley we are both close enough to gross injustice not to forget; but far enough away, and set well enough apart, so as neither to despair nor simply to merge into the common blight. Furthermore, ours is not a commuter school; the students live here at least part of the year. This makes possible a continuing community such as would be impossible at UCLA for example. This community, with a great deal of internal communication, has been essential to the development of political consciousness. And there is a good deal for the students to communicate to one another. Over ten per cent of the student body has taken part *directly* in civil-rights activity, in the South or in the Bay Area. These three thousand, all of whom have at least walked picket lines, are a leaven for the campus. And many more can be said to have participated vicariously: there is great and widespread interest in what those who "go South" have done and experienced. Of course, there is a natural receptivity for politics at Berkeley simply because this is a state-supported university: a good percentage of the student body comes from lower-middle-class or working-class homes; many who can afford to pay more for an education go, for example, to Stanford.

Now for those problems which have their origin within the university: the tale which follows is strictly true only for undergraduates in their first two years; there are some improvements during the second two years; but only graduate students can expect to be treated tolerably well.

It is surprising at first, after taking a semester of undergraduate courses here—except in the natural sciences or mathematics—to realize how little you have learned. It is alarming at the same time to recognize how much busy work you have done: so many papers hastily thrown together, superficially read by some graduate-student teaching assistant. Even if you want to work carefully, it is difficult to do so in each of five courses, which often have unrealistically long reading lists—courses with little or no logical relationship to one another. Perhaps in the same semester, the student will "take" a superficial survey of all the major (and many minor) principles of biology, *and* a language course a good part of which is spent in a language "laboratory" very poorly integrated into the grammar and reading part of the course, a laboratory which requires its full hour of outside preparation but which benefits the student very little in terms of speaking ability in the foreign language. Perhaps, ironically, the semester's fare will include a sociology course in which you are sure to learn, in inscrutably "scientific" language, just what is so good and only marginally improvable in today's pluralistic, democratic America.

If you are an undergraduate still taking non-major courses, at least one of your subjects will be a "big" lecture in which, with field glasses and some good luck, you should be able, a few times a week, to glimpse that famous profile giving those four- or five-year-old lectures, which have been very conveniently written up for sale by the Fybate Company anyway. The lectures in the flesh will not contain much more than is already in the Fybate notes, and generally no more than will be necessary to do well on the examinations. Naturally, it will be these examinations which determine whether or not you pass the course. Such an education is conceived as something readily quantifiable: 120 units constitute a bachelor's degree. It is rather like the outside world —the "real" world—where values are quantified in terms of the dollar: at the university we use play money, course units. The teacher whom you will have to strain to see while he lectures will be very seldom available for discussion with his students; there is usually an hour set aside, in the course of each week, during which all of the students who want to speak with him will have to arrange to do so. In the face of physical impossibility, there are generally few such brave souls. If more came, it would make little difference; this system is rarely responsive to individual needs. There are too few teachers, and too little time. Indeed, if the professor is one of those really famous scholars of whom the university is understandably proud, then the primary reason there is not enough time for the problems of individual undergraduates is that the bulk of the professor's time (other than the six or eight hours spent in the classroom each week) is devoted to "research" or spent with graduate students. The moral of the piece is: if you want to get an education, you will have to get it yourself. This is true in any case, but it is not usually intended to be true in the sense that getting it yourself means *in spite* of the work at school. There are just too many nonsense hours spent by American students, hours to "do" much as one "does" time in prison.

In the course of one semester, doubtless, there will be several opportunities for each unlucky student to come into contact with the administration of the university. This may be to request an exception from some university requirement. However formal the requirement may be, invariably at least once a semester, the student finds he cannot be excepted, not because the requirement is important but simply because it happens to be a *requirement.* Well, that is a problem common to bureaucracies of various kinds, but one wonders if this is the sort of thing that should be regularly encountered at a university. Yet this ordeal is what a large part of American college-age youth have to endure. We should ask not whether such intellectual cacophony and bureaucratic harassment are appropriate at universities—for certainly they are not—but rather, whether these local "plants" in what Clark Kerr calls the "knowledge industry" deserve the name university at all.

This is a somewhat overdrawn picture of life at Berkeley. The students are aware of meaningful activity going on outside the university. For there is some meaningful activity going on in America today—in the civil-rights movement, certainly. At the same time, but much more dimly, each student is aware of how barren of essential meaning and direction is the activity in which he is primarily involved, as a card-carrying student. I write "each student is aware" but I realize that this is to express more hope than fact. In less than a tenth of the students is this "awareness" a "consciousness." This consciousness of the poverty of one's immediate environment is a difficult thing to come by. In most it must remain a dim awareness. It is far easier to become aware of (and angry at) the victimization of others than to perceive one's own victimization. It is far easier to become angry when others are hurt. This is so for a number of reasons. Fighting for others' rights cannot engender nearly so great a guilt as striking rebelliously at one's own immediate environment. Also, it is simply easier to see the injustice done others—it's "out there." Many of us came to college with what we later acknowledge were rather romantic expectations, perhaps mostly unexpressed at first, about what a delight and adventure learning would be. We really did have unanswered questions searching for words, though to say so sounds almost corny. But once at college we quickly lose much of the romantic vision; although, fortunately, some never give in to the disappointment. Discovering that college is really high school grown up and not significantly more challenging, many console themselves with the realization that it is not much more difficult either.

The revolt began in the fall semester of 1964 as an extension of either vicarious or actual involvement in the struggle for civil rights. It was easy to draw upon this reservoir of outrage at the wrongs done to other people; but such action usually masks the venting, by a more acceptable channel, of outrage at the wrongs done to oneself. I am far from propounding a psychoanalytic theory of politics, yet most people whom I have met who are committed to radical political innovation are people who have experienced a good deal of personal pain, who have felt strong frustration in their own lives. This mechanism made possible the *beginning* of one pint-sized revolution on the Berkeley campus. The university set about denying students access to those facilities and rights on campus which had made possible student involvement in the civil-rights movement in the previous few years. Yet very rapidly the concern of the movement shifted from Mississippi to much closer to home; we soon began doing an awful lot of talking and thinking about the limitations of the university, the "Multiversity," the "knowledge industry"—these metaphors became ever more a part of the rhetoric of the movement. Civil rights was central in our fight because of business-community pressure on the university to crack down on campus-launched campaigns into the surrounding community—which had proven all too effective. University spokesmen have acknowledged that the need to respond to such pressures was the only "justification" for the ban on political activity. Nevertheless, the focus of our attention shifted from our deep concern with the victimization of others to outrage at the injustices done to ourselves. These injustices we came to perceive more and more clearly with each new attack upon us by the university bureaucracy as we sought to secure our own rights to political advocacy. The political consciousness of the Berkeley community has been quickened by this fight. The Berkeley students now demand what hopefully the rest of an oppressed white middle class will some day demand: freedom for all Americans, not just for Negroes!

**A word about the author of this book:**

"Don't trust anyone over thirty" became a motto of the Free Speech Movement when Jack Weinberg was quoted to that effect. Hal Draper is one of the few "over thirty" who were familiar with the events of the struggle from the very beginning, and who understood well enough to take the students seriously. He has always been ready with encouragement, but has consistently refrained from giving inappropriate and unsolicited "vintage 1930" advice. This is far from common with our "fathers." A pamphlet Hal wrote, *The Mind of Clark Kerr,* contributed mightily to the movement's understanding of the extent and depth of the injustice by which the "multiversity" runs.

He has been a friend.

## *Foreword*

This story of the "free speech" uprising on the Berkeley campus of the University of California was begun in the conviction that an extraordinary event, in an historical sense, had taken place before our startled citizenry; and that it should be described for history as it was. This is the way it was.

"Historical"? This episode did not change history, but it did reflect an aspect of current history which is easily overlooked, and will continue to be overlooked until further explosions impel retrospective glances. This aspect is the molecular—"underground"—crystallization of currents of discontent, dissent and disaffection among a people which in its large majority is one of the most politically apathetic in the world (even after we take into account the "great exception" in America, the Negroes' fight for freedom now).

Judging by its frequency, the unexpected in social history is what should be expected; but that we should actually do so is too much to expect. The "suddenness" of any outburst in nature or society is, of course, only a function of our ignorance. The next big earthquake in the San Francisco Bay Area will be sudden, but the geologists tell us to expect it in anywhere from seven weeks to seventy years; they chart the fault lines and record the small slippages that occur daily. In society, however, it is one of the functions of the Establishment scientists to paper over the fault lines and explain away the slippage jolts.

Fault lines now run through many sections of our tranquilized society. There is, for instance, in many places an "underground" labor movement dual to the official one, unacknowledged by any of the bureaucracies and unknown to the Ph.D. theses in industrial relations. The disparate social forces frozen in the Johnsonian consensus are marked with fine crack-lines like old pots. This was the case also among American Negroes at the moment before the Birmingham battles, after which the earth yawned. It is the case among the students now, and everyone knows it today only because of Berkeley.

*This is the way it was:* but I make no claim to impartiality. Like everyone else in Berkeley who has written about these events, I have taken sides. Because of a dim view of the academy's habit of clothing bitter polemic in bland "objective" jargon—a form of institutionalized hypocrisy which has great advantages for both the writer and his butt but none for the reader who wants to know what the argument is about—there is no pretense here to the colorless detachment of the uninvolved historian. We were all involved.

On the contrary I have tried to convey something more than the events: something of the inner "feel" and flavor of the students' movement (I mean: that which moved the students). I have inserted my personal impressions at some points, as a participant; but I think these are clearly distinguished as such.

Objectivity is another matter. As a non-student member of the university community—its library staff—I had no obligation or pressure to take sides except as the issues demanded it. My participation, like many others', was peripheral; I never attended, even as an observer, any of the meetings of the FSM leading committees, and viewed its day-to-day operation from the outside, sometimes highly critically. What I did commit myself to, actively, was defense of the Free Speech Movement before the university community, both at FSM rallies and at other meetings on and around the campus. I do not think that such engagement is inconsistent with the demands of objectivity, certainly not more than the involvement of others who damned the FSM in private and publicly wrote "scientifically objective" hatchet-jobs.

Factual accuracy is still another matter. Virtually all accounts of the Berkeley movement that I have seen, on all sides, are peppered with errors of fact, often quite untendentious. More than once, in checking points of detail with people who were on the spot, I was able to confirm the famous lawyers', historians' and psychologists' principle that few people remember accurately what happens before their very eyes.

The account in this book has been read and checked, in whole or in part, by a number of FSM activists, and to these students' corrections and suggestions I owe a debt of gratitude for scores of changes and modifications, especially but not only on the factual side. They were: Ron Anastasi, Barbara and Marvin Garson, Joel Geier, Arthur Lipow, Michael

Parker, James Petras, Michael Rossman, Martin Roysher, Mario Savio, Michael Shute, and Stephan Weissman; and to this list Prof. John Leggett of the Sociology Department must also be added. Of course none of these bears any responsibility whatsoever for the present form of this book or any opinions expressed in it.

I also attempted to get the manuscript checked for factual accuracy by representatives of the university administration. Mr. Richard Hafner, public relations officer for the Berkeley administration, kindly answered a number of specific factual questions, and also agreed to read the manuscript; but arrangements for this reading went awry through no fault of his and to my regret. In contrast: for the state-wide administration, Vice President David Fulton, the highest officer in charge of public relations under President Kerr, promised very amicably both to answer specific questions and to read the manuscript, but subsequently declined even to acknowledge reminders; I presume this decision in public relations was not his own. In addition, there is a long list of participants whom I have interviewed on specific points.

Three rich sources of documentary material consulted should also be mentioned; as far as I know they have not been previously tapped for this purpose: (1) The scores of reels of tape, made daily on the scene throughout the events, by Pacifica Radio, station KPFA, for the use of which I am indebted to Mr. Burton White of this unique listener-supported institution; (2) The transcripts of the trial of the FSM sit-in defendants; (3) The "FSM Archives," a depository of documents, leaflets, clippings, etc. kindly made available to me by Mr. Marston Schultz.

The problem of selection in the second part of this book, "Voices from Berkeley," has been difficult because of lack of space to include everything that demanded entrance. The aim of this section is to give the reader an insight. into how the *students* thought and felt, through their own writings and through writings which reflected them. It is obviously one-sided in terms of the controversial questions; I hasten to point this out. But this concentration on the students' side of the picture has been made easier by the knowledge that there has been more than plentiful ventilation of the other side (or sides) in the nation's newspapers and magazines as well as in others books published this year. There is probably no one in the Berkeley community—not even myself—who would give unqualified agreement to everything between these covers; these students are an exasperatingly independent-minded lot with a prejudice *against* unanimity. But it will be satisfying enough if at the end you say: "I remain unconvinced that what the students did was right; *but I understand.*"

To this end there are two supplements to the material in this book which need mention: (1) An illuminating photographic history with running text, *The Trouble in Berkeley,* edited by Steven Warshaw (Berkeley, Diablo Press, 1965); (2) The text of the only debate on the FSM controversy which took place on the Berkeley campus, between Professor Nathan Glazer and myself, on January 9, 1965, as part of a conference sponsored by the Independent Socialist Club (the full transcript, including most especially the cross-discussion and summaries, has been published in the quarterly *New Politics,* Vol. 4, No. 1).

The most dangerous nonsense about the Berkeley uprising is represented by the cries foretelling the destruction of the university unless the students are forthwith bullied and bashed into submissive quiescence. Everything that has happened has made many prouder than ever to be associated with the University of California (a term not synonymous with any administration)—not in spite of what has happened, but because it was able to happen here. The intellectual vitality and ferment which produced it, and which it produced in turn, add a new dimension to one of the great universities of the world, and a new criterion by which to judge others. By this standard Berkeley stands as a beacon light for American students. The university can indeed be destroyed, but only if its own administration and Regents try to stifle the breath of life that has blown through its halls.

HAL DRAPER
*Berkeley, July 1965*

P.S. While this was being written, the trial of the FSM sit-inners ended with the judge's decision in favor of conviction, on grounds of trespassing and resisting arrest (by going limp); the charges of unlawful assembly were thrown out. The cases will be appealed, in order to test important points of law, but a great deal of money will be needed. It can come only from people who believe that hundreds of dedicated students should not be crucified for their success in stopping an attack on campus freedoms. Ten per cent of the author's royalties on this book is going to the defendants' Legal Fund. It is to be hoped that there will be sufficient support to see this through.

## 1. *"A New Generation of Students"*

From the middle of September 1964 until the end of the year, followed by an armistice-like lull in January, the University of California campus at Berkeley was the scene of the largest-scale war between students and administration ever seen in the United States. It was also the scene of the largest scale victory ever won in such a battle by students, organized as the Free Speech Movement.

It had everything in terms of American superlatives: the largest and longest mass blockade of a police operation ever seen; the biggest mobilization of police force ever set up on any campus; the biggest mass arrest ever made in California, or of students, or perhaps ever made in the country; the most massive student strike ever organized here. It was, in sum, by far the most gigantic student protest movement ever mounted in the United States on a single campus.

There must have been a reason—an equally gigantic reason. Berkeley gets the most brilliant students in California, by and large, and a good portion of the best from the rest of the country. In turn, the FSM included a good portion of the best at Berkeley.

"The real question," said the head of the university's History Department, Professor Henry May, "is why such a large number of students—and many of them our best students, who have engaged in no prior political activity—followed the Free Speech leaders."

A professor who thought the FSM's sit-in tactics were "anarchy," Roger Stanier, nevertheless admitted that the state's governor was wrong in thinking that "the dissident students constitute a small radical fringe." He declared, "This is simply not the case. Some of the most able, distinguished students at the university are involved in this matter."

The chairman of the university's Classics Department, Joseph Fontenrose, wrote to a daily paper that "The FSM leaders represent a new generation of students . . . They are good students, serious, dedicated, responsible, committed to democratic ideals."

*Life* magazine's columnist Shana Alexander seemed rather surprised to report from the field that "the FSMers I met were all serious students, idealists, bright even by Berkeley's high standards, and passionate about civil rights. Although, regrettably, they neither dress nor sound one bit like Martin Luther King, they do *feel* like him." (Jan 15, 1965.)

In a survey of the FSM students who were arrested in the mass sit-in of December 3, it was found that:

> Most are earnest students of considerably better than average academic standing.... Of the undergraduates arrested, nearly half (47 %) had better than 3.0 (B) averages; 71 % of the graduate students had averages above 3.5 (between B and A). Comparable figures for the undergraduate and graduate student bodies as a whole, according to the Registrar's Office, are 20% and 50%, respectively. Twenty were Phi Beta Kappa; eight were Woodrow Wilson fellows; twenty, have published articles in scholarly journals; 53 were National Merit Scholarship winners or finalists; and 260 have received other academic awards. Not only are these students among the 'brightest in the University, but they are also among the most advanced in their academic careers. Nearly two-thirds (64.3%) are upper-division or graduate students. *(Graduate Political Scientists' Report.)**

A similar result was found in a survey of student opinion made in November under the supervision of a sociology professor, Robert Somers.

> Of those interviewed who had a grade point average of B+ or better, nearly half (45%) were pro-FSM, and only a tenth were anti-FSM; but of those with B or less, over a third were anti-FSM and only 15% were pro.**

---

* This is the short title of the following document: *The Berkeley Free Speech Controversy (Preliminary Report).* Prepared by: A Fact-Finding Committee of Graduate Political Scientists (E. Bardach, J. Citrin, E. Eisenbach, D. Elkins, S. Ferguson, R. Jervis, E. Levine, P. Sniderman), December 13, 1964. (Mimeo.) The viewpoint of these graduate students is pro-FSM, but their work is a valuable compilation of information and data.

** We shall refer to this again as Somers' November survey. He based his (continued...)

We shall also see later that the "elite" of the graduate students, those given jobs as Teaching Assistants and Research Assistants, had a far higher proportion of commitment to the FSM than the graduate body as a whole. In terms of student quality, the higher a student stood in accomplishment

These are rather mind-shaking facts for those journalistic or professorial commentators whose reflex reaction to the outbreak of Berkeley's Time of Troubles was to derogate the "trouble-makers" as "a bunch of rowdies," "unwashed beatniks," "forlorn crackpots" or with other profound epithets.

Perhaps more surprising to some is the fact that, in spite of some feeble efforts at McCarthy-type redbaiting—by University President Clark Kerr, by Professor Lewis Feuer, and by some local politicians—even lunatic fringe elements apparently decided that the FSM was really and truly not Communist led. At one FSM rally the local fuehrer of Rockwell's American Nazis held aloft a placard with the announcement "Mario Savio Is a Dupe of Communism," which translated means that the FSM leader could not possibly *be* a Communist. Of course, to hand the Communist Party (which is insignificant in influence in the Bay Area) credit for a great democratic student movement would be an ultimate commentary on the self-destructiveness of the American obsession with "anti-Communism" as a substitute for politics.

A student revolt of these massive proportions is a phenomenon of national importance. It demands to be studied, analyzed, and understood, whether by students who want to go and do likewise, or by educators who want to remedy the conditions which produced it, or by observers who want to grasp what is happening to the Great Society of the sixties.

---

(...continued)
report, issued in January, on "a carefully drawn sample of 285 students representing the whole student body."or level of training, the more likely was he to be pro-FSM to one degree or another.

## 2 . *The Liberal Bureaucrat*

To some it is a mystery that the Berkeley revolt should have broken out against the "liberal" administration of President Clark Kerr, in the state-wide university, and of Chancellor Edward Strong as chief officer of the Berkeley campus. Both are liberals, to be sure, as liberals go nowadays; but what is most clearly liberal about them is their pasts.

In his student days, indeed, Kerr was what is now sometimes called a "peacenik," and even joined the socialist Student League for Industrial Democracy. Liberalism is the direction *from* which Kerr has been evolving. In his 1960 book, *Industrialism and Industrial Man,* Kerr intimates quite clearly that he has been going through a process of changing his "original convictions," but this does not necessarily involve any conscious abandonment of liberalism as the framework for his rhetoric. What he has been superimposing on this framework is a newly embraced concept of bureaucratic managerialism as the social model to be accepted. The bureaucratization of Kerr's thought has been held in balance with liberalism only in the sense that he looks forward to a Bureaucratic Society which retains adventitious aspects of liberalism in the *interstices* of the social system.

I do not know how long this social world view had been growing on Kerr; but its first publication occurred in an article on "The Structuring of the Labor Force in Industrial Society" (written in collaboration with A. J. Siegel), published in January 1955. Since his central concept is the role of the bureaucracy (for Kerr, the bureaucracy is the Vanguard of the Future in the same sense, he tells us, as the working class was for Marx), it is interesting to note that Kerr himself definitely rose into the upper ranks of the Multiversity bureaucracy in mid-1952, when he became chancellor at Berkeley, after directing the Institute of Industrial Relations since 1945. The article mentioned was written within two years after this ascension. The fuller flowering of this world view in his subsequent book came within two years after his further ascension to the presidency in 1958, when he became (in his own term) "Captain of the Bureaucracy."

People who think of Kerr as a liberal, but who have not paid attention to his most recent societal lucubrations, tend to be incredulous when told that the new Kerr views systemic and systematic *bureaucratism* as the new revelation. The population living under his Multiversity, however, had to take this as seriously as does Kerr himself.

Failure to understand the theoretician of the Multiversity is one source of the myth that the student revolt burst out against a particularly liberal administration. Another source is misconception of what has happened on the Berkeley campus under Kerr's administration.

## *3 . Behind the Myth of Liberalization*

The previous president, Robert G. Sproul, had been a reactionary bureaucrat, not a liberal bureaucrat. It was in his reign, of course, that Berkeley had gone through the shattering "Year of the Oath"—the subjection of the faculty to a McCarthyite loyalty oath; the long fight of the faculty against this indignity, to which most ended up by capitulating; the loss of some of the most eminent men on the faculty, who left rather than disgrace themselves and their profession. (Kerr in those days played a role much appreciated by the faculty, not as a militant non-signer but as a mediator, and this strongly influenced his accession as chancellor in 1952.)

One of the by-product virtues of a reactionary is that you are more likely to know just where you stand with him. Sproul's stand on political discussion and social action as far as students were concerned was straightforward: it was all banned, except at the pleasure of the administration. In accordance with his notorious "Rule 17," even Adlai Stevenson could not speak on campus, and Norman Thomas was likewise not permitted to subvert the state constitution by speaking inside Sather Gate.

As the nation and even California emerged more and more from the miasma of the McCarthyite era, as the "Silent Generation" of students became vocal, this blunt knownothingism became more and more intolerable, i.e., was obviously leading to a blowup. In fact, the rule was eased in the fall of 1957 under Sproul himself and after Kerr became president the next year, an entirely different tack was taken to keep political discussion and action under control on the campus. The key was not a brusque ban but administrative manipulation accompanied by libertarian rhetoric. The "Kerr Directives" of 1959 liberalized some aspects of Sproul's regime (no difficult achievement) but, even with later modifications, *actually worsened* others.*

During the next five years of Kerr's regime, student activists complained of a long series of harassments. Here are some highlights:

♦ The student government (ASUC—Associated Students of the University of California) was forbidden to take stands on "off-campus" issues, except as permitted by the administration, and was effectively converted to a "sandbox" government.

♦ Graduate students-over a third of the student body were disfranchised, excluded from the ASUC, by a series of manipulations.

♦ Political-interest and social-issue clubs were misleadingly labeled "off-campus clubs" and forbidden to hold most organizational meetings on campus, or to collect funds or recruit. ("On many campuses all student groups can use equally the offices, equipment, secretarial staff and other facilities provided by their student governments. At Cal these privileges are

*A fully documented study, *Administrative Pressures and Student Political Activity at the University of California: A Preliminary Report,* edited by Michael Rossman and Lynne Hollander, was issued by the FSM in December 1964. The introductory summary was distributed separately; the complete report is a thick document made up of forty studies, mostly on issues during Kerr's administration, but also taking up the loyalty-oath fight of 1949-58. Also see the article "Yesterday's Discords" by Max Heinrich and Sam Kaplan, in the *California Monthly* (alumni magazine), February 1965.

reserved for non-controversial groups such as the hiking and yachting clubs," explained *FSM Newsletter, No. 1.)*

♦ Groups like the Republican "Students for Lodge" and "Students for Scranton" could not even put the names of their candidates on posters.

♦ Club posters were censored on other grounds of political content.

♦ Outside speakers were not permitted except on a 72 hour-notification basis.

♦ Clubs could not, in practice, schedule a connected series of discussions or classes at all.

♦ Off-campus activities could not be announced at impromptu rallies. ,

♦ Malcolm X, then a Black Muslim leader, was at first banned from speaking on campus, and eventually permitted to speak only after an uproar.

♦ Students for Racial Equality were forbidden to use $900 collected to establish a scholarship for a Negro student expelled from a Southern university.

♦ The clubs were forbidden to hold campus meetings in support of a Fair Housing Ordinance on the ballot in the city of Berkeley.

♦ In 1960, virtually the whole staff of the *Daily Californian* resigned in protest when a docile ASUC, instigated by the administration, clamped down on the newspaper's endorsement of Slate candidates and its attention to "off-campus" issues.

So it went. This is the campus which some, later, claimed to be "the freest campus in the country."*

In a somewhat different field, it is relevant to note that in 1962 the California Labor Federation (state AFL-CIO)—under one of the most conservative state leaderships in the country adopted a convention resolution condemning the university administration and Regents for their "antiquated labor relations philosophy" which, it said, "lags far behind the standards established through collective bargaining in private industry." The resolution cited experiences with the "countless roadblocks" thrown up by the administration against union activities. The unions' complaints about treatment by the university are remarkably similar to the students'.

## 4 *The Myth: Two Showpieces*

There are two showpieces of Kerr's administrative liberalism, a consideration of which will complete the picture. Kerr supporters constantly cite these two items, in addition to equating the decline of McCarthyite pressures with advances in liberalization.

---

* On this claim, cf. the *California Monthly* article "Yesterday's Discord," reporting on the 1962-63 academic year: "The ASUC, while continuing to abide by the Kerr Directives, sought .. . to learn whether schools similar to U.C. had comparable regulations. It found in a survey of 20 schools with student bodies of more than 8,000 that only one, the University of Arizona, had similarly restrictive rules." For a similar report, see the summary in *Time,* December 18, 1964, beginning: "By and large, restrictions are the mark of small, church-affiliated colleges intent on serving in *loco parentis,* while freedom for students, defined roughly as the rights and curbs of ordinary civil law, is the goal at big, old, and scholastically high-ranking state and private universities." After a survey it concludes: "Berkeley students have blown off the lid. It now remains for them to follow the tradition of schools that have long allowed a wide range of undergraduate freedom." In the Bay Area itself, even San Francisco State College, operating under the same state legislature as the more prestigious university, imposed none of the restrictions against which the Berkeley students revolted.

In 1960 occurred the famous student "riot" or "demonstration" (depending on your view) at the San Francisco City Hall, against the House Committee on Un-American Activities hearing. Discriminatory exclusion of students from the hearing room helped to turn the demonstration into a shambles; then the police opened up powerful water hoses to batter the students down the City Hall stairs. Mass arrests followed.

When right-winger called for the expulsion of the arrested students, Kerr replied that they had acted in their capacity as citizens and were not liable to the university for their conduct. For this he was cheered by liberals.

It was not much noticed at the time that Kerr inserted a basic qualification into his stand. If the action had been planned on campus, he indicated, then university disciplinary action *would* be in order. In 1964 he was going to put sharp teeth into what had seemed in 1960 to be a principled defense of liberalism.

There was a sequel to the HUAC episode, particularly involving the notorious film *Operation Abolition.* The administration evidently had expended so much courage in refusing to expel the anti-HUAC students that there was little left in the next pinch. The law students' club at Berkeley proposed to show *Operation Abolition* together with a talk on it by Professor John Searle. Searle was forbidden to speak unrebutted, on the ground that his speech would be controversial; yet the administration was willing to allow the pro-HUAC film to be shown by itself, presumably because it was *not* controversial. After the student "party," Slate, produced a record ("Sounds of Protest") as a reply to the film, the administration began a harassment campaign which resulted in Slate's losing its "on-campus" status—as the California McCarthyite, State Senator Burns, had predicted in advance. The harassment of the *Daily Cal,* which resulted in the mass resignation of its staff, was also in part due to the attention which the newspaper had paid to the HUAC issue.

The second showpiece was the Regents' removal, in 1963, of the ban against Communist speakers on campus. Kerr was later (January 1965) going to use this move as proof that "Demonstrations do not speed administrative changes," for, he argued, the Communist-speaker ban was removed without FSM rallies, sit-ins or strikes.

In this capsule-history Kerr omitted the long series of student protests, rallies, polls, ASUC and club petitions, and other pressures organized against the ban after 1960 in Berkeley, especially in 1962. He also ignored the increasing realization, even by conservatives, that the ban only served to ensure big *off-campus* audiences for the Communist speakers banned, as well as misplaced sympathy. Moreover, in February 1963 the faculty itself was gravely embarrassed when the administration forbade even the History Department from listening to the Communist Party writer Herbert Aptheker, who had been invited to give an academic talk in the field of Negro history. It was becoming ridiculous.

Even so, the Regents were not induced to "Ban the Ban" until a court test, started by a Riverside campus student group, threatened to bring a ruling from the State Supreme Court which would force their hand. They then finally agreed to end the ban voluntarily, rather than risk reversal by the courts, and the suit was dropped.

But this is not the end of this story of administrative liberalism. In the same action which abolished the special ban on Communist speakers, Kerr proclaimed new harassing rules aimed against *all* "controversial" speakers. Henceforth, the administration could require, at its pleasure, that any meeting with an outside speaker be chaired by a tenured professor, allegedly in order to ensure its "educational" character. The purely harassing intent of this regulation was adequately expressed by the proviso (tenure) which excluded even assistant professors from fulfilling the requirement. There has never been an explanation of why a meeting is less "educational" if chaired by an assistant professor than by an associate or full professor.* As a result, many

---

* But a revealing modification of the tenured-professor rule was later (December) instituted at UCLA. New regulations required a tenured chairman

(continued...)

a meeting had to be canceled or transferred off-campus when no tenured professor could be induced to spend an evening of his time satisfying Kerr's "liberalized" rules.

By combining this nuisance rule and some minor ones with the much-praised abolition of the Communist-speaker ban, so that the former went through with little notice among the chorus of amens that rose over the latter, Kerr showed a mastery of administrative manipulation which merits admiration. He received more than admiration: he was given the Alexander Meiklejohn award by the American Association of University Professors for contributions to academic freedom.

Nor was the tenured-professor stratagem the only rule thrown at "controversial" speakers. Around the spring of 1964 the administration invented the practice of assigning policemen to "protect" meetings deemed to be "controversial" —even though not requested and not needed—and then charging the sponsoring club from about $20 or $40 up to $100 for the privilege. (At the same time, the club was forbidden to take any collection to pay for this hard blow to its usually meager finances.) As Campus CORE put it in a leaflet reproducing such a bill: "forcing people to pay for protection from non-existent dangers is extortion . . . The administration is pushing us off campus with its protection."

But it was not any of this that led directly to the explosion. All of this was, so to speak, *routine* administrative harassment of free speech and political activity.

---

(...continued)

only "in the case of speakers representing social or political points of view substantially at variance with established social and political traditions in the U.S." Thus the conditions for "free speech" are here *officially* made dependent on a speaker's support of or disagreement with the American Party Line.

## *5. The Power Structure Triggers the Conflict*

The storm was brewing from another quarter.

This is the place to make clear that one would be wrong to conclude from the preceding history that President Kerr himself had any dislike for "controversial" speeches, student political activity, or "free speech."* On the contrary; he is, after all, a kind of liberal. When he writes his eloquent addresses about not making "ideas safe for students, but students safe for ideas," etc., he means every word of it. It is a Great Ideal, and he firmly believes it should be talked about on every possible ceremonial occasion.

But Kerr is sensitive to the real relations between Ideals and Power in our society. Ideals are what you are for, inside your skull, while your knees are bowing to Power. This is not cynicism to Kerr; he has a theory about the role of the Multiversity president as a mediator among Powers. It is no part of a mediator's task to dress up as Galahad and break a lance against dragons. In fact, if a Galahad does show up, he may only be an annoyance to the mediator, since this introduces a third, complicating party to the dispute between the dragon and his prey.

The students' onslaught against HUAC had stirred up dragons—forked-tongue monsters from Birchites to Republican assemblymen—breathing fire against the university authorities who were "protecting" all those "Communist" students. Holding the fort against these made one feel like a courageous liberal; and if a Professor Searle was going to take up the lance, he would only enrage the animals—slap *him* down.

In 1963 and 1964, from the viewpoint of the University mediator, a frightening thing was happening: there was a growing movement on campus devoted to systematically provoking and stirring up every dragon within fifty miles. This was the civil-rights movement.

---

* Throughout this account, "free speech" (in quotation marks) is used as a shorthand term for the range of student demands on freedom of political activity and social action, as well as free speech in the narrow sense.

The Friends of SNCC were collecting money for Mississippi project workers. But Campus CORE and Berkeley CORE were engaged in local projects: for example, picketing and signing fair-hiring agreements with the Shattuck Avenue (central Berkeley) merchants, and with Telegraph Avenue (campus district) businessmen. Then there was the Ad Hoc Committee to End Discrimination, not a campus group but supported by many students.

In November 1963 came the first mass-picketing of a commercial firm charged with discrimination in hiring, Mel's Drive-In restaurants on both sides of the bay. Many university students were involved when police arrested 111 in San Francisco. Berkeley CORE engaged in Christmas picketing of campus-district stores. In February, Campus CORE (formed the previous September) took on the local branch of Lucky Supermarkets, as part of an area-wide campaign against the store chain, using a new tactic, the "shop-in." The company signed an agreement. Then a series of picket lines at San Francisco's Sheraton Palace Hotel, marked by over 120 arrests (about half of them U.C. students), culminated on March 8 in a picket line of 2000 and a lobby sit-in. Of the 767 demonstrators arrested for blocking the lobby, 100 were U.C. students. The Hotel Owners' Association signed an agreement. Later the same month, anti-discrimination picketing began at the city Cadillac agency (100 arrests, about 20 from U.C.) and eventually spread to other Auto Row agencies (another 226 arrests). The courts were jammed with cases; some got jail sentences and fines. In June, Campus CORE sponsored a sit-in at the U.S. District Attorney's office to dramatize federal inaction on the Mississippi murders, and the demonstrators were forcibly carried out. Bay Area CORE started preparing for an assault even on the octopodous Bank of America.

Then, on September 4, the Ad Hoc Committee launched a picket line against one of the biggest dragons of all, the Oakland Tribune, run by William Knowland, Goldwater's state manager, a kingpin in the entire power structure of the East Bay, especially Alameda County (which includes Berkeley).

It was clearly inevitable that a civil-rights movement which sought to erase all discrimination in hiring would come squarely up against the power structure of the Bay Area. Of the various civil-rights groups in the area, only Campus CORE and Friends of SNCC were university clubs, but a big action, especially if it were militant, could count on a good part of the "troops" coming from the campus.

That summer, the picture was complicated by another factor. The Republican convention was going to meet in San Francisco: Goldwater versus the "moderates" Lodge, Scranton and Rockefeller. For the first time within man's memory, the Berkeley campus became a hotbed of political activity not only by radicals but also by conservative students. Supporters of the various GOP contenders began to organize for work at the convention. Campus CORE also organized an anti-Goldwater demonstration at the Cow Palace.

Some time in July, a reporter for the Oakland *Tribune* (which was boosting Goldwater, of course) noted that pro-Scranton students were recruiting convention workers at a table placed at the Bancroft entrance to the campus, the then-regular place for this type of activity. It appears that he, or someone else from the *Tribune,* pointed out to the administration that the table was on university property and violated its rules. An official report by Chancellor Strong* later admitted that "The situation [regarding political activity at Bancroft] was brought to a head by the multiplied activity incidental to the primary election, the Republican convention, and the forthcoming fall elections," and that administration officials began taking up the question on July 22 and 29.

But Strong himself was out of town till early August and nothing was done. Then on September 2 the Ad Hoc Committee announced it would picket the Oakland *Tribune.* On the 3rd the *Tribune* appeared with a front-page "Statement" personally signed by William Knowland, denouncing the move. On the 4th, the picketing started. The same day the Berkeley administration again took up the question of campus political activity, for the first time since July 29 (according to the dates given in Strong's report).

---

* His report (mimeo.) to the Academic Senate, dated October 26, 1964.

Flat statements that the crisis was originally touched off by Goldwaterite complaints against pro-Scranton recruitment appeared later both in the Hearst daily, the S. F. *Examiner,* of December 4, and in the S. F. *Chronicle* of October 3 and December 4. Two affidavits by students were later sworn out stating that, in September, Chancellor Strong told a number of people at a campus meeting that the Oakland *Tribune* had phoned him to ask whether he was aware that the *Tribune* picketing was being organized on university property, i.e., at the Bancroft entrance.

According to this account, then, it was the Goldwaterite forces of Knowland's *Tribune* who put the administration on the spot with respect to the toleration of political activities at the Bancroft sidewalk strip. Strong's official report admits that some, though not all, of the campus officers did know right along that this strip was university property, not city property, but that up to this time they "considered no action to be necessary."

Now action was demanded. Knowland, who was not much of an idealist but was very much of a Power, was on the administration's neck, and something had to be done. An extra urgency was added by the fact that the university was very anxious that a bond issue (Proposition 2) be passed at the November 3 election; it wanted no anti-university publicity which might turn votes against it, let alone a press campaign led by the *Tribune.*

The outside pressures were mounting. Many believe that the Bank of America also had a hand in the pressure, but the bank's president, Jesse Tapp, was also one of the most important members of the Board of Regents, and any pressure he chose to apply or amplify need not have been exerted from the outside.

One of the most unique features of the Berkeley student revolt is that from its beginning to its climax it was linked closely to the social and political issues and forces of the bigger society outside the campus. At every step the threads ran plainly to every facet of the social system: there were overt roles played by big business, politicians, government leaders, labor, the press, etc. as well as the Academy itself. This was no conflict in the cloister.

## *6 The Administration Clamps Off the Safety Valve*

The Bancroft sidewalk strip became the first battleground because the administration had designedly left this small area as the sole safety valve for much of student political activity. The explosive forces become concentrated there.

Traditionally the "free speech" arena at Berkeley used to be at Sather Gate, but in 1959 the block between the gate and Bancroft Avenue was turned into a plaza connecting the new Student Union on one side with Sproul Hall (the administration center) on the other. This plaza, called Sproul Hall Plaza (or Upper Plaza), is going to. figure as the next battleground of our story; at this point it had definitely become a part of the campus.

The Bancroft Avenue sidewalk, just outside, had been regarded as city property, not under the jurisdiction of the university. Hence all the activities which the "Kerr Directives" had banned from campus could find an outlet only here. Here clubs set up folding card tables, displaying their literature or other publications, collecting funds, and selling bumper strips or buttons and such. Here students might stop to talk with the "table-manners" (who are not to be confused with Emily Post's subject). In this way tables were used to "recruit" pro-Scranton students for the Republican convention, or to "recruit" for CORE civil-rights actions.

But in fact the Bancroft sidewalk was not all city property. A line marked by plaques separated it into a 26-foot university strip running along the campus and a smaller city strip running along the curb. As mentioned, the administration always acted as if it were all the city's; as late as the spring of 1964, the dean's office was directing clubs to get city permits to set up their tables.

To be sure, the administration had in 1962 formally set up an official "Hyde Park" (free speech) area on campus, in the Lower Plaza. It was out of sight of the main line of student traffic in and out of the campus, and, the students felt, this was why the administration found it suitable for the purpose. By the same token, the students generally ignored it, and it was largely unused. The *de facto* "Hyde Park" was the Bancroft sidewalk.

*Then on September 14 the dean's office announced that even this safety-valve area was going to be closed:* tables and their activities were banned. They had fired on Fort Sumter.

It must be said for Dean of Students Katherine Towle that she did not conceal the basic motivation. Speaking to protesting club representatives in the following week, she openly referred to the "outside pressures." Also, the *Daily Cal* reported on September 22:

> ... Dean Towle admitted [Sept. 21] that the question came up in the first place because of the frequent announcement of and recruitment for picket lines and demonstrations going on in the area in the past.

But this was not so much an "admission" as it was an appeal or plea: *Please understand our problem with these outside pressures, and don't push us too hard.*

What was supposed to happen from here on was pretty much cut-and-dried: The students would protest bitterly; the administration would explain that rules-were-rules-and-it-had-no-alternative; perhaps some minor concessions would be made; the protests would peter out; and the new setup would be an accomplished fact by the time the students had settled into their new classes for the semester.

President Kerr had articulated this somewhat bored view of student protests in a passage of his 1963 Godkin Lectures which was eliminated from the text when they were published as *The Uses of the University:*

> One of the most distressful tasks of a university president is to pretend that the protest and outrage of each new generation of undergraduates is really fresh and meaningful. In fact, it is one of the most predictable

> controversies that we know—the participants go through a ritual of hackneyed complaints almost as ancient as academe, while believing that what is said is radical and new.

The following January, Kerr was going to tell newsmen: "They took us completely by surprise." Something went wrong with the predictability of the hackneyed complaints. Instead there was a "protest and outrage" that was "fresh and meaningful" and therefore even more distressful to the president.

## 7. *"What's Intellectual About Collecting Money?"*

When Kerr finally gave the public his history of how the fight all started (interview of January 5), his account went as follows:

Returning from a trip abroad on September 15, he found that, the day before, the Berkeley administration had closed the Bancroft political arena. He thought this was a mistake, but, instead of correcting the mistake, he suggested that Sproul Hall steps be made a "Hyde Park" area. "I thought," he said, "we could get things back into channels of discussion if we showed reasonableness, but it didn't work." The interview adds: "Instead of reasonable discussion Kerr got the Free Speech Movement."

We shall see the administration's view of reasonable discussion.

The edict of September 14 was handed down, a week before classes started, with no consultation of the student clubs affected. There was likewise none even with the ASUC, the "sandbox" student government. The administration ignored the impotent ASUC as fully as did the student protesters.

"Off-campus politics will be removed from its last on campus stronghold," interpreted the *Daily Cal.* "The boom has been lowered ... on off-campus political activities within the limits of the Berkeley campus," reported the Berkeley *Daily Gazette.*

In addition to banning the use of tables (and posters) at Bancroft, the September 14 announcement also specifically prohibited fund-raising, membership recruitment and speeches, and the "planning and implementing of off-campus political and social action." The reason given for banning the tables was their "interference with the flow of traffic." The clubs offered to conduct a traffic-flow survey, but without result.

The ban on the activities was based on Art. 9, Sec. 9 of the State Constitution which reads: "The University shall be entirely independent of all political or sectarian influence and kept free therefrom in the appointment of its regents and in the administration of its affairs . . ."

Many pointed out in the ensuing three months that the best way to insure the university's independence of "political or sectarian influence" was to permit free speech and advocacy of. *all* views on campus, not to bar any.*

Although the September 14 regulations were presented as the "historic policy" of the university—historically winked at —a second and new version of the "historic policy" was disclosed a week later, on September 21, after student protests spread. Following a conference with Kerr and Strong, Dean Towle met a group of club representatives and announced some "clarifications":

(1) Sproul Hall steps would be the new "Hyde Park"—the concession suggested by Kerr—but no voice amplification would be allowed.

(2) A number of tables would be allowed at Bancroft; presumably it had been ascertained in the meantime that they would not block traffic.

(3) But at the tables there could still be no fund-raising, no recruitment, and no advocacy of partisan positions. Only "informative" material, not "advocative" or "persuasive," could be distributed for or

* Even Kerr later admitted that "by the fall of 1964, certain of the university's rules had become of doubtful legal enforceability."
(Calif. Monthly, February 1965, p. 96.)

against a candidate, a proposition or an issue; but no urging of "a specific vote" or "call for direct social or political action."

Chancellor Strong added: there could be no "mounting of social and political actions directed to the surrounding community."

The student representatives tried to find out where the line was being drawn between informing and advocating, and ran into the Semantic Barrier. The dean offered the interpretation that "information" about a scheduled picket line would be considered "advocacy."

This abstruse distinction between "information" and "advocacy" had to be partially scuttled within the week, after a discussion on September 24-25 between the campus officers and Kerr. The third version of the "historic policy" was announced on September 28 by Chancellor Strong. "Advocacy" would be permitted of a candidate or a proposition currently on the ballot, but that was all.

And the chancellor announced at the same time that discussion on the matter was over: "no further changes are envisaged. The matter is closed." So much for "reasonable discussion".*

By this time it was quite clear that the administration could not possibly believe it was merely enforcing the state constitution. It would have been difficult to claim that the constitution smiled on advocacy of Goldwater after he had become the candidate but frowned on advocacy of Scranton before a candidate had been chosen. Nor would a battery of lawyers have undertaken to prove that it was the constitution that banned "information" about a scheduled picket line. Nor could the constitution explain why fund-raising on campus was allowed for the World University Service, for schools in Asia, while SNCC was barred from collecting for "freedom schools" in Mississippi, or CORE for tutorials in Oakland.

---

* Three days later, a statement by the chancellor asserted that the new policy "is now and has always been the unchanged policy of the university. . . . No instance of a newly imposed restriction or curtailment of freedom of speech on campus can be truthfully alleged for the simple reason that none exists."

But these interpretations had the undeniable virtue of giving the "outside pressures" what they were demanding. At the same time the new version eased an embarrassing contradiction: the university was spending taxpayers' money to mail out propaganda in favor of Proposition 2 (the bond issue) while it cracked down on students for collecting nickels for "No on Proposition 14" (the anti-fair-housing measure). It had taken two weeks and Kerr's best advice to work out this highly selective gloss on the state constitution, which would give substance to Power and rhetoric to Ideals.

(Version 4 of the "historic policy" was going to come in November.)

Students and some faculty members reacted sharply on educational grounds to the prohibition of "mounting social and political action." A statement by the clubs, for example, spoke of an "obligation to be informed participants in our society—and not armchair intellectuals." Kerr took up another challenge:

> In an apparent retort to the history professors who joined the student protests on the Berkeley campus earlier this week, Kerr said: "If action were necessary for intellectual experience we wouldn't teach history, since we cannot be involved with the Greeks and Romans." (S.F. *Chronicle,* Sept. 27.)

Since we cannot learn through acting in Greek history, is it proper for an educational institution to discourage acting in our own history? The implied argument did nothing to improve the intellectual respectability of the administration's stand in the eyes of the university community. It did not help that Kerr also added: "What's so intellectual about collecting money?" Only the civil-rights workers in Mississippi could have replied adequately.

## 8. The Clubs Fight Back

The "off-campus" clubs formed a United Front on September 17 to protest the new rules. It consisted of some 20 organizations: civil-rights groups, radical and socialist groups, religious and peace groups, Young Democrats, and all three Republican clubs (including Youth for Goldwater) plus another right-wing conservative society. The conservatives' campus publication *Man and State* later summarized:

The new regulations were immediately opposed by all campus political organizations.... The initial conversations with the administration left no doubt but that the regulations were a result of outside pressure and were intended to stop any political activity on campus.... The negotiations failed.

Right across the political board from left to right, not one of the clubs felt that the administration was set on "reasonable discussion."

Next day, the United Front submitted a request to the dean for restoration of the tables, agreeing to a number of conditions regulating their use. On the first day of classes, September 21, Dean Towle met with them and unleashed Version 2 of the regulations. The student representatives thanked her for the improvement and replied that it was not enough. By noon that day the first protest demonstration unrolled before Sproul Hall: a picket line of 200 carrying signs such as "Bomb the Ban" and "UC Manufactures Safe Minds."

> The most surprising aspect of yesterday's picketing was the relatively large numbers of non-activists who joined the picket line, took a few turns in front of Sproul, and then turned their sign over to others. *(Daily Cal,* Sept. 22.)

In addition, tables were set up (with permits) but proceeded to offer "advocative" material in defiance of the order. All the clubs had agreed on the previous evening that no one of them would move its table to the city-owned strip-now labeled the "fink area." Even the conservatives agreed on this measure of solidarity, though not on setting up tables in violation of the rules. *A Daily Cal* editorial warned, "Campus administrators are making a mistake," though it urged moderation in protest. The next day even the ASUC Senate addressed a request to the Regents "to allow free political and social action," etc.

On the night of the 23rd there was a "Free Speech Vigil" on Sproul Hall steps, beginning 9 P.M.—about three hundred strong. In response to a report that Kerr and the Regents were meeting at University House, the group decided, after a quarter-hour discussion and a vote, to march there, walk around for five minutes and leave. "The single-file procession stretched a quarter mile, and was called remarkable for its orderliness," reported the *Daily Cal.* (This note, surprise at the self-disciplined orderliness, was to be struck by all unbiased observers from here on.) All Regents having left, except the secretary, a letter of appeal to the board was composed and left. Back at Sproul Hall, some 75 students composed themselves till morning, when they greeted the arrivals with singing.

On September 28 the United Front opened the throttle a little more. "Advocative" tables were set up at Sather Gate itself, since the new rules were supposed to be campus-wide now. At 11 A.M. Chancellor Strong was scheduled to open an official university meeting to present awards, in the Lower Plaza. The United Front held a rally in Dwinelle Plaza to group its forces, and then marched as a picket line to the chancellor's meeting (where, incidentally, Strong unexpectedly announced Version 3 of the rules). Against the instructions of one of the deans, the picket line went down the aisles as well as around the perimeter.

It was a strange scene: there were at least 1000 picketers—1500 according to one paper—and there were probably not quite that many students attending the official meeting. Two of the student leaders, including Mario Savio of SNCC, were threatened with disciplinary action; some of the clubs were given warnings.

On September 29 the dean's staff began making hourly checks of violations, and at first found the students "cooperative," with the exception of one Slate student. In the afternoon SNCC set up a table in violation of the rules.

## *9. The First Sit-in and the Eight Suspensions*

On Wednesday, September 30, the dean's checks continued, but this time they ran into a stiffening resistance. By afternoon five students—Brian Turner, Donald Hatch, David Goines, Elizabeth Stapleton and Mark Bravo—who had refused to back down on what they insisted were their constitutional rights, were summoned to the dean's office at 3 o'clock. The deans quit taking names when they realized that their list might run into hundreds. Hastily written petitions were circulated among the students gathered in the Sather Gate area, and some 400 of them signed statements on the spot, like the following:

> We the undersigned have jointly manned tables at Sather Gate—realizing that we were in violation of University edicts to the contrary, and that we may be subject to expulsion.

At 3 o'clock over 500 students showed up at the dean's office together with the five cited. Their spokesman was Mario Savio, not one of the five. He told the dean: all the students present had equally violated the rules; they wanted equal disciplinary treatment and were not going to leave till assured of it.

> . the administration explained that it was punishing only observed offenses, an explanation which under the

> circumstances struck the student community as disingenuous .. . *(Suggestion for Dismissal, p. 5.)* *

Right there, instead, three more students were added to the cited list—Mario Savio, Art Goldberg and Sandor Fuchs making eight in all.

Originally scheduled for 4 P.M. had been another meeting between the administrators and the club representatives; but at this point the administration unilaterally canceled the parley on the ground that "the environment was not conducive to reasonable discussion." Did the chancellor consider that his own intimidation campaign of the past two days, preceding this scheduled meeting, had been "conducive to reasonable discussion?" At any rate, the students were inaugurating a principle they never dropped: *When they try to pick off a few leaders, hit 'em with all you've got.* As Kerr was later to write retrospectively about the FSM activists: "They have a remarkable sense of solidarity among themselves . . ."

The students, swelling eventually to several hundreds, stayed in the halls and turned the sit-in into a mass "sleep-in," till early morning. Shortly before midnight, after conferring with Kerr, Chancellor Strong issued a statement announcing that the penalty of "indefinite suspension" was being assessed against the eight students.

It was characteristic of the panicky virulence with which Strong and Kerr moved to strike that they fixed on a penalty which did not even exist in the very university regulations which they were presumably defending. But this was only one detail. For an assessment of this fateful

---

* *A Suggestion for Dismissal* [of the case of the People of the State vs. Mario Savio *et al.]. Submitted by: Certain Faculty Members of the University of ' California, Berkeley, January 1965.* This document was signed by 255 professors and submitted to the court considering the case of the sit-inners arrested on December 3, 1964. It includes an able review of the controversy as well as a discussion in depth of some of the issues.

decision which was made by the chancellor in conference with the president, we must look ahead to the judgment finally rendered in mid-November by a faculty committee appointed by the Academic Senate, usually called the Heyman Committee after its chairman, a professor of law:

> The procedures followed were unusual. Normally, penalties of any consequences are imposed only after hearings before the Faculty Student Conduct Committee. Such procedure was not followed here with the result that the students were suspended without a hearing . . . in hindsight, it would have been more fitting to announce that the students were to be proceeded against before the Faculty Committee rather than levying summary punishments of such severity. We were left with the impression that some or all of these eight students were gratuitously singled out for heavy penalties summarily imposed in the hope that by making examples of these students, the University could end the sit-in and perhaps forestall further mass demonstrations.

In the case of six students out of the eight, even the administration admitted to the Heyman Committee that the table-manning offenses would normally have been considered "innocuous" but that the draconic penalty was imposed for the "context." The Heyman Committee disagreed, since it saw the context as a sincere belief by the students that their constitutional rights were at stake.

> Moreover, we believe [went on the Committee] that these students viewed their actions in operating the tables as necessary to precipitate a test of the validity of the regulations in some arena outside the University . . . [the

> Chancellor had] made it clear that the President and the Regents had rejected in final form the request of the ASUC Senate for changes in the rules to permit solicitation of funds and membership and organization of political and social action campaigns on campus. The door was thus seemingly closed to any negotiations on these central points.

We should note two things in connection with this very important passage. (1) Later on, the ASUC Senate was going to decide, unanimously, to force a court test of the regulations through an arranged violation of them-that is, it decided to do exactly what the rebel students were suspended for doing. (2) The last two sentences give an official quietus to Kerr's later claim that all he wanted was "reasonable discussion." At every crucial point the administration systematically struck the attitude "Not negotiable!"*

This persistent intransigence made sense in terms of the usual bureaucratic calculation: insofar as the students could be induced to give up all hope of moving the administration, they could the more easily be discouraged from even making the attempt. It is a usually effective approach; the only reason it failed in this case is that the administration confronted a student leadership which was not ruled by "possibilism." This indeed was going to be the FSM's main offense in the eyes of a number of dogmatically "possibilist" academics, who were going to "project" the Administration's indubitable intransigence onto the militant students.

---

* Cf. the later summary statement by Chancellor Strong: "During the days leading up to the fateful evening of October 2, the position was stated and restated for all to hear that the university would never negotiate with individuals who were at the time engaged in unlawful behavior . . ." (Confidential report to Regents, dated December 16, 1964. Published in *S.F. Examiner,* March 13, 1965.)

Regarding the sit-in at the dean's office, the Heyman Committee observed as follows, naturally unaware of the full future import of its remarks:

> In retrospect, the University's best tactic might have been to carry on operations in Sproul Hall as usual, leaving the students where they were until the demonstration ended naturally through the weariness of the demonstrators.

And here is its general summary on the suspensions:

> ... the procedure by which the University acted to punish these wrongdoings is subject to serious criticism. The relevant factors are: first, the vagueness of many off the relevant regulations; second, the precipitate action taken in suspending the students some time between dinner time and the issuance of the press release at 11:45 P.M.; third, the disregard of the usual channel of hearings for student offenses—notably hearings by the Faculty Committee on Student Conduct; fourth, the deliberate singling out of these students (almost as hostages) for punishment despite evidence that in almost every case others were or could have been easily identified as performing similar acts; and fifth, the choice of an extraordinary and novel penalty—"indefinite suspension"—which is nowhere made explicit in the regulations, and the failure to reinstate the students temporarily pending actions taken on the recommendations of this committee. *[The last remark is ahead of our story.]*

"We do not believe or suggest that the administration was motivated by malice or vengeance," the Committee assures us, expressing "confident faith that the university administration will be as desirous as we are of correcting [the shortcomings]." Alas, chancellor, president and Regents were going to reject the Heyman Committee's recommendations about as summarily as. the eight students had been suspended.

The administration does not always act so precipitately in putting regulations into force. For example, in connection with its laudable decision to abolish racial discrimination in fraternities, the administration gave frats a period of five years to get into line. The long delay may have been justifiable; it is the contrast that tells the story.

## *10. A Couple of Rebels*

For each student involved, this last week in September was also a personal crisis.

For example, there was Brian Turner, 19-year-old sophomore in economics, who had joined SNCC little more than a week before. On the 29th the "little deans" had approached him, as others, and asked if he knew he was breaking the rules.

> "I backed down on Tuesday because I didn't want to go alone," he said. "I folded up the table and went home. But I thought about it overnight and I went back. When they came up to see me again, my own principles prevented me from leaving. I had decided that the freedom of 27,000 people to speak freely is worth the sacrifice of my own academic career at Cal." *(S. F. Chronicle,* Oct. 3.)

Turner's background was only mildly liberal (and in fact he was going to become one of the "moderates" in the FSM spectrum) but in one short week he had to educate himself fast on the most fundamental characterological question in politics: In confrontation with oppressive Power, do you adapt discreetly or do you go over into opposition?

Mario Savio, a junior, who had become the spokesman of the group on September 30, was a different case: he already knew who he was. This was perhaps his main title to the mantle of leadership which did in fact fall on him.

Not a glib orator, retaining remnants of a stutter, rather tending to a certain shyness, he yet projected forcefulness and decision in action. This was the outward glow of the inner fact that he was not In Hiding—he was in open opposition, and he had no doubts about it. He became the recognized leader of the FSM not in a contest but mainly because there was no other eligible student around who was morally as ready and capable of assuming the burden.

Still under 22 when the fight broke out, Mario Savio had been a high-grade student in three colleges: Manhattan College (Catholic), Queens College (New York City), and Berkeley. He had moved from absorption in physics and mathematics to a major in philosophy. He had spent his summer in 1963 on a do-gooder project in Taxco, Mexico; then in the summer of 1964 he became a SNCC voter-registration worker in Mississippi. He saw a co-worker beaten. Most important, he saw Mississippi, where the relationships between Ideals and Power quiver out in the open like exposed nerve endings.

When at summer's end he returned to Berkeley, from a state where Law and Order meant the legally organized subjection of a whole people, the administration greeted him with the news that Law and Order meant he could not even collect quarters to aid those people. He knew all about this kind of Law and Order.

## *11. The Police-car Blockade Begins*

On the morning of October 1, a student phoned me to ask whether I would speak at a "Free Speech Rally" which the United Front of clubs was organizing for noon in Sproul Hall Plaza. The eight students had been summarily suspended the night before. Three different leaflets calling for the rally were being distributed at the entrances to the campus. Students and faculty were asked to demand a lifting of the suspensions and equal treatment for all the student rule violators, as well as the original demands for rescission of the new regulations.

About that same time in mid-morning, shortly after 10, the first table appeared at Sather Gate; then others—about ten in all before long. At 11 o'clock the tables moved over to the foot of Sproul Hall steps. For the next 30-40 minutes the "table-manners" industriously violated regulations, particularly by asking for contributions. In two large knots of students lively debates on the issues went on between articulate proponents.*

At about a quarter to 12, Deans Murphy and Van Houten emerged from the building together with the campus police chief, and approached the tables. The Campus CORE table was perhaps the largest in size—a door panel on supports with eight or ten people operating it. Dean Van Houten approached the loudest of the group and asked: "Are you prepared to remove yourself and the table from university property?"

He wasn't. "I must inform you," said the dean, "that if you are a student, you are violating university regulations; and if you are a non-student you are violating the trespass law. Will you identify yourself? ... You leave no alternative but to ask Lieutenant Chandler to arrest you. Lieutenant Chandler, put him under arrest."

When the police chief said, "Will you come peacefully, or if not, we'll take you," the cry went up, "Take all of us!" The cop went off to get help.

The CORE member now under arrest was in fact temporarily a non-student. Jack Weinberg, 24, had been a graduate student in mathematics but had dropped out about November of the previous year. He had then gotten himself deeply involved with CORE's "Shattuck Avenue project," and mathematics (as he put it to me later) "no longer meant that much"

* This and the next scene are based on the tapes made on the spot by the ubiquitous reporters of Pacifica Radio, station KPFA.

to him. He was going to rethink his personal perspective.* In the meantime he had become a veteran of three arrests at Bay Area civil-rights actions: the Sheraton-Palace sit-in, the Cadillac agency picket, and a demonstration at Mel's Drive-In. Being "bugged" by the police was not a novelty.

While waiting for the police reinforcements to return and with the "little dean" patiently standing by, Weinberg addressed himself to the growing crowd of students, in what turned into a little speech:

> I want to tell you about this knowledge factory, while we're all sitting here now. It seems that certain of the products are not coming out to standard specifications. And I feel the university is trying to purge these products so that they can once again produce for the industry exactly what they specify. This is a Knowledge Factory; if you read Clark Kerr's book, these are his words.... This is mass production; no deviations from the norms are tolerated. Occasionally a few students get together and they decide they are human beings, that they are not willing to be products, and they protest; and the university feels obliged to purge these non-standard products.

---

* This describes a very typical example of the "non-students" who were soon going to be denounced by the authorities and the press as if they were outside agitators imported from Caracas. Indeed, official recognition of some "non-students" as rightful members of the university community was later registered when the UCLA administration adopted new regulations in December on the basis of the lessons of Berkeley: the definition of "student" specifically included ""those who have been regularly enrolled in the preceding semester (or quarter) and who in addition are eligible to return at their own option." A similar proposal was made by a Berkeley faculty committee, inconclusively. Unofficially, recent alumni and drop-outs of even more than one semester ago are socially and psychologically an accepted part of the university community.

Weinberg was here taking off from a talk I had given for the Independent Socialist Club that week on "Behind the Ban: Clark Kerr's View of the University as a Knowledge Factory." A number of other FSM activists-to-be had been at the meeting too. But in any case the idea was in the air: twice during the preceding week the *Daily Cal* had published letters from students which were along similar lines even though without reference to Kerr's theory at all.

A hostile student asked Weinberg why the advocacy of social action was so important to the protesters.

> It's very simple [replied Weinberg]. We want to see social change in the world in which we live. We want to see this social change because we are human beings who have ideas. We think, we talk, we discuss, and when we're done thinking and talking and discussing, well then, we feel that these things are vacuous unless we then act on the principle that we think, talk and discuss about. This is as much a part of a university education as anything else.

He continued:

> We feel that we, as human beings first and students second, must take our stand on every vital issue which faces this nation, and in particular the vital issue of discrimination, of segregation, of poverty, of unemployment; the vital issue of people who aren't getting the decent breaks that they as individuals deserve ...

That was as far as he got. A police car had been driven right into the middle of the plaza, and the police now informed him that he was under arrest for trespassing. As he went limp they prepared to carry him into the car. Even as they were doing so, some students started to sit down between the table and the car, in the way of the harassed policemen as they carried their prisoner across.

There are almost as many claimants for the honor of being "the first to sit down around the police car" as there were cities claiming to be Homer's birthplace, but in this case the explanation is different. People unacquainted with the civil rights movement believe that "someone" must have launched the move, but in point of fact it is almost a reflex action among experienced civil-rights activists, of whom there were many within ten feet. The same thing had been done when the paddy wagons had rolled up for the Cadillac agency demonstrators that spring.

Literally in less time than it has taken to tell, the police car into which Weinberg had been bundled was surrounded by sitting students. For a while the engine was kept running as the police stolidly waited for them to give up. But it was going to be 32 hours before that car moved.

## *12. Second Sit-in and the Greeks*

A student named Jamie Burton pushed his way into the hubbub around the car. "I've been upstairs talking to Dean Williams ... As long as there is trouble down here, we can't talk in good faith," he expostulated.

Mario Savio replied, "Here's a compromise for the dean: release the guy, don't bother the people on the tables, and we'll quietly disperse till the end of negotiations."

After an interchange, Burton shrilled in indignant exasperation: "You're a bunch of *fools*. Look, you're asking too much!"

This student was the very first of a long line of personages of all degrees of eminence who were going to say the same thing. In this case, the immediate response to Burton's agonized cry was a mass chant: *"Let him go! Let him. go!. .."*

Savio started to speak to the crowd, now quickly swelling by hundreds as the noon hour struck and classrooms poured out. The better to be seen, he hoisted himself on top of the car, taking his shoes off; the policemen made no objection. From this position, he suggested a sit-in at Sproul Hall.

The president of the ASUC, Charles Powell, newly arrived, asked for the "floor" (i.e. the car top), took off his shoes, and climbed up. "If you let me speak for you, I'll ask the deans that this boy here be allowed to go free . . ." Students roared back, "What about the other eight?" Powell replied, "This one is the immediate problem; all right?" There were shouts of "No." Weinberg leaned out of the car window and cried, "I'm not the immediate problem; we're all together." Powell tacked: "I'll ask at the same time about the other eight. Meanwhile I ask you that you give the [ASUC Senate a week's time . . ." (There was that note again: *Go home: let us leaders settle it for you ...*)

Savio announced that he would go immediately with Powell to see the deans, and introduced me as the next speaker. I had arrived some minutes after 12, just before Powell spoke, and had barely learned what had happened. There were perhaps a couple of hundred actually sitting down, but by this time the crowd seemed to extend as far as the eye could see in every direction around the car, a few thousand in number. On one side, the broad steps of Sproul Hall acted as a convenient grandstand for a thousand or so, and Savio and Powell had instinctively faced in this direction.

It was a tense situation, but what was more vivid at the time was a peculiar fact: this was my first speech in stockinged feet. Or from the top of a police car. There was no loudspeaker, but the immense crowd was amazingly quiet and orderly, except for weak heckling that soon died away. By the time I had spoken for fifteen minutes about the basic issues in "mounting social and political action" that had led to the suspensions and this protest, my voice was breaking.

A succession of speakers followed, for hours, many of them club representatives who related their attempts at negotiation with the administration.

After Savio returned and reported on his fruitless conversation with the administration—who were standing pat on the formula "Not negotiable!"—sentiment turned toward the sit-in proposal that had been thrown out earlier. Toward 3 o'clock, about 200 students went in, leaving enough sitters behind to keep the car immobilized.

Meanwhile, some faculty members had been trying to mediate the dispute, even though administration spokesmen kept telling them as well as the students that the issues were "not negotiable." (The tale about seeking "reasonable discussion" had not yet been invented.)

Several professors undertook to convince the students to give up the Sproul sit-in as an earnest of good will, to make it easier for them to mediate with Kerr. Under this pressure, most of the sit-inners left the building temporarily as a unilateral concession. But Kerr could not be contacted, even by the faculty members.

When the guards started locking the doors of the building about 6:30, the students rushed back in, and there was a short scuffle with the police. By about 8, almost all pulled out again; but they quickly found that this brought no change of attitude on the part of the administration (except, perhaps, to convince it that the students could be bullied by a hard line).

Faculty members were taken aback by the realization that Kerr and Strong were following a course of tough intransigence. A student proposal that the police-car blockade would be ended if the administration turned the eight suspensions into citations before the Faculty Committee on Student Conduct (as the Heyman Committee later decided *should* have been done anyway) evoked no interest from the authorities.

The vigil around the police car went on in the darkness; the speeches went on, more desultory; the roof of the car became one large dent, and eventually speakers stopped taking off their shoes. The prospect seemed a quiet night, when, around 11 in the evening, the plaza was invaded by a phalanx of fraternity boys who had been mobilized out of the Greek-letter houses.

Estimates of the "Greek" contingent run from 100 to 200 (I think it was nearer 100), but this was more than enough if the aim was to touch off a riot in order to involve the police. Arriving from the Bancroft side, the "Greeks" made for the main body of the sitters, but the intervening standees linked arms, swayed a bit, and held. Late as it was, there were still thousands in the plaza, and what was visible at this point was that the mass were decisively with the demonstrators even though not sitting down themselves.

Their first rush turned back, the frat boys began to express their opinions by hurling lighted cigarettes and eggs at the sitters, an amusement which they continued sporadically for the next couple of hours. Their main body then took up a station on the Sproul steps "grandstand" and tried to drown out speakers by systematic noise-making—the noises being demands for observance of law and order. When the demonstrators asked them to listen to and reply to the "free speech" case against the regulations, they raucously chanted, "We Want Our Own Police Car!"

Finally, one of the invaders did mount the police car and speak, making a respectable defense of Law and Order as an absolute, only to be shouted down by his own "Greek chorus" almost as rudely as were the demonstrators. Meanwhile the latter, tightly repressing any tendency to reply in kind to the provocations, were successfully frustrating the invaders' intentions. An uglier note began to creep into the "Greek" insults.

By this time, however, a sort of rescue mission had arrived. An ASUC vice-president took the rostrum with a direct appeal to the frat boys to leave, in the name of the law and order they were invoking. A dean did likewise, and even this symbol of Law and Order was jeered, as was also the information that the police themselves (Law and Order incarnate) would prefer that they go home.

It was not until Father James Fisher of Newman House made a solemn appeal to them that the mood changed. When the immediate hush was broken by a raucous jeer from one of the Greeks, the crowd grasped the situation as if of one mind. The thousands of demonstrators maintained an absolute pin-drop silence without a word of instruction, and the now isolated shouts by a few frat yell-leaders began to make even their own troops squirm. It was not long before the whole platoon slunk away.

The official report later made by Chancellor Strong described these fraternity hooligans as "student counter-action in maintaining law and order on the campus."

The student blockaders settled down. It was a mild night.

## *13. Whose Law and Order?*

That day, the argumentation swirling in knots around the car and the campus had naturally tended to shift away from the "free speech" issues to the derivative issue of "Law and Order." Assuming that the administration was wrong in imposing the new restrictions, as an overwhelming majority of the campus agreed, was this the way to fight it? asked anxious students, turning over the crisis in their minds.

There were undigested rhetorical platitudes on both sides. On the one hand, what would society be without Law and Order? On the other hand, one could read, in a local guidebook to the East Bay area, that President Kerr was a great civil-libertarian who had loftily proclaimed:

> I would urge each individual ... to teach children, in the home and in the school, "To be laws to themselves and to depend on themselves," as Walt Whitman urged us ... for that is the well-source of the independent spirit.

"Laws to themselves!" This Whitmanesque anarchism went far beyond what the students were demanding. It appeared that, in his character as a Liberal Philosopher, Kerr called on students to be Independent Spirits, but in his character as Responsible Administrator he had to punish them if they took him seriously.

Although "Law and Order" seemed to be an indivisible phrase like "hue and cry," the events of this day and subsequent days suggested a cleavage. Whatever indignities the law was suffering, the mass of students went through the entire three months of sharp conflict with a regard for order, orderliness and individual self-discipline that was phenomenal. The scuffle that day around the Sproul Hall doors was a minor exception, but even such an incident did not recur. On the night of October 1, it had been the touters of Law who were the flouters of Order.

The CIO sitdown strikes of the thirties had been clear violations of law too. As a result they had brought a measure of democracy and human dignity to the shops and assembly lines. Many who denounced the students' sit-ins seemed to think the students had invented the tactic. Nor did they ask themselves how "criminal" it could be if the Berkeley halls of learning suddenly produced such a multitude of criminals. If several thousands of the brightest scholars in California had been driven to measures so heinous, didn't this suggest there might be something dreadfully wrong with what the administration was doing, that it had pushed them to desperate recourses?*

---

* The same point has been made about the American colonists of 1776. In this connection, interestingly enough, Governor Brown has revealed that he isn't. at all sure but that Sam Adams & Co. were a bunch of troublemakers like the FSM. Here is his discussion of civil disobedience in a radio interview (KPFA, March 28, 1965) : "I spoke to Mario Savio on the telephone and he said, 'Would you have opposed the Boston Tea Party?' and I said, 'Well, I don't know whether I'd have opposed the Boston Tea Party or not. But I do know that the colonial government sent representatives to the court of King James in order to achieve—or King George—I forget who it was—King George, that's right—to achieve their proper objective, and they only resorted to that as a last resort. Now I wouldn't be prepared to say that under certain circumstances where rights are denied an individual that he might not feel he can achieve it is by revolt *[sic]*, but if he does revolt then he'd better be prepared to either win or suffer the civil consequences

(continued...)

The students that day heard many abstract appeals to the sanctity of law, but the "law" itself did not seem to behave so abstractly. It was certainly not blind. Instead of impartially punishing all "lawbreakers," the administration was openly and "gratuitously" singling out leaders for punishment ("almost as hostages," as the Heyman Committee put it.) It was acting as if interested not in enforcing blind law but rather in beheading a mass protest.

The issue was put most provocatively from the top of the police car as dusk was falling. We have mentioned that a number of professors had been trying to act as mediators between the demonstrators and President Kerr. One of them climbed on top of the car to tell the crowd of students not only that it was useless to expect concessions from Kerr but also that the police-car blockade was antidemocratic and immoral.

This was Seymour Martin Lipset, one of the most upwardly mobile of the sociology professors, who had recently been honored by Kerr with the directorship of the Institute of International Studies, an academic entrepreneur of notable talent in channeling government and foundation grant money, who was himself then engaged in research on foreign student movements for the Air Force (which was presumably interested in a bird's-eye view of the question).

Lipset charged that the students were acting "like the Ku Klux Klan," for did not the Southern segregationists also believe in violating the law when they didn't like it, instead of obeying decisions adopted in a democracy? (Kerr was going to echo this line later.)

An impromptu debate broke out as students called out rebuttals. The most obvious answer was that the university community was not even theoretically a democracy, even though it existed *within* a democracy (just as any factory is an authoritarian regime within the larger society). Kerr

---

(...continued)
of what he does."—Or in better-known terms: the Patriots are the side that wins.

openly wrote of the Multiversity's government as a "benevolent bureaucracy." Although one of the easy platitudes of the day was the advice that the students should "exhaust all channels" before resorting to drastic protest, there were in fact no "channels" open to the students that had not been available to the sans-culottes under Louis XVI, such as the right of petition. Precisely when the students had sought to appeal to the larger democracy in which the university was embedded—"to precipitate a test of the [constitutional] validity of the regulations *in some arena outside the university,"* as the Heyman Committee said—the Benevolent Bureaucracy inside the university had reacted violently with the *coup de force* of the summary suspensions.

Others stressed that "democracy" in the situation meant acting only through the so-called student government, ASUC.*

This argument assumed that ASUC was indeed "student government." But as we have mentioned, the most advanced one-third of the students were excluded from it, and the simulacrum of government which did exist was firmly circumscribed by the administration itself. No one, including the administration, took ASUC seriously as a government, especially since the 1959 disfranchisement of the graduate students. "Acting through ASUC" usually had the operational meaning of waiting while Charles Powell and his "sandbox" colleagues sparred with the administration, or else of waiting for the next election—but in any case doing nothing *now*. (But when the next election took place, the rebel students did "act through ASUC" to the extent of winning the most smashing group victory in the history of the student government.)**

---

* Cf. Lewis Feuer, "Rebellion at Berkeley-II," *New Leader,* January 4, 1965.

** Later, the ASUC vice-president, not an FSM'er, "explained the actions of the [ASUC] Senate are frequently ignored by the faculty and administration on the grounds the government is not respected by the students. The students,

(continued...)

But fundamentally the students' demands did not merely depend on proving that a majority supported them. The number of students themselves interested in "mounting social and political action" was admittedly a minority, but the majority (it was contended) does not have the right to exclude this minority from the possibility of acting. Democracy, of course, does not mean "majority decision" without the maintenance of the rights of minorities. If a majority passes a law to gag you, you have the moral and political duty of fighting back with every means left. Thus went the students' case.

So much for the context of democracy. The Lipset analogy with the KKK went further. The Klan do not like the Supreme Court's directives and wish to violate them; and so, skulking in the dead of night with hooded visages, they terrorize—not the Supreme Court itself (which would take some courage) but defenseless Negroes, by beating them, burning churches, murdering civil-rights workers. And this even though as' citizens they have full rights (denied to their victims) in helping to determine the law.

The case of the students was just the reverse. In the microcosm of the university community, the students were informed—by an administration in which they had no say, by a Power Structure in which they had no vote—that *they* (not their "victims") were being deprived of some basic freedoms of campus life. They were also informed that the issue was "not negotiable," that they had no further recourse. They responded, in

---

(...continued)

he stated, do not respect the government because its actions are not honored by the faculty and administration." *(Daily Cal,* Feb. 4, 1965.) The usual number of students voting in an ASUC election was less than one of the smaller FSM demonstrations. On October 1, ASUC President Powell issued a formal statement jettisoning the ASUC position of September 22. He now informed the students that nothing could be done about the ban on recruitment and fund-raising because "the prohibition ... is not a ruling of the chancellor or of President Clark Kerr. It is, in fact, a State law." (This, of course, was untrue.) "I ask," he concluded, "that you not oppose the administration—the administration can do nothing to meet the demands being made."

the open light of day, with civil disobedience. They did not beat up their "victims," the administration; on the contrary, it is they who were eventually roughed up. Yet they were told that they were "just like the Ku Klux Klan."

What is the meaning of civil disobedience? It deliberately violates a law, with as great an insistence on open publicity as the Ku Klux Klan and other criminals insist on clandestine evasion, because the act has meaning only as an appeal to the public conscience. Its aim is to put the *authorities* on the spot. It says: We hereby put our bodies on the line publicly and openly, and challenge you to enforce your Law and Order. *We wish to compel you to take the consequences of arresting us* .. .

All this is the exact opposite of criminal violations of law, even if these are politically motivated violations like the Klan's. "The consequences of arresting us" concentrate public attention on the concrete evil which is under attack. "We" do not meekly collapse under arrest; we vigorously protest the step. A strange argument is frequently made: if you challenge arrest and do in fact get arrested, "you have no right to complain." On the contrary: "complaining" (protest) is the whole point of civil disobedience.

Lipset was finally pushed by the give-and-take to admit that civil disobedience might be all right in the South because of the lack of democracy there; yet, in terms of his own analogy, he did not conclude that Ku Klux Klan lynchings were all right in the South (or anywhere else) because of the special circumstances. The new Berkeley chancellor, Martin Meyerson, was later to concede, also, that civil disobedience might be legitimate "as a last resort"; but presumably Lipset would not agree that Ku Klux Klanism could be legitimate in any resort. By fathering the "Ku Klux Klan" charge against the student protest, Lipset became known as one of the prominent adversaries of the movement among the faculty.

## *14. "You Can't Win!"*

The next day, Friday, was the hottest October 2 in local history. The temperature was in the middle eighties when the noon rally opened, still from the top of the car. The crowd again overfilled the plaza; but now there was a loudspeaker too (for which I was grateful). Sproul Hall was closed to all except "authorized persons."

In the morning, arriving students were greeted by the 200 or so who had remained around the car all night, in blankets or sleeping bags, some trying to study by a feeble light, others singing around a guitar. They were also greeted by a leaflet issued by the United Front of clubs, demanding reinstatement of the suspended students and dropping of charges against Jack Weinberg, as well as restoration of "freedom of speech" and the right to political activity that did not "interfere with the normal functioning of the university." It urged students to wear a black armband, obtainable at Sather Gate, to show agreement with the demands. The following thirteen clubs signed to show support for these aims:

University Young Democrats
University Young Republicans
Campus CORE
California Students for Goldwater
Campus Civil Liberties Union
Slate
Young Socialist Alliance
Independent Socialist Club
W.E.B. DuBois Club
Berkeley Young Democratic Club
Students for a Democratic Society
Friends of SNCC
Women for Peace

However, the attitude taken by the Goldwaterites and other conservatives was that while supporting the aims, they would join only in lawful actions. "But let no one mistake our intent," one of them warned. "The United Front still stands."

On top of the car the microphone was turned over by the demonstrators to opponents and critics of the protest as well as to supporters, in an attempt at a dialogue with skeptical or antagonistic students. Efforts at mediation by faculty members intensified as the day wore on

> ... but the administration told them, and told the students as well, that the issues of the rules and the disciplinary measures were not negotiable. (Administrative officers consistently refused to discuss the issues in dispute as long as regulations were being violated, thereby abdicating their power to alleviate a situation of growing intensity.) (*A Suggestion for Dismissal.)*

Kerr, in a scheduled speech that noon at an American Council on Education gathering in San Francisco, interpolated a tough attack on the students as "a mob ... assembled on the Berkeley campus":

> The rules will not be changed in the face of mob action. The penalties already assessed against certain students will not be removed in the face of mob action.

At a press conference he "flatly ruled out any possibility of compromise," and with "uncompromising tone," said, "There is no possibility whatsoever that we will remove the penalties imposed on certain students." (S. F. *Chronicle,* Oct. 3, under the headline: "Before the Agreement: Kerr Ruled Out Compromise!")

From every side it was dinned into the students' ears that "You can't win; give up." The *Daily Cal's* senior editorial board ran a special editorial assuring that:

> The administration has drawn the line at what it believes is the last concession on the university level. We completely believe they are telling the truth. Those who espouse oversimplified concepts of the issues and solutions will tell you otherwise. The university has drawn the last line it can.

There was an especially powerful "mediators' backlash." Kerr, an experienced labor mediator himself, was well aware that a skillful negotiator can turn mediators into instruments to convince the other side to yield, by first convincing the mediators that any further retreat on his part is out of the question. The mediators then go to the other side and say, "Look, we'll tip you off ..."

The mediator who particularly played this role actively was Professor Lipset, who took every opportunity to assure the student leaders that Kerr could not possibly afford to compromise since he would be fired from the presidency if he did so. Professor Nathan Glazer pressed the same argumentation, and had also spoken from the top of the car the day before with advice to surrender the blockade. In the middle of October 2, Lipset however abandoned his mediator role and was not involved when the actual *rapprochement* took place.

Early that morning, President Kerr and Chancellor Strong both agreed on mobilizing the police for action against the students. By 10:30 A.M., ranking officers of the campus police, Berkeley police, Oakland police, state Highway Patrol and the Alameda County sheriff's office were in Sproul Hall "at a three-hour session to hammer out the master plan" (as the Oakland *Tribune* said) for "the massive police effort." At five minutes to noon, direct representatives of Kerr and also of Governor Brown joined the session. The police were to be armed with pistols, billy-clubs and tear gas, and some were called in from as far as Vallejo. The largest number were from the Oakland police-known for what is called "toughness" by friends and "sadistic brutality" by critics-and from the

Highway Patrol, provided by the governor. This was a fairly wide United Front too.

An agreement was reached among the university representatives and police strategists for a 6 P.M. deadline, at which time Chancellor Strong would read a statement calling for dispersal—or else ... (It should be noted that a later tale, that this deadline was leveled by the police *against* the university, was not true.)

So the administration was all prepared, with a tough no compromise stand and with the police, clubs and tear gas to implement it. Tomorrow, Saturday, was—as luck would have it—to be "Parents Day," when the proud papas and mamas were due to overrun the campus to inspect the place where their progeny studied so hard. Kerr and Strong had to get the "mob" out of the plaza before then, one way or another. Their army of cops started mobilizing against the nonviolent army around the car.

But not all the mediators had given up, and new ones had gone to work in the morning. In addition to faculty members, the problem had reached local Democratic politicos. The latter were concerned as individuals, but in addition the Democratic administration in Sacramento was in it hip-deep. What would happen to the Liberal Image of the governor if this regiment of police were loosed on the kids in the plaza, with unpredictable consequences?

From the beginning Governor Brown had lined up with both feet—with both feet in the mouth as usual, some thought—on the side of the tough fire-breathing policy: "This is not a matter of freedom of speech on the campus," he claimed on Thursday, but "purely and simply an attempt on the part of the students to use the campus of the university unlawfully by soliciting funds. . . . This will not be tolerated." (Brown seemed to think there was *a law,* rather than a campus regulation, against soliciting funds.) Speaking at the American Council on Education meeting, he vowed that he was in favor of freedom of thought and would maintain it, adding: *"Even if we have to expel a few students from time to time."* He issued a statement that he "supports fully" the suspension of the eight students.

All through this tense Friday, Kerr remained in close telephone contact with the governor. A couple of Democratic politicos in the East Bay, informed by students that they wanted to deal with Kerr but could not get to him, seem to have had a hand in bringing about the negotiations that ensued, after considerable phoning around the state to party stalwarts. . The informal faculty group had been working in the same direction on campus. As late as 3 P.M. Strong still told the professors that he refused to negotiate with the students. But around 4 o'clock the students were given to understand that Kerr would finally deal with them, and a meeting at University Hall was set up for 5. The students were already prepared with a negotiation committee, chosen the previous day and now enlarged. The committee that went to see Kerr were, in terms of their personal affiliation, from: CORE, Independent Socialist Club, Slate, SNCC, Students for Democratic Society, Women for Peace, Young Democrats, Young Peoples Socialist League, Young Republicans—nine in all. In addition, the administration brought in the ASUC president, the *Daily Cal* editor, and representatives of the Inter-Faith Council.

The faculty mediators had drafted points for a pact, and the parley between the dual powers got under way.

## *15. The Pact of October 2*

By this time Kerr was facing the deadline he had helped to set.

Sproul Hall had become a seething fortress of armed men in uniform, who started crowding into the usually staid halls at the same time that Kerr began the meeting with the students. They were going to wait in the hot, stuffy corridors for two and a half hours, shedding their jackets from time to time, adjusting their riot helmets, giving their holsters a hitch. All of them were on overtime pay and the operation was costing from $2500 to $3000 per hour. The official word was that there were 450—500 police, but only the San Francisco *Examiner* (Hearst) reporters made a physical count and they reported almost a thousand—965 to be exact. Sheriff's buses and paddy wagons were lined up to take away the bodies.

If this army had been given the word to go against the mass of students in the plaza outside, it would not only have been a question of the hundreds sitting down, who would of course go limp when arrested. The best guess is that the battle plan which had been laboriously worked out called first for opening up a wide corridor between the building entrance and the car, so that the' arrested students could be carried into Sproul (where they would then be handled very much as in the proceedings of December 3, which is still ahead in our story).

This corridor would have had to be cut through an intervening crowd of a couple of thousand students, who were not themselves sitting down but who were jammed in between the building doors and the sitters, and who would be compressed even more by the movement of other thousands in the plaza toward the scene of action. If the thousands of standees were not all definitely sympathetic with the sitters, they were yet likely to be antagonistic to the armed police descending on them. The potentialities were further darkened by the incredible decision of the authorities that the police should carry this off with guns at hand, not to speak of tear gas.*

This was the picture that Kerr faced, and he did not like it. Perhaps the original decision to call in the police that morning had seemed like the routine thing to do; but this was the reality. The issues became

---

* Dr. Sidney Hook was going to raise his hands in horror at this situation in the *N.Y. Times Magazine* (Jan. 3, 1965), since it showed (my italics) "the extremism of the *student leaders,* the lengths to which *they* were willing to go—at one point, bloodshed and possible loss of life seemed imminent ..." How extremist of the students to compel the police to attack them carrying guns and tear gas! As the French saying has it: "Cet animal est si méchant: Quand on l'attaque, il se défend!" or "This animal's vicious, and that's a fact: He defends himself when he's attacked!" The *FSM Newsletter* later had a more philosophical comment: a cartoon showed a phalanx of burly cops, clubs at the ready and hands on gun-butts, giving the students the following advice: *"De ends don't justify de meansl"*

"negotiable" after all; compromise became possible after all; he found he had to talk with the "mob," or else face an even more unpleasant decision.

Meanwhile, back on the plaza, word of the impending action began to spread soon after 5. When I arrived about 5:30, the air over the plaza was electric. There were perhaps 300 sitting down now, in an irregular free-form area around the car; these were prepared to be arrested. The crowd was a solid wall circling this theater-in-the-round. The top of the car had been turned into a lecture platform on what to do till the policeman comes. Civil-rights veterans gave instructions on going limp, advised on what to get rid of (wrist watches, earrings, etc.), warned against linking arms or struggling with the cops. A lawyer gave information on legal rights. And time and again, student leaders would emphasize that no one should sit down unless he had really thought it through. Foreign students were advised not to join in; so were students of juvenile-court age (under 18). It was not being made easy to sit down.

The picture later drawn of this "hard core" as a legion of hardened radicals is good for a wry smile. My wife and I talked to the students sitting nearby with us: they had never been arrested, they had never participated in any political activity. Had we ever been arrested and what was it like? they asked apprehensively. We assured them we had, as if it were routine—though in fact we each had been arrested only once, in strikes.

They were sitting down only because they felt that they had to, that they would not be able to live with themselves if they did not. Yet everywhere we read afterward in the press that the students were in this for a lark ("civil rights panty raid"), or for a jape against the older generation.*

---

* A questionnaire was later distributed to those who had taken any part in the October 1-2 demonstrations, not necessarily by sitting down. Only 618 were filled—not a reliable cross section and probably weighted toward the more committed individuals. The results: over 70 per cent belong to no campus

(continued...)

Around 6:30, in response to appeals from the car top, a new wave of students who had been standing around the periphery decided to sit down. The irregular outline of the sit-down area extended a pseudopod closer to the police fortress that had once been the administration building. The sitters now numbered about 500. Night was falling.

In University Hall, the students' negotiating committee was considering a proposed agreement and adding a couple of points to those drafted by the faculty mediators. Kerr and Strong were in one room, the students in another discussing among themselves, and the faculty people literally acted as go-betweens.

One of the moves by the president had been to threaten the student negotiators with the unleashing of the police: at one point he gave them ten minutes to sign. This backfired; and Kerr assured them he would request the police not to move until the negotiations were over and the students had returned to the demonstration to report. But he insisted that he did not control the police, that the chiefs were restive, and that they might decide at some point to overrule him.*

Point 1 as drafted originally read: "The student demonstrators promise to abide by legal processes in their protest of university regulations." The students rejected this unlimited promise, and compromised on a statement which merely meant that the *present* demonstration would be lifted: "The student demonstrators shall *desist* from all forms of illegal protest against university regulations."

---

(...continued)
political organization; half had never before participated in any demonstrations.

* Among the errors in the Lipset-Seabury article in *The Reporter,* Jan. 28, 1965, was the statement that Kerr "had authority over them [the police]." Kerr himself stressed that this was not so. What is involved here is the argument by some faculty people like Professors Lipset and Feuer that the FSM demands would open the campus to the police. They ignore the fact that police invaded the campus twice, with authority not subject to the administration.

In return for this, three concessions were accepted by the students:

> 2. A committee representing students (including leaders of the demonstration), faculty and administration will immediately be set up to conduct discussions and hearings into all aspects of political behavior on campus and its control, and to make recommendations to the administration.
> 3. The arrested man will be booked, released on his own recognizance and the university will not press charges.
> 4. The duration of the suspension of the suspended students will be submitted within one week to the Student Conduct Committee of the Academic Senate.

Point 4 stated that the suspension cases would be put in the hands, not of the administration-appointed "Faculty Committee on Student Conduct," but of a committee of the Academic Senate which is autonomous of the administration. In addition the faculty mediators orally assured the student negotiators that it was understood the suspensions would be lifted right away.

Two more points were added to the agreement:

> 5. Activity may be continued by student organizations in accordance with university regulations.
>
> 6. The President of the University has declared his willingness to support deeding certain university property at the end of Telegraph Avenue to the City of Berkeley or to the ASUC. [This refers to the 26-foot sidewalk strip on Bancroft.]

Nine student signatures were affixed to the pact plus the signature of Clark Kerr. (Chancellor Strong did not sign.) The opposing sides, with their respective armies mobilized outside on the field, had signed a formal armistice—administration and students in "eyeball to eyeball" confrontation. It is doubtful that a similar scene had ever been enacted on an American campus before.

It was now 7:30, an hour and a half past the deadline originally set by the planners of the operation. The negotiating committee returned to the plaza, and Mario Savio, now in the glare of television camera lights, mounted the police car for the last time to present the Pact of October 2, to explain its provisions and why it had been accepted. Indicating serious dubiety in the minds of the student committee about the terms of the pact, he announced that there would be an open discussion meeting in Sproul Hall Plaza on Monday where views would be aired. Then he asked the students to leave the area "with dignity."

The police code 938 (cancel assignment) was flashed to the waiting units; the Oakland motorcycle cops roared away; the sheriff's troops formed ranks in Barrows Lane in the cool night air. The sitters arose and stretched. The crowd broke up and disintegrated, but knots of students gathered to discuss whether the pact should have been accepted. A couple of blocks away at the campus Greek Theater, a concert by Joan Baez was due to start after eight. We had bought tickets a week before, and the pact had come in the nick of time. In the open-sky circle of the theater, Joan Baez came on stage and said: "It's a fine night. The students have won. And I'm glad."

## *16. Enter Redbaiting*

> This new generation of student activists also has a new tactic—civil disobedience. The technique was developed for Alabama and Mississippi but is easily transferred. I misjudged the FSM's willingness to use

> this tactic. When we didn't give in to their early demands, they went to civil disobedience like that! They set up tables, they blocked the police car, they sat in. They took us completely by surprise. (Clark Kerr, in Jan. 5 interview.)

What took the administration completely by surprise, then, was the unexpected militancy and unconventionality of the students' fighting style. But there was far more about the "new generation of student activists" that the administrators did not understand. And it was even more of a mystery to the newspaper commentators who could oscillate only between "college kids on a tear" and "sinister Communist plot."

> Many administrators, like the press and the outside community, saw the protest as not much more than "a civil rights panty raid," as one administrator put it. The bearded, sandaled, longhaired students in the protest took on a great prominence in their eyes. Their rebellion against the administration, they believed, was no different than their rebellion against the conventions of dress and appearance. They did not take the political motives of the demonstrators very seriously. Some members of the administration, on the other hand, saw the demonstrations as anything but frivolous. In fact, they saw in them wider implications and broader goals than the students' professed aim of free speech. They saw them as the beginning of an attempt to turn Berkeley into a Latin American style university, where the students have a major, if not a predominant, say in determining all aspects of university life and policy. The leaders of the FSM, they believed, wanted to harness the student movement and the university itself to the

> cause of the particular social and political changes they sought. *(Graduate Political Scientists' Report.)*

Newspaper readers who saw only the specter of "beatniks" and "Communists" can be forgiven, since the press fed them little else. Photographers in some cases deliberately sought out the one or two bearded, longhaired students in a group; this was "color," and the majority of "respectable" looking boys and girls in the crowd were not news. That the administrators operated on basically the same intellectual level, however, was a more serious matter.

Relations between the administration and the students immediately after the Pact of October 2 were severely complicated by the redbaiting in which Kerr engaged.

Two San Francisco dailies quoted him on October 3 as saying that "Forty-nine per cent of the hard-core group are followers of the Castro-Mao line," but Kerr denied the accuracy of this quotation when asked personally and also later (December 1) denied it in the *Daily Cal;* there is no record, however, that he ever sent a public denial to the papers themselves. He had the benefit of letting the Hearst press's readership think him a properly "hard" Communist slayer while shaking off responsibility for the slander before the campus community.

To citizens sending in letters, he replied by enclosing an editorial from the Los Angeles *Times* as "a good analysis of a complex situation." The editorial charged that the demonstrators "were doing their best to embarrass the university and create `martyrs' for a cause that probably had little to do with the issue of free speech or the right to petition," and that "about half [of the activist group] reportedly weren't students at all, but off-campus meddlers." This editorial, which Kerr personally circulated, would leave little doubt of what off campus meddlers' "cause" was being hinted at. Kerr was also quoted in the press—accurately—as saying that "some elements have been impressed with the tactics of Fidel Castro and Mao Tse-tung." (He went on to add: "There are very few of these, but there are some." This was literally true: there were very few;

but in that case, what exactly was the point? There were also "very few" Goldwaterites, for example.)

A student neatly answered Kerr's implication that the students' tactics were borrowed from Castro or Mao, in a letter to the *Daily Cal.* He was glad to learn, he said ironically, that the Castroites had won in Cuba because they merely "picketed Batista's headquarters, set up illegal tables on the streets of Havana, and held sit-down demonstrations in front of tanks, singing freedom songs while waiting for the police to take them away." As we have seen, Kerr later found out that the students' tactics had been transferred from "Alabama and Mississippi."

On October 6 in Los Angeles, Kerr continued the barrage by telling a news conference that "up to 40 per cent of the hard-core participants" came from off-campus; he identified them as "very experienced and professional people ... tied in with organizations having Communist influences." These baseless charges were repeated on Kerr's authority by others, such as the president of Stanford University, and by the state and national press.*

The relation of radicalism to the FSM will be considered later, but it may be pointed out here that the real meaning of Kerr's esoteric reference to Mao and Castro followers was not generally appreciated. What it meant implicitly was that Kerr knew and admitted that the *Communist* Party—the minuscule one existing in the Bay Area, not the one in Cuba or China had decisively nothing to do with the outbreak of the student movement.

---

* Kerr later exonerated himself of the redbaiting charge in the following disingenuous terms. Replying to the "claim" that "the administration engaged in making improper charges," he answered: "I did say in October that, among the outsiders who turned up, some had been sympathetic with Communist causes. I consider this a statement of fact." But the pretense that this was all he had said, is not a statement of fact.

What many students resented particularly was the idea that the Communists should be given the credit for what they themselves had accomplished. It was another example of the fact that the Communists could depend on the redbaiters for their biggest boosts.

With the exception of Kerr and of the inevitable hoarse cries from Birchite and Republican-rightist politicians and editors, there were remarkably few in the situation who even hinted at "Communist domination" of the FSM. Even the *Reporter* account by Professors Lipset and Seabury limited itself to the insinuation that "the use of illegal tactics was part of a conscious effort by extremists to undermine faith in the democratic system." The main exception was Professor Lewis Feuer, who, swinging from the floor, charged that political and social activism on the campus was "a melange of narcotics, sexual perversion, — collegiate Castroism, and campus Maoism," in the best style of Billy Hargis, and that the FSM was a "Soviet-style coalition." But then, Feuer even came close to redbaiting Kerr himself, whose view of the Multiversity he dislikes: Kerr, he wrote, is "almost a 'neoMarxist' in his conception of the modem university's development," and his basic theory "converges strikingly with dialectical materialism"!*

But this runs ahead of our story.

## *17. The FSM Is Formed*

Up to this point, the student protest had been organized and led by a United Front of clubs. On the weekend after the pact, representatives of the clubs met and constituted the Free Speech Movement.

It was conceived of as a temporary fighting formation, not a permanent organization. The body of club representatives became the Executive Committee, and a smaller Steering Committee was elected as the day-to-day leadership. All were students, including suspended students, with the exception of Jack Weinberg.

---

*Feuer, "Rebellion at Berkeley," *New Leader,* December 21, 1964

To provide representation to the large number of students participating who were not members of any of the constituent clubs, a meeting was called for "Independents," attended by several hundreds, who elected representatives. A meeting called specifically for graduate students also elected representatives, and evolved into the Graduate Coordinating Committee. Separate recognition was accorded to the supporting non-students (largely student drop-outs) in the campus community, who were called to a meeting and got a representative too. Representatives were added also from religious organizations.

The Steering Committee, from October 10 on, consisted usually of ten to twelve members; the composition of the Executive Committee, with a membership in the fifties, also tended to fluctuate with the vicissitudes of the movement, as individuals dropped or assumed activity, and as groups (such as the Republicans) popped in and out of the structure. At the time the FSM was formed, the conservatives refused to join, although invited into both the Executive Committee and the Steering Committee.

The organizational work and life of the FSM was as fine an example of the organized—disorganized—unorganized as it is possible to imagine. The description of the movement as "highly efficient" by Lipset-Seabury and others is a testimonial to the impact of the FSM on the campus, but the knowledgeable description would have been only "remarkably effective." Especially at critical junctures, the organization of the FSM was often spontaneously ordered chaos.

The pattern of October 1-2 was partially operative even after the FSM was formally constituted. There were remarkable feats of what-appeared-to-be-organization accomplished during those two days: obtaining, setting up and servicing various items of loudspeaker equipment; canteen services; mass telephone campaigns; fund-raising (over $800 was collected right in the plaza), etc. But there was virtually no over-all organization.

Things were accomplished because hundreds of students threw themselves into the work spontaneously and somehow did it in clots of organization, with a furious amount of talk but also with overweening energy and will. Anyone could become a "leader," and the process was very simple and very visible: you *led,* and if you seemed to be doing any good, others followed with a will. This was true not only in the background tasks but also up front, on top of the car.

After the first week of the FSM's formal existence, the many jobs to be done were decentralized into separate working units called "centrals," set up in various students' apartments or other places. In the course of time there were Work Central, Legal Central, Press Central, Information Central, Newsletter Central, Archives Central, Picket Central, Command Central—and I seem to remember talk of a "Central Central." The speedy expansion of the FSM "bureaucracy" was a standing joke among the students, but, in my own contacts with the result, "efficiency" is the last word that would occur to me. A better approximation of the ambience can be gained from reading parts of John Reed's *Ten Days That Shook the World.*

The word "revolution" has been mainly applied to the Berkeley events by appalled observers rather than by FSM supporters, but the kernel of truth in the phrase lies in this: there was a massive upheaval from below, mounting in waves from the police-car blockade to the December sit-in and strike, which hurled hundreds and at some points thousands of newly energized students, previously non-political and nonactivist, into the conflict. It was literally *a rising,* if some overtones of this word are eliminated. Outsiders are likely to consider this a literary exaggeration, but, as the quotations preceding this history indicate, the authorities on the spot are not among them.

All of this was financed mainly through "passing the hat" among students, faculty and university staff, plus some parents and local businessmen. "The total expenditure of the FSM, from its organization on October 3 to the present (December 10)," says the *Graduate Political Scientists' Report,* "was approximately $2,000," spent almost entirely on publications, leaflets and other printing, loudspeaker equipment, meeting places, telephone, postage. This does not include the sums later collected by faculty people for bail money, nor the still later defense funds necessitated by the mass arrests.

As revolutions go, it was not expensive, except of time and heart.

## *18. Some Lessons in Good Faith*

By the Monday after the pact, October 5, when the promised discussion mass meeting assembled in Sproul Hall Plaza at noon, the sparks of student opposition to the settlement had faded and the meeting was more like a celebration. (Over 2000 attended even though Hubert Humphrey was speaking elsewhere on campus.) In the evening, too, there was no important opposition registered at a discussion meeting held by the Independent Socialist Club with Mario Savio, Jack Weinberg and the club's representatives to the Executive Committee; but there was considerable concern at both meetings with possible exaggeration of the interim "victory," since it was clear that the main battle was still ahead.

That this was a sober appreciation had already been underlined by the first move of the campus administration, made while everyone was still breathing a sigh of relief over the bloodless ending of the Friday confrontation. On Sunday it became known that Chancellor Strong had decided on the arrest of Mario Savio and the other suspended students if they spoke at the Monday noon meeting called for the very purpose of justifying the pact which they had signed with Ken.

It was an extraordinary decision, based on the equally remarkable premise that the suspended students were "outside speakers" who required 72 hours' notice and would be "trespassing" otherwise: a clear augury of the future course of the administration. Now that the "mob" had demobilized, Strong calculated, it was time for the authorities to use the iron fist.

Through the small hours and into most of Monday morning, a group of faculty members worked on Strong to call off the planned provocation, but it was not until 20 minutes before the noon meeting opened that the administration agreed to a "special waiver" of the rules to let the suspended students talk. (The next day, the waiver was continued indefinitely.) Meanwhile the FSM Steering Committee had decided that Mario Savio and the others should *not* speak if threatened with arrest, but greeted the reversal as a "substantial victory."

It is undoubtedly true that heavy pressure was being exerted from the outside for a tough line by the administration. Local politicians were striking "anti-Communist" poses, and the Hearst press openly called for expulsion of the student leaders. Governor "Pat" Brown, despite his "liberal image," was also understood to be nettled at the failure of the administration to unleash the police army on the students, and showed his disgruntlement publicly in a statement about "the rule of law" and a prickly exchange of notes with Kerr.*

On the other side, outside support for the students came from a statement by James Farmer, national head of CORE, from sympathy demonstrations and statements by groups at other colleges throughout the country, and, most important at the moment, from the Association of California State College Professors. The latter declared:

> The Executive Committee of the ASCP believe that student participation in social action is consistent with our constitutionally guaranteed freedoms and contributes to the educational process. Therefore, whether it is political or non-political, it ought not only to be permitted, but to be actively encouraged, so long as it does not interfere with the regular instructional program, even if it involves persons from off-campus who are invited to participate by students and faculty members. Consequently, the

* Months later, Brown was asked in a radio interview (KPFA, March 28) why there had been no arrests on October 2, in contrast with the mass arrest on December 3. "I don't know why they weren't arrested [in October]," he answered. "They [the authorities] didn't call on me for any help or they might have been."

> Executive Committee of the ASCP supports all University of California students and student groups, whatever their social or political commitments, in their efforts to bring about the repeal of these rules against political action.

The threatened arrests, on the heels of Kerr's disturbing public statements, made the students increasingly suspicious of the administration's good faith. Next came what seemed to the students, and others, an open flouting of Point 4 of the Pact of October 2. This had called for the suspension cases to be "submitted within one week to the Student Conduct Committee of the Academic Senate."

The administration now announced that such a committee did not exist: there was no such committee of the Academic Senate, even though it had been suggested by faculty members in the course of the October 2 negotiations! Of course it was not the students who could have been expected to know that the suggested committee was a figment.

This was bizarre enough, but the remedy was clear: the Academic Senate need only establish such a committee in order to fulfill the agreement. But the administration immediately announced that, since the committee named did not exist, the suspension cases would be taken up by the only committee which did exist—namely, the same administration appointed committee on student conduct which the pact had pointedly *not* assigned to the task.

A personal incident may help here to underline the meaning of this administration claim. When the blockade was lifted on Friday and before we hurried away to the Greek Theater concert, I had gotten into a short exchange with some students whose immediate reaction to the pact was "Sellout!" Arguing on the spot that the agreement was an acceptable victory-for-the-moment, I was able to dwell on Point 4. While it was obviously a compromise—the suspensions were not thereby lifted—it was important that the case was being taken out of the hands of the administration and handed to the Academic Senate instead. Now the administration was claiming that this compromise had never really been made.

Even the *Daily Cal* denounced the administration stand and pointed to the obvious solution. A very large number of faculty members were incensed. The American Civil Liberties Union intervened on this point too. The suspended students refused to appear before the chancellor's committee. Their immediate reinstatement was urged by a petition signed by 88 faculty members.

Kerr publicly took the floor to back up the campus administration's stand. In a statement issued October 8 he maintained that the committee name used in the Pact of October 2 was "a misnomer . . . I did not catch the misstatement at the time, nor did anyone else," and he asserted that Strong was acting in "good faith." However, Kerr had stood listening when Mario Savio, reading the terms of the pact from the top of the car, had stressed in so many words that the cases were *not* being referred to the administration appointed committee. Apparently he did not catch this statement either. It looked as if both Kerr and Strong were going to insist on putting the thing across.

But they buckled within the next week in the face of the gathering wave of disapprobation. Ironically perhaps, one factor in bringing this about was a move by Professors Lewis Feuer and Nathan Glazer, who were going to become two of the bitter-end enemies of the FSM.

Having been among the faculty mediators who had helped arrange the pact, and considering the Kerr-Strong stand as a piece of needless stupidity if not bad faith, Feuer and Glazer composed a joint letter to the *Daily Cal* which, among other things, spread on the record a fact most embarrassing to the administration. The letter testified that, during the negotiations on the pact, *the faculty mediators had assured the students that, even though it would not be written down, the agreement meant that the suspensions would be lifted pronto.*

Rather, the letter would have spread this on the public record if it had been published. But, immediately on sending the letter to the paper, the two authors were subjected to personal pressure—by Professor Lipset, for one—to withdraw it or at least postpone publication until it could be ascertained whether Kerr had known of the assurances. The letter itself was never in fact published, but its existence undoubtedly provided additional reason for the administration to back away from its stand.*

This was so because publication of the letter would have undercut more than the administration stand on the immediate question of "Which committee?" It would have set up at least a moral obligation to lift the suspensions right away, and would have borne strongly on the recommendation to do exactly that, later made by the Heyman Committee, which the administration summarily rejected. The revelation in this letter was never made known to the university community by any of the faculty mediators who on October 2 had used those assurances to pressure the student negotiators into signing. The FSM itself never tried to make any capital out of this, but a history of the affair has a different obligation.

The upshot was that, over Chancellor Strong's objection, Kerr finally decided to capitulate to the proposed solution the assignment of the suspension cases to an *ad hoc* committee to be established by the Academic Senate—but with the proviso that this committee would be advisory to the administration. It was accomplished in the form of a communication by Kerr (not Strong) to the October 15 meeting of the Academic Senate; a motion by Professor Arthur Ross to the effect was

---

* This account is based on Feuer's statements to me around the time the letter was sent. Lipset maintains that he urged Feuer only to postpone the letter till Kerr could be contacted. The editor of the *Daily Cal* says that, to the best of her recollections, the last instructions from Feuer were to hold up the letter till further notice, which never came. Glazer thinks this might possibly be so. Feuer insists that he postponed but never withdrew the letter, and expected publication from day to day. However, he admits that he never complained about or followed up the non-publication of the letter. Neither the authors nor the *Daily Cal* office can now find their copies of the letter. According to Feuer, Kerr had indeed known about the assurances, but this question is obscure.

passed without dissent. The committee so established was the Heyman Committee.

## *19. Standoff on "Fee Speech"*

A parallel tug of war with the administration went *on* during the same two weeks over the implementation of Point 2 of the pact: the joint student-faculty-administration committee to make new proposals for the regulation of political activity on the campus, that is, of the basic "free speech" aspect of the conflict.

The first hang-up can be summarized in the complaint formulated in an FSM leaflet:

> President Kerr assured us [in the October 2 negotiations] that he would consider carefully our recommendations for members to sit on this committee, and told us that we had to have some trust in the administration ... yet when the FSM tried to contact him during the weekend with its recommendations, he was consistently unavailable. Monday morning [October 5] the names of the committee members appeared in the newspapers.

Both Kerr and Strong, the students charged, refused to discuss with them any questions about the committee's composition, structure, procedures, powers, etc. Instead, unilaterally and without consultation, the administration went ahead to appoint not only the four administration representatives on the committee, but also all four of the faculty representatives, and two out of four of the student representatives, leaving two places for the students who represented the committee's reason for existence.

There was undoubtedly bureaucratic precedent for this, within the framework of the administration's habitual mode of operation, but for a campus community which was beginning to take a second look at precisely these modes, the action touched off a strong reaction. Besides the claim of the students that the decisions as a whole should have been taken after consultation with them, there were two other questions about the administration's position that it had to appoint faculty and student representatives. Shouldn't representatives of the faculty be named by the faculty, organized in the Academic Senate, and if the Academic Senate could not do even this, what meaning did it have? Shouldn't student representatives be named by the student government, at least in the opinion of those who claimed that the ASUC had meaning as student government?

The FSM's claim to be consulted was also formulated in the following "trade union" terms:

> It was only through massive pressure that the university finally recognized representatives of the student demonstrators as bargaining agents. The FSM is, in essence, seeking to continue as a bargaining agent on behalf of the students, in defense of the first amendment. *(FSM Newsletter, No. 1.)*

Instead, the administration announced in the press that the Committee on Campus Political Activity (CCPA) would meet the next day on October 7. Instead of designating two representatives, an FSM delegation read a statement at the meeting and walked out. The statement refused to recognize the legitimacy of the meeting, on the ground that the administration was insisting on being the sole arbiter and unilateral judge of the interpretation and implementation of an agreement which, after all, had been made between two parties. An FSM leaflet declared that the behavior of the administration was *de facto* proof that the committee was being set up simply as a formal fulfillment of the pact but would not engage in meaningful negotiations.

The following Monday a meeting between FSM representatives and the chancellor got nowhere. The next day, October 13, saw an evening "open hearing" called by the administration-appointed CCPA to give all students an opportunity to discuss the work of the committee simply by signing up to testify. Several hundred attended (variously estimated at 300-500). Out of fifty students who spoke, all but one echoed the FSM position. Mario Savio received an ovation when he urged the committee to disband, attacking the administration's regulations on political activity as the "symbolic embodiment of the paternalism that we must fight at every step."

It looked like a standoff.

On October 13 also, the Academic Senate (Berkeley Division) met for the first time since the fight began. Its performance was not stirring.

A very general motion was adopted directing its Committee on Academic Freedom to inquire into the issues in conflict, together with an obeisance in one direction to "maximum freedom for student political activity," and in the other a bow to the administration ("general improvement in recent years in the atmosphere," etc.). A more significant action was the defeat of two attempts to amend in the direction of implied condemnation of the students' demonstration, particularly the defeat of a motion by Professor William Petersen to qualify "maximum freedom" by "within the law." The rationale was a refusal to take any "action which might be construed as condemnation or condonation of any action" in the conflict, say the minutes. However, a Lipset-Petersen motion was passed which did imply condemnation of the FSM's refusal to participate in the CCPA.

The meeting was adjourned until the 15th. If the students had had any hope that the faculty would come in to save the situation, there was little ground for further illusions.

As a matter of fact, the next session on the 15th effectually reversed the one vote of the 13th which might have cheered the students. It had become known that Kerr was "disturbed" by the vote of the Academic Senate turning down the qualification "within the law" after "maximum freedom." He also let it be known that he felt this vote was a repudiation of his policy and that it should be reversed. A couple of days of busy work ensued to line up votes for such a reversal, by Lipset and others. Sure enough, on the 15th, a motion was introduced by Professor Frank Newman, referring to the previous motion and adding: "Whereas the attitude of the Division has been widely misunderstood as condoning lawlessness, Now therefore this body reaffirms its conviction that force and violence have no place on this campus." This resolution against sin was carried, and Kerr was appeased. But in between the two sessions there *had* been a break in the apparent impasse. On October 14 the FSM decided that it was through with the run-around which, it felt, it had been getting from the administration; that it was high time to end the moratorium on direct action. It prepared a proclamation for the next day which began, "Where does the FSM stand today?" and answered:

> With great reluctance, the FSM Executive Committee must announce that we've just about had it. For almost two weeks now we've been shuffled back and forth through the maze of the university's bureaucracy and have encountered nothing more than a clear indication on the part of the administration that they are willing to do nothing more than keep us shuffling .. .

And after a two-page account of the run-around, it concluded:

> We have been playing the administration's game: it's called bureaucracy, and we're *it.*
> *Unless we get some clear indication by 5* P.M. *today [i.e.* Oct. 15] *that the administration is not playing, we cannot but conclude that we have been taken.* What would constitute a clear indication? Almost anything substantive, almost anything that is not just another stall. Even if we just get permission to present our case to the Regents

> tomorrow, are granted just one hour of their time, we will be appeased, at least for the moment. If, however, all doors remain shut, we cannot but conclude that *the pact of October 2 has been voided.*

The reference to the Regents was to the fact that the board was going to be meeting in Davis (near Sacramento), and the FSM was planning a car and bus "caravan," followed by a student vigil outside the meeting, to help put its viewpoint before the body.*

The very fact that the FSM was starting to move toward direct action got a galvanized response from administration circles even before the end of the day, that is, even before the drafted proclamation came out as a leaflet. (The reaction came, probably, via one of the professors who had tried that afternoon to argue the FSM committee out of its intentions.) Late that night, Professor Arthur Ross, a long-time associate of Kerr's, phoned to present himself as a mediator, and, beginning after midnight and through the night, met with the FSM committee to essay a compromise.

We have already mentioned that, at the Academic Senate session of October 15, it was Professor Ross who made the motion which set up the Heyman Committee on the issue of the suspensions, once Kerr had capitulated on the nature of the committee. But the more difficult issue was the refusal of the FSM to recognize the CCPA as the arena in which to work out the substantive questions of "free speech" on campus. The upshot of Ross's mediation on October 15 was an agreement to revamp and enlarge the CCPA.

---

* There has been no clear report of what took place at this Regents' meeting, though the secretary to the board, a Miss Woolman, did tell reporters two months later that "It was a rather wild one, I'll have to admit." In violation of its own regulations, the Regents' meetings were not open to the public or press.

The new CCPA would consist of six (instead of four) from each of the three sides represented. The student delegation would consist of the two named by the administration plus *four* named by the FSM. The two additional faculty representatives would be appointed by the Academic Senate, not the administration; and the two additional administration men would represent the state-wide administration. The FSM also got the right to have five observers and an attorney present but silent. All findings and recommendations would be by consensus of the three blocs.

Encouraged to believe that something might now come of the negotiations, the FSM called off the caravan sortie to the Board of Regents and issued an optimistic leaflet headlined "A Major Battle Won." After all, the administration had been educated to one thing at least: less than two weeks before, it had unilaterally set up the old CCPA with a fine disdain of going through the motions of consulting the students on implementation of the pact. Now, at least, even if through the back door of Professor Ross's mediation, it had recognized that it could not get away with such an approach.

Another crisis had been surmounted, but the optimism did not last long.

## *20. Hidden Battle over Civil Rights*

Students' hopes that there would be any real change in the administration's style were dashed by a number of minor things and one big thing, in the course of the next two or three weeks.

The eight suspended students were still suspended. On October 21 the Heyman Committee of the Academic Senate, charged with the cases, addressed a letter to the chancellor requesting temporary reinstatement of the students pending a decision. The request of the committee was summarily denied. (This, even though by this time there could be no doubt that the administration was fully aware of the assurances which had been given by the faculty mediators in the October 2 negotiations.)

There was a two-day furor over a science club, Particle Berkeley, which decided to send delegates to the FSM. The administration toughly announced that this act would force it off-campus; then, in the face of general indignation, reversed itself, mainly because its technical argument would have had to be that "free speech" on campus was an "off-campus issue."

The *FSM Newsletter,* No. 4, cited another case. Campus CORE was told by the dean's office that it could not use any "Hyde Park" area: "By a new clarification, we find that they are intended for impromptu speeches by individuals, not recognized campus groups." When CORE informed the dean that it was going to hold the rally, . anyway, permission was granted.

In the course of his mediation efforts on October 15, Professor Ross had assured the FSM that Kerr would issue a public statement indicating an intention to give careful consideration to the findings of the new CCPA. Instead, the only statement issued by Kerr was another blast about non-students and Communists in the FSM. Ross declined to take any responsibility for setting the record straight about the agreement, and the FSM denounced this as an abdication of his moral responsibility.

In fact, instead of Kerr's looking forward to the work of the new CCPA at all, the FSM charged, "Our attorneys have since discovered that the Regents have had legislation drafted which would make certain forms of demonstrations on campus misdemeanors, and that President Kerr has already had the regulations governing political activity on campus completely revised—before the CCPA has made any recommendations!"

The latter charge was based on the disclosure (through a photostatic copy obtained by the FSM) that the university's general counsel, Thomas Cunningham, had prepared a letter, signed with Kerr's typed name, which proposed the following new regulation: "University facilities may not be used for the purpose of recruiting participants for unlawful off-campus action." Kerr had not signed it but it was under discussion. Although dated October 13-before the CCPA got under way-it was essentially this formulation which was later adopted by the Regents, as we shall see.

Within the new CCPA, a proposal that *all* substantive matters be decided by consensus only was voted down; so also were a proposal to set up temporary regulations on political activity for the duration of the negotiations, and a proposal that FSM counsel be permitted to question witnesses on points of law.

The students began to feel entrapped "in a widening and deepening morass of red tape, committees and *ad hoc* negotiations" (as the FSM's October 28 leaflet said). What ensured the next crisis, however, was the course of the CCPA discussions on the basic "free speech" question, that is, the regulation of political activity on campus.

The administration delegation unveiled a new version (Version No. 4) of the "historic policy." The originally invented distinction between "advocacy" and "information," which had largely led to the whole imbroglio, was as dead as a mutton. Nor was there objection any more to "mounting social and political action on campus" for off-campus purposes, as such. The whole administration position of September, which had been insisted on as "non-negotiable," "historic," and constitutionally fixed, was now down the drain.*

The formulation supported by the students in the CCPA went like this:

---

* For example, Chancellor Strong had stated on October 1: "Some students demand on-campus solicitation of funds and planning and recruitment of off-campus social and political action. The university cannot allow its facilities to be so used without endangering its future as an independent educational institution." This, like all the policy statements of that period, was unqualified as to unlawful action. It was not the unlawfulness of a particular action that the administration was then concerned about, but the politicalness of any action. By November, the administration had learned that political action on campus did not endanger the university; but its spokesmen, from Kerr down, never made an attempt to explain how this discovery took place. We can assume that they did not become converted to this opinion simply by listening to the speeches from the top of the car.

> The advocacy of ideas and acts which is constitutionally protected off the campus should be protected on the campus. By the same token, of course, speech which is in violation of law and constitutionally unprotected should receive no greater protection on the campus than off the campus.

They specified, in terms reflecting the position of the American Association of University Professors and the American Civil Liberties Union:

> In the area of First Amendment rights and civil liberties, the university may impose no disciplinary action against members of the university community and organizations. In this area members of the university community and organizations are subject only to the civil authorities.

The administration, however, needed something else: some ground for holding the threat of *university* penalties (e.g.,expulsion) over students engaged in off-campus political action of the kind they wished to stop. Its formulation went through different versions, but the last one in the CCPA was this:

> If acts unlawful under California or federal law directly result from advocacy, organization, or planning on the campus, the students and organizations involved may be subject to such disciplinary action as is appropriate and conditioned upon fair hearing as to the appropriateness of the action taken.

The difference involved was fairly stated by the following summary in the *Graduate Political Scientists' Report:*

> Now advocacy would be permitted, but the university reserved the right to discipline students if speech on campus led to illegal acts committed off the campus. The administration reserved the right to decide whether the speech on campus led to the illegal act off campus. The students argued that the courts were the only ones who could decide whether the speech itself was illegal; if it were, the civil authorities were justified in taking action; if the speech itself were not found to be illegal, then the university would not be justified in disciplining a student. The students feared that the university would press charges against speakers on far less substantial grounds than would a court of law; they believed that even with a full measure of due process written into administrative hearings the full range of case law as applied in the courts would not be applicable. At no time did the students demand the right of illegal speech, as the administration at times charged. They rather demanded that the courts alone be left to judge whether speech was or was not protected under the Constitution.

Further formulations by administration people tightened up one aspect of their position. The question was raised whether they would themselves presume to determine that a given off campus action was illegal or wait for determination to be made by the courts. An interpretation by the chancellor on November 7 conceded the latter alternative. "There will be no prior determination of double jeopardy," he stated.

But would it mean posterior determination of "double jeopardy"? The term was widely used by the students, and just as often shown to be legally inapplicable, since (it was pointed out) a crime and a conspiracy to commit the crime are technically two separate acts and separately punishable. Be that as it might, the double punishment (by both the courts and the university) seemed unfair and vindictive to many.

The concession that the off-campus act had to be determined as unlawful by the courts did not, of course, erase the basic vice of the administration position from the students' viewpoint. How would it be determined whether the unlawful action off-campus "directly resulted" from on-campus planning? If a CORE meeting on campus advocated that the Oakland *Tribune* be picketed, and if an unlawful act later occurred at the picket line, could the administration take the opportunity (if there were enough outside pressure on it) to penalize anyone connected with CORE or its meeting? Or suppose the CORE meeting advocated a sit-in at the Bank of America, would that be enough for the chancellor to crack down, even though sit-ins have not been found by the courts to be illegal *ipso facto?*

At this point, the whole conflict came down from the clouds of legal and administrative abstraction and into a simple framework: Wasn't it true, then, that the administration's main aim, through all of its shifting versions, was to prevent students from carrying out civil-rights direct action in the community?

A public answer in the affirmative was given by Professor Lipset (notoriously close to the administration, particularly to Kerr, who leans upon him as a brain truster) and Seabury in their *Reporter* article: the administration and Regents insisted on their "right to prohibit *organized* efforts to prepare illegal off-campus activities—a restriction aimed primarily at the organization of civil-rights sit-ins." The authors seem to assume that sit-ins are necessarily illegal.*

---

* The same assumption was implicitly made by Governor Brown, in a radio interview (KPFA, March 28, 1965) in which he revealed that he was against sit-ins even in the South. Sit-ins, said the liberal image of the California Democratic Party, should not be advocated "by any student at the university. Now what form of discipline it should take I don't know, but if they want to advocate any illegal act they should get off the campus ..."

It was also publicly charged by Mario Savio, at a campus meeting, that in the CCPA the administration spokesmen—particularly Vice-Chancellor Searcy—had stressed one argument:

> that the university is subject to external, extra-legal pressures and that it must have some way of responding to these pressures so that it be protected. That means to me [Savio went on to say] the due process you get or the consideration given the hearing by the chancellor, or both, will vary roughly inversely as the external pressures.*

In this connection the FSM leader also quoted another administration representative, Dean Kidner, who told an ASUC meeting: "I am not here to defend either the wisdom or the justice of this position but only to present this position." (When he found that radio station KPFA was taping the session and had recorded his remarks, he insisted on having the tape sequestered for editing.)

The clear stand by the FSM that any actions on or off campus were subject to the civil authorities—in fact, their insistence that in the area of First Amendment rights political action be subject *only* to the civil authorities—did not stop detractors from charging it with just the opposite. Professor Lewis Feuer wrote that "The student activists . . .

---

* For example, the following statement by the vice-chancellor on October 29 is recorded in the incomplete minutes of the CCPA that are available: "The major point is opportunity to mount political action from the campus. You want to be able to use campus facilities for meetings and go from meetings to form picket lines in some nearby area on some point that you feel strongly about. You cannot do that without involving the university in the eyes of the community. This makes it very difficult for the university to abstain from interfering with your rights." So the administration preferred to interfere with student rights rather than resist pressure from the community. There is also a relevant statement by Searcy in the minutes for October 28.

insisted that the university grounds should be available for organizing illegal activities." In truth the student activists insisted on just the reverse: accountability for illegal acts on campus to the civil government and the courts. Besides, this charge contradicts another of Feuer's complaints: that the FSM policy meant opening the campus up to the police, who would have to come in to enforce the civil authority as demanded by the students.

*Life* magazine (January 22, 1965), on the other hand, probably did not know what it was about when it paraphrased Kerr as saying that the FSM would make the university "a sanctuary for fugitives from the police, as so often has happened at Caracas." The editorialist was perhaps taking off from a statement made by Kerr in a January 5 interview, but Kerr had been more canny:

> "We cannot allow conspiracies to commit illegal acts off campus to be organized on campus," Kerr said. "The campus cannot be a sanctuary, but the question is whether punishment should be by the courts or by campus authorities."

One can see why his ambiguous formulation confused the *Life* editorialist into making his boner.

The reality behind all these charges was, however, simply the threat of civil-rights actions by students. And the administration wanted to be able to scotch this threat by constituting itself the legislature, executive, judge, jury, and . hangman, all in one.

## *21. Return to Direct Action*

By the beginning of November, the FSM was thoroughly disillusioned with the results of what it had hailed in mid-October as "A Major Battle Won," the Ross compromise:

> We do not know how long the already established committees will take and we do not even know that the administration will listen to their decisions. But let it be known that we can be stopped only by so many detours before the road begins to lead nowhere, and then there will remain only one road, that of direct action.
>
> We continue to meet in growing frustration and with deepening doubts as to the value of the committee proceedings .. .
>
> Perhaps we should not have moved on October 2. Perhaps our subsequent demands should have been stronger, our subsequent position firmer. If our greatest weakness was letting our hands be tied, then we must make this greatest weakness our greatest lesson.
>
> We repeat: when the morass of mediation becomes too thick to see through, action must let in the light. *(FSM Newsletter,* No. 3, Nov. 2, 1964.)

On November 5 an FSM picket line of a few hundred was before Sproul Hall protesting the administration's policy. During the course of the CCPA meetings, the administration declared that its position was "final, that is, that there was no longer any possibility of meaningful negotiations. The administration was reverting to take-it-or-leave-it. The FSM reacted accordingly:

> When it became apparent that the administration was not prepared to allow for these [constitutional] rights [of the 1st and 14th Amendments], when we realized that continued negotiations would make for little gains but for much time, when days turned into weeks and disagreements into deadlocks, then it became necessary

> to return to the power of numbers, of voices, of action.[*]
> (*FSM Newsletter,* No. 4, Nov. *17,* 1964.)

After much debate at a meeting on November 7, the FSM decided to return to direct action on November 9, that is, to exercise its constitutional rights on campus directly, as it saw fit. For the first time since October 2, the students once again set up tables in deliberate violation of the still extant regulations against fund-raising, recruiting or mounting off-campus political action—regulations which had been impugned by all sides in the CCPA but which were still officially in force.

There were eight or ten tables lined up at the foot of Sproul Hall steps, set up by clubs participating in FSM. At noon, occupying approximately the spot where 'the police car had tarried, was a battered chest-of-drawers serving as a rostrum, from which we addressed the crowd on what was happening. There were three professors among the speakers that day. One was Professor John Leggett of Sociology: taking off from Kerr's rumblings about "Maoists" among the students, he showed the basic analogy between the Mao regime's repressions of intellectuals and the Kerr regime's attitude toward campus political activity.

At 12:25 Mario Savio was speaking from the improvised podium when he interrupted himself to say, "I see a couple of little deans coming. Welcome, gentlemen!" Assistant deans Rice and Murphy returned cursory nods and walked to the end of the line of tables. As each "table-manner" was interrogated, the conversation went something like this, in outline:

* Or as Thomas Paine had put it, "Every quiet method of peace hath been ineffectual. Our prayers have been rejected with disdain; and have tended to convince us that nothing flatters vanity or confirms obstinacy in kings more than repeated petitioning..." This had been quoted in *FSM Newsletter, No. 2.*

Dean: Are you manning this table?
—: Yes.
Dean: Are you collecting money?
—: I'm accepting contributions.
Dean: Do you have a permit?
—: No.
Dean: Do you know that you are violating a school rule?
—: I know that the school rule is unconstitutional.
Dean: Will you cease this action?
— No.
Dean: Will you identify yourself?

In almost all cases, the table-manner identified himself, but exceptions were *not* arrested that day. As soon as his name was taken, someone else took his place, and the performance was repeated. After taking some 75 names, and even though lines were still formed to replace the cited students at the tables, the deans refused to take any more and retired.

Over eight hundred students signed statements declaring that they too had manned tables.

This was probably the first time that a dean's interrogation was broadcast as it took place. For the first few interrogations, the microphone which had been used by the speakers was brought over to the table with the action, so that the crowd could hear what was going on, while a student MC'd the proceedings. Then the rally continued. Distinguished visitors present were involuntarily, introduced to the assembly, including some gentlemen from the Berkeley "Red Squad," the district attorney's office and the FBI, as well as Berkeley's mayor.

On the following day, November 10, a new wave of "direct constitutional action" hit the plaza. The reinforcements consisted of nearly 200 Teaching Assistants and graduate students (a substantial proportion of the TA staff), who manned tables in the area with placards identifying themselves by the various departments they represented. This action had been decided on the day before at a meeting of the Graduate Coordinating Committee.

This time no deans appeared; but the students carefully sent a list of their names to the administration. The signers were insisting on equal responsibility for violating the rules. "They must either take all of us or none of us," argued Mario Savio. The tables were set up in the plaza on the following days also. A set of provisional "Regulations Governing the Use of Tables on Campus" was distributed by the FSM, with the explanation: "The legitimacy of these regulations is based on the consent of those that they govern."

The immediate reaction of the administration (Kerr and Strong jointly) was to declare the CCPA dissolved on the ground that the Pact, of October 2 had been broken, and to threaten "penalties." Then on the evening of November 11 the chancellor's office announced that disciplinary action was planned against those table-manners whose names had been taken. On the 11th, a meeting of 300 TA's discussed the organization of a TA trade union (which was going to come into being, in fact, toward the end of December), and on the 16th the dean's office rumbled that the graduate students who had listed themselves as manning tables would receive letters.* Attention began to concentrate on the Regents' meeting scheduled to take place on the Berkeley campus on November 19-20.

But at this point a flashback is necessary to "another part of the forest."

The FSM's return to militant action had not been achieved without a serious internal crisis. As frustration and dissatisfaction with the administration run-around mounted in the FSM leadership, a bifurcation

* The letters turned out to be an effort by the administration to shelve the problem. The student was told that if he did *not* respond, he would be assumed innocent Hence the mass response of the recipients, insisting that they had violated regulations, was a reiteration of solidarity.

between "moderates" and "militants" showed itself—a division which cut across many other lines of political differences and club affiliations.

The issue at this point was concrete: whether to continue in the maze of negotiations and committee-mongering with the administration, or to go to direct action (open violation of the rules at the tables). The moderates, led by Brian Turner and the Young Democrats, wished to prolong the status quo without alarms or threats. The militants argued that the movement was visibly bogging down, losing its steam; that by the time the negotiations were exhausted without result the energies of the students would be exhausted too; the fight would peter out in a cloud of red tape and technicalities; the FSM had to return to the weapons of militancy before it was too late.

At its November 7 meeting, the FSM Executive Committee re-examined the whole question of tactics, before deciding on the return of the tables. It also re-elected its Steering Committee, in order both to drop members who had seldom come to meetings and to strengthen the militancy of its composition in accordance with the policy adopted. Some known for moderate tactical views failed of election, and the balance swung strongly to the militant wing.

In this alignment, political views were only a partial factor. It was notorious in the FSM that the leadership of the DuBois Club (pro-Communist) leaned strongly toward moderate tactics, though a representative went along with the militant line; SNCC too was split (Mario Savio vs. Turner), as were other groups to one extent or another, not to speak of independents. Slate was mainly moderate; SDS (Students for Democratic Society) was divided. On the other hand, CORE was quite homogeneously militant, along with the Independent Socialist Club (left-wing socialist) and the Trotskyist club. At the other end of the spectrum, the leaders of the Young Democrats, the Young Republicans, and the Young Peoples Socialist League (right-wing social-democratic on this campus) were consistently moderate.

Two dissentient moves developed out of this internal crisis. The moderate wing, feeling that the reactivation of the tables on November

9 would lead to disaster (a draconic crackdown by the administration and possibly mass expulsions, etc.), demanded an emergency meeting of the Executive Committee. The meeting took place on the morning of the 10th and, after a stormy discussion, decisively upheld the Steering Committee policy, 29-17.

More dangerous, however, was another move, by a part of the moderate group who, precisely at this delicate juncture, held two secret meetings with Kerr in an attempt at a deal with the administration behind the backs of the FSM Steering Committee.

When they came out of the bitter November 10 meeting at which the moderates were defeated, the social democrats (YPSL and Democratic Socialist Club) went to Professor Lipset with their view of the state of affairs. Lipset phoned Kerr and set up a meeting for later the same day. At this meeting at Lipset's house, with the social democrats and a Young Democrat leader, Kerr urged the moderates to precipitate an open break in the FSM so that he could have a "realistic" group to deal with. The moderates replied that they were willing to undermine the FSM provided Kerr gave concessions on the "free speech" issue. They left the meeting believing that Kerr had agreed to or was seriously considering concessions, happily planning how to put the deal across in the FSM or else split it. But at a second meeting the next day—comprising ten moderates, this time including Young Republicans also, meeting with Kerr and Vice President Bolton—they discovered in considerable disillusionment that Kerr talked as if there were no concessions to be made at all. As one of the social-democratic participants said indignantly afterward: "He wanted us to sell out without even offering anything!"*

Nothing came of the episode after all, except the discrediting of the participants among FSM supporters.

---

* The facts in this account are based on information supplied to me by participants: Lipset, R. Roman, Jo Freeman.

The threatening breach in the FSM, however, was repaired by the end of the week, especially since Kerr and Lipset had not proved capable of taking advantage of the situation. The change may have been triggered by the fact that, just at this juncture, the Heyman Committee issued its long awaited report, dated November 12 and made known the next day. At the FSM's noon rally in Sproul Hall Plaza on the 13th, there were tones of gratification and optimism for the first time in weeks.

The Heyman Committee not only sharply criticized the procedures and policies of the administration in imposing the eight suspensions on September 30 but recommended that the record of six of the students be changed to show merely censure, not suspension. (It was noted also that the committee directed its report to the Academic Senate which had established it, not to the administration. Kerr and Strong condemned this, and the committee back watered on the 17th.)

The day after the report came out, the S.F. *Chronicle* reported:

> The Free Speech Movement, which normally criticizes the administration, was meanwhile expressing optimism that the dispute ... would be settled.
> Savio told a noon rally . that . . . Kerr "is finally seeing our side of the question. Maybe we can settle this and dissolve the Free Speech Movement."

By the end of that week, FSM unity was shored up when the Executive Committee restored one moderate to the Steering Committee and added another moderate and a conservative.

Even the ASUC president issued a statement affirming that "The ASUC Senate supports the ideals and freedoms sought by the FSM" and that it was "in substantial accordance" with its objectives, though it disagreed on the means employed (violation of regulations). The Student Association of the campus law school overwhelmingly approved a statement condemning the administration's rulings on political activity:

"Where the choice is between expediency and freedom of speech, a nation of free men can have no choice," they said, 402-170.

But once again, the optimistic hopes were due to be dashed.

## *22. The Regents Throw a Time Bomb*

Even when the Heyman Committee announced its report, there were ominous rumblings from the chancellor's office which were not fully appreciated at the time. The Heyman Committee had limited its consideration to disciplinary charges through September 30, and the campus community assumed that the Pact of October 2 meant the administration would *not* consider penalties for the infractions of October 1-2. But on November 13 Strong referred pointedly to the problem of "serious misconduct" *after* September 30 and promised "immediate filing of charges"—a promise which was going to be put into effect by Kerr and the Regents a week later, with fateful consequences.

The long-awaited Regents meeting came, to take up the two substantive questions that had so long been chewed in committee: new regulations for "free speech" and political activity on the campus, and the case of the eight suspended students.

As mentioned, the Regents habitually violated their own formal rules by conducting their decisive discussions in secret sessions. In this case it is generally understood that by the end of their private meetings of November 19, the important decisions had already been made. The formalization of these decisions took place at an afternoon session on November 20, held on the edge of the Berkeley campus, open to the press and attended by an FSM delegation as the "public."

The request of the students for the right to present their case to the Regents was rejected; it is one of the suggestive features of the whole conflict that at no time did the Regents ever concede that students had a right which even absolute despots habitually granted in their courts.

But the FSM delegation did not come alone. At noon, one of the largest rallies yet assembled, about 5000 strong, had gathered in Sproul Hall Plaza to listen to the singing of Joan Baez (who now appeared for the first but not the last time in support of FSM demonstrations); to speeches setting forth the issues before the Regents; to cheers for the Cal football team which was facing the "Big Game" with Stanford on Saturday; and to instructions on forming lines of march which would cross the campus to University Hall—where the Regents were pretending to deliberate the questions they had decided the day before.

By about 2, proceeding in complete order, the parade lines converged at the West Gate, and the vast sea of students subsided on the lawn across the street from University Hall, unaware that the Regents had chosen to meet for the occasion in a room without windows.

At this public session in the room without windows, the agreed-on motions concerning the suspended students were presented in a document signed by Clark Kerr (beginning "Chancellor Strong and I recommend as follows") and were duly adopted by the board. The recommendations of the Heyman Committee, which had so cheered the students the week before, were not publicly acted on; that is, they were silently rejected.

Where the Heyman Committee had asked that the penalty for six of the students be changed to censure and the suspensions expunged from the record, the Kerr-Regents decision was to confirm the suspensions to the current date. Where the committee had proposed that the penalty of the other two be limited to the suspension, Kerr and the Regents added an additional probation for the rest of the semester. All the suspensions, however, were ended as of that day.

There were three points in the Kerr document presumably intended to ameliorate similar difficulties in the future. There is perhaps nothing in our story so symptomatic of the administrative approach.

There across the street were 5000 of the best students in the state, waiting for a word of understanding and of human sensibility from their mentors. What they got was Kerr's Point 6: a request to the Regents that the Berkeley campus enlarge the staff of its Police Department and Dean's Office to handle violations, and of the General Counsel's office, "since a more legalistic approach is being taken towards student discipline." They got Point 5: that regulations be made clearer, "more detailed and legalistic," with explicit penalties. They got Point 7: that the ability of university authorities to force identification of individuals be assured.*

And there was another point in this Kerr document, one which was going to blow the lid off the whole campus before the month was up. Yet, unexplainably today, hardly anyone paid attention to it at the time.

This was Kerr's Point 4: "*New* disciplinary proceedings before the [administration-appointed) Faculty Committee on Student Conduct will be instituted *immediately* against certain students and organizations for violations *subsequent* to September 30, 1964." (Emphasis added.)

This meant that the administration had to move immediately to rake up the violations committed during the police-car blockade (or afterward) and to reinflame the situation which everyone believed had been settled by the Pact of October 2believed by everyone except the administration and the Regents.

In retrospect it is widely assumed in the university community that this decision was the result of a deal made in the secret sessions of the Regents'

---

* On the eve of this Regents meeting (November 18), Strong had written a letter to Kerr which illustrates the thinking behind such proposals to beef up the policing arm of the administration. In this letter Strong pointed with some dismay to the Heyman Committee recommendations, which would encourage the FSM to continue its "defiance of duly constituted authority." Then Strong refers to a decision, apparently already made, to announce that Sproul Hall Plaza is no longer a Hyde Park area: when this announcement is made, he writes, "we can expect further demonstration in this area." The authorities then must "declare an unlawful assemblage and clear the area." Moreover, there are the table-manners of November 9-10 who are rejecting discipline. "How do we proceed effectively to control and penalize further acts of civil disobedience with which we will be confronted?" Answer: probation followed by summary expulsion at the next violation. Then this "will produce further defiance." In response the administration must "stand absolutely firm" and make no "concessions, retreats, and compromises." (Summary from Strong's confidential report to the Regents of December 16.) This was the prescription for a sort of martial law on campus which, when it became known, made Strong the darling of the Hearst-Knowland press.

meeting: that the Regents would vote for "liberalized" regulations on political activity provided that the administration served up the heads of those "certain" student leaders who had been responsible for forcing them into this concession, and punished "certain" clubs which had been instrumental in carrying on the fight.

Although it is the name of Clark Kerr, and no one else, which is signed to this fateful motion, it is not necessarily true that it was he who initiated it in the secret session. This provocative instruction may have been insisted on by the right-wing Regents, abetted by Chancellor Strong, whose term of high administrative office had turned him into a martinet. In the upshot, the odium clung to Strong, who executed the decision.

The *quid pro quo, such* as it was, was provided by the Regents' concession

> that certain campus facilities, carefully selected and properly regulated, may be used by students and staff for planning, implementing, raising funds or recruiting participants for lawful off-campus action, not for unlawful off-campus action.

This was the same language which, the FSM had charged, the administration's General Counsel had drawn up before the revised CCPA had even begun its work—suggesting ex post facto the empty role which that committee had played. At the best interpretation, the language endorsed the position which the administration had taken in the discussions of the past weeks over "double punishment." Furthermore, the Regents gave no public sign of having even considered alternative proposals that had been made by groups of faculty members and by the ASUC Senate as well as by the FSM.

A follow-up statement by Kerr was carefully ambiguous in answering the question: who would decide the unlawfulness of an advocated action. He said, "In the usual case you'd wait for the courts to decide. It would then go to the Faculty Committee on Student Conduct." This avoided saying that the administration would accept the court's decision; let alone the further question of who would decide that the on-campus activity had been "for" (or had led to) the "unlawful off campus action."

Later on, when the Regents under further pressure had modified their stand at their December 18 meeting, Professor Ross was going to admit that "the November 20 ruling was obscure as to where the Regents stood on speech and advocacy." That is, their "liberalization" was obscure, but it was perfectly clear that they had rejected the students' "free speech" position. The "liberalization" was one only in comparison with the September version of the administration's "historic policy."

## *23. The Abortive Sit-in*

When the FSM delegation came back from the room without windows and reported to the throng of students spread over the great lawn across the street, the prevailing reaction was stunned distress. Some girls wept; all were overcome with gloom.

It is hard to say now why they should have expected much from the Regents, and perhaps it was not really illusory hopes that were at stake; for now the big question that stared them in the face was: *Where do we go from here?* They did not know that the administration was going to solve this problem for them shortly, that in fact one' decision of the Regents had already started the wheels turning.

Then and there, a segment of the FSM leadership favored an immediate sit-in, but the majority, including Mario Savio, decided to adjourn any action till Monday. That weekend while another segment of the student body met a defeat, this time the football team at the hands of Stanford—the FSM Executive and Steering Committees suffered through marathon meetings tensely arguing what to do.

It was not all like that: at the Saturday night post-Big-Game parties there was a burgeoning of what the S.F. *Chronicle's* jazz columnist, Ralph Gleason, called "the new folk music of the FSM movement":

> There even exists a rough libretto for a Free Speech musical, which is sprouting up in true folk music fashion. ... some of the best songs of the FSM have been written to melodies of the Beatles. "If I negotiate with you" is one, a satirical version of the Beatles' "If I Fell in Love with You." Rodgers and Hammerstein are equally honored. "There are five thousand Reds on the Plaza" is the opening line of the FSM version of "Oh What a Beautiful Morning." And "Won't You Come Home, Bill Bailey" has been rewritten to tell of Jack Weinberg's vigil in the police car, and there's a devastating version of "Twelve Days of Christmas."*

The students were pulled two ways. The FSM cadres were frankly tired—indeed, Mario Savio had told the crowd on the lawn: "Last week I said that if the Regents don't come down with too horrendous restrictions, then I guess, for a while anyway, we're going to have to fold up shop. . . . [We're] damned tired . . ." although this was a prelude to concluding that such moods had now to be thrown aside for a return to combat. And the end of the semester was getting nearer, with its pressure to start studying to make up for all the time spent fighting the administration; for it must be remembered that these were good students. And, above all, what *could* be done now?

The argument in the FSM leading committees was over the advisability of launching a sit-in on Monday in Sproul Hall. Although some wanted an all-out sit-in, the proposal at this time was for a "moral witness" sit-in, not obstructive or disruptive—one that would allow the more or less normal operation of the building. The Executive Committee finally decided, in a rather close vote after an acrimonious discussion, to

* A number of FSM-inspired songs were later issued in two records produced by students: "Joy to U.C." and "FSM's Sounds and Songs of the Demonstration." (A third record, produced by KPFA, entitled "Is Freedom Academic?" is limited to prose.)

authorize the Steering Committee to launch it; and the Steering Committee, also badly divided, voted to do so, 7-4. Both sides were going to be presented to the noon rally on Monday.

The rally that Monday, November 23, was one of the most peculiar yet seen in the plaza. It was going to see an open intra-FSM debate; but first the administration took its turn at the goings on.

The oratory opened with a united presentation by FSM spokesmen of their case against the Regents' decisions. After a little of this presentation, carried over the plaza by excellent loudspeakers, the doors of Sproul Hall opened and a custodian trundled out a small loudspeaker setup, which he placed on the top of the steps facing the FSM rostrum.

Vice-Chancellor Searcy emerged, took up a stand at the new loudspeaker, and, directing himself to the rally, requested the floor for a statement by the chancellor. The students gave the administrator the floor—in fact, urged him in vain to use their loudspeaker system since his own could not be heard well. Searcy wanted to read the complete text of the statement which Strong had issued the night before, explaining that the *Daily Cal* had failed to carry it *in toto;* and to add color to the proceedings, launched into a peppery attack on the student paper—which, incidentally, had consistently supported the administration against the FSM.

This strange interlude over, it turned out that the chancellor's statement was a vague amplification of the Regents' motions on "free speech." Searcy turned to go, but was induced to stay and listen to FSM comments. A brief one-sided debate followed between the two unequal loudspeakers, but since the vice-chancellor had never intended to get into an impromptu confrontation before live students, he soon fled.

After farce, tragedy. Before a smaller assembly of students the FSM meeting continued as a discussion on the moot question of the proposed sit-in.

For the proponents of the sit-in, the dominant motive was clearly a feeling of angry despair. The main driving force was the felt need for a moral gesture of defiance, not reasoned considerations of strategy.

For this reason, the internal line-up departed widely from the previous moderate-militant split. The dividing line was not only militancy but generalship. Some of the militants felt that it was not *always* the best militant tactic to bugle for a cavalry charge at the center, especially if it were a futile one.

The alternative, distasteful as it might be, was to gird loins for a new period—of continuing the illegal tables and challenging a crackdown, of feeling out the scope of the new regulations, perhaps setting up legal .tests of students' rights, mobilization of community and national support, publication and research on the issues—in short, standing fast and regrouping. This would have required not only militancy but tactical flexibility.

Experience was to show indeed that the sit-in tactic was not best fitted for the use proposed. The "spectacular" forms of civil disobedience were most effective in the course of the Berkeley revolt when they were used *defensively*—in clear reaction against overt crackdowns by the administration. On October 1-2, the massive sit-down around the police car was a direct riposte to the provocative arrest; on December 2, we are going to see that the sit-in was the response to the provocative move of the administration toward expelling the FSM leaders. But on November 23 the sit-in was proposed as a means to force new campus regulations. While the Regents' decisions which spurred it were, to be sure, unacceptable to the FSM, still they were not of the same immediately provocative character as arrests or threatened expulsions.

At the discussion in the plaza, Jack Weinberg put the case for a sit-in in moral (or as he liked to call it, existential) terms:

> [It is] a plea, sort of an existential cry: Listen to my voice; you haven't heard me before; you ignore me.* I

* How literally true this was of Chancellor Strong was brought out in his (continued...)

> came out in 5000, and you didn't recognize me. You didn't even mention me. I sent in petitions; you didn't read them. I put forward platforms: you didn't study them. You cannot ignore me any longer; and I'm going to put myself in a position where I cannot be ignored, because you're going to have to look at me. You're going to have to look at me as you go about your business, and you're going to have to take me into account. This was our majority decision ...

This was moving, and it expressed an inner urge of the greatest importance, but it did not deal with an evaluation of external effectiveness and consequences.

The result was a near disaster for the FSM, known as the "abortive sit-in." In the course of the debate in the plaza, it was no clear whether the sit-in would last only till 5 (office closing time), or would go on till the Academic Senate meeting scheduled for the next day, or would be indefinite. The sit-in's chief proponent, Mario Savio, put it that "how long we will sit-in depends on individuals," that is, would be up to each individual's conscience. This invited a process of splintering.

Led by Savio, about 300 students moved into Sproul; many of these had opposed the sit-in but now went in with the others, in order to minimize the effects of a divided policy or else to ensure that the sit-in would at least not drag out to catastrophe.

Inside, as the demonstrators lined the corridor, a continuous debate went on. One of the most fascinating of the tape-recording made by the

---

(...continued)
testimony at the later trial of the FSM sit-inners. He admitted under questioning that he had never stopped to listen to a single FSM rally in the plaza during the whole period of the dispute. Other evidence brought out how seldom, and with how much difficulty, he could be gotten to discuss the issues with students.

KPFA reporters is the record of this discussion; it ranged over most of the problems of the "free speech" fight and its strategy, and its level of serious thought and controversy puts to shame the contemporaneous deliberations of the Academic Senate.

While this discussion was going on, the Steering Committee was also debating the question, on an upper floor, and finally voted 6-5 to recommend ending the sit-in at 5 o'clock. This was done. The abortive sit-in was over, but the question still remained: what to do?

## *24. Back to the Wars*

The Academic Senate meeting which took place the next day, November 24, seemed like just another toll of the bell. By a close vote, it defeated a motion to limit the university's regulation of political activity only to the extent "necessary to prevent undue interference with other university affairs." It also defeated a motion to establish a committee to deal with questions of student political conduct.*

This week the FSM hit perhaps its lowest point. Tables were set up again in the plaza but the dynamism was out of it.

As Mario Savio had mentioned on November 20 about a previous occasion, the FSM leaders began to talk in terms of "folding up shop," or "putting FSM on the shelf for a while." Another leader, Steve

---

* But the faculty did come to grips with the administration on another question, which perhaps contributed to its wormturning two weeks later. The faculty's much-valued control over the hiring and firing of professors was at stake. Chancellor Strong, summarily rejecting recommendations by both the German Department and an Academic Senate committee, refused an assistant professorship to Eli Katz. In 1958 Katz had refused to answer questions about Communist Party membership put by the House Un-American Committee, and, while making clear he was not a Communist, refused to do this for Strong too, on the ground that he had already signed the Levering (AntiCommunist) Oath required by the state constitution. On November 24 the Academic Senate condemned the administration 267-79 "for its disregard of and contempt for" the Senate in handling the case.

Weissman, has also testified that at this point the FSM was ready to "let things go along." It is not accurate to say, as Professor Henry May did later, that "As we went into the Thanksgiving weekend the movement seemed to be dying out," but it certainly seemed to be losing its steam.

The movement would undoubtedly have continued in some form, but with more normal and longer-range perspectives.

We are now at a turning point in the story. From this low low point in its existence, the FSM was going to zoom up *in a week* to the zenith of its militancy; in another half week it was going to sweep up the support of a clear majority of the campus for the first time since it started, and be more solidly united than ever before.

And the transition from one phase to the other took about three minutes. This may be an exaggeration, but I say it on the basis of a personal memory.

On Saturday evening of the Thanksgiving vacation weekend, November 28, some of us were chatting casually about what to do while the FSM was "on the shelf." The phone rang with news: Mario Savio and others were up for expulsion! Two of the FSM leaders—in fact, the two who had been put on probation by Kerr and the Regents, Mario Savio and Art Goldberg—had received letters from Chancellor Strong, dated November 25, instituting disciplinary action before his own appointed committee for their actions during the police-car blockade. "On October 1 and 2, 1964," said the letters, "you led and encouraged numerous demonstrators .. ." etc. (In addition, Savio was charged with biting a policeman in the leg during the October 1 scuffle around the Sproul doors—an act which he admitted to be "excessive" and informally explained as due to momentary irritation at having his head trampled by policemen's heels.)

The full text of the letter was read over the phone. The conversation went on, but now it was about how to mobilize the campus.

There were good reasons for the quick redressment of the FSM's ranks, their speedy adjustment to the new crisis. For one thing, by this time few had any illusions about that favorite subject of breast-thumping:

the administration's "good faith." For another thing, the "FSM on the shelf" mood had spread but had not yet sunk in; it was easy to snap back. Lastly, there was little or no uncertainty about the meaning of such an attempt to decapitate the movement by striking at a few leaders.

Two others got similar letters that weekend, making four in all; and in addition the administration sent letters to a number of clubs.

There were few other moves by the administration which could have so thoroughly united all the diverse elements of the FSM. The four were being singled out as "hostages" (as the Heyman Committee had complained about the September 30 suspensions) for acts in which a very large number of students had equally shared. It had been true from the very beginning of this movement—vide the tactics of mass violations for table-manning as well as the sit-down around the police car-that solidarity with the victimized was almost a reflex action, as was true among civil-rights activists generally. This was a basic key to the movement's strength.

The four "Thanksgiving letters" were signed by Strong as chancellor, and almost every article that has appeared on the Berkeley rebellion has pointed the finger of blame at him for the "unexpected," "provocative" and "hasty" charges. But this gross injustice has been due, as mentioned, to general amnesia about the public fact that it was Kerr and the Regents (with Strong's concurrence, to be sure) who decided on this move in advance. Kerr's Point 4, moreover, had read "immediately," and Strong was carrying out the scheme. The letters, in fact, were prepared by the Regents' counsel. It is true that Strong had been pushing for such a hard policy right along, but he could hardly have carried it through on his own say-so.

At bottom, the blame for the debacle must be laid not on any individual's personality but squarely on the Regents, out of whose meeting the explosive spark came. Within this body, an allocation of blame can be only speculative, but it is probably safe to say that, despite all the right wing big businessmen on the board, Governor Brown (ex-officio Regent) could have put his foot down if he wanted to.

Unfortunately, Brown's record in this affair suggests rather that he may have been foremost among those crying for blood.

To many who had never been sympathetic to the FSM at all the Thanksgiving letters seemed like a gross provocation too. Some had just finished hailing the Regents' decisions as "liberalizing" and pacificatory; and since the Regents themselves had just reinstated the suspendees, the letters seemed like a gratuitous act of war declared from the chancellor's office against a newly found chance of peace. (This widespread opinion did not understand that the contradiction was the Regents', not Strong's.)

Furthermore, even many faculty members who had been anti-FSM could, in this situation, appreciate the wrath of the students against a betrayal of trust—one which not only singled out four leaders from hundreds or thousands who had violated regulations and laws around the police car, which not only came two months after acts which were by then assumed to be dead issues, but which was vindictively directed against these leaders after they had been tacitly justified by the very action of the authorities in changing the regulations which had provoked the violations. "Understandably, I think, the students felt tricked," wrote Professor Henry May later.

After all, on signing the Pact of October 2 with some of these same students, Clark Kerr had told the press: "I look upon this [settlement] as a triumph for common sense, decency, democracy, and faith in our fellow men." There is a wide-open question suggested here, which I put later (in a talk at a noon rally during the following week's strike) in these terms:

> You remember what happened on October 1-2; there was an eyeball-to-eyeball confrontation; Kerr negotiated with these FSM leaders, presumably in good faith. He agreed on a pact with these same leaders. He hailed it as a "decent" settlement, and the FSM negotiators signed it. Now I want to know: On October 2, when Kerr was (metaphorically) shaking hands on the pact with these

> FSM leaders, did he, or Strong, already have in mind that he would move to expel them, just as soon as things quieted down? On October 2, when Mario Savio was announcing the pact to the students, did Kerr, or Strong, already know that there was another "plank" in the pact which he hadn't yet divulged? that the following month he was going to say in effect, "Oh-uh-we forgot to mention on October 2 that the students with whom we arrived at this 'decent' settlement have got to be expelled, because of the part they played in extorting this decent settlement from us?" Or did they think this up later?

Of course they thought it up later, for on October 2 it would have been unthinkable. For most of the campus it was just as unthinkable at the end of November. The administration had thrown a bomb, and it got an explosion.

## *25. The Big Sit-in*

For two days following the holiday—Monday and Tuesday, November 30 and December 1—the FSM tried to enter into negotiations with the administration. Some members of the administration who said they had opposed the action assured them, however, that it could not be rescinded. From other quarters the students were again told that there was no "free speech" issue at all to negotiate, nothing to discuss.

Two lines of action began to be planned. On Monday the Graduate Coordinating Committee (affiliated with FSM) issued a leaflet calling for a meeting of graduates and TA's the next day to discuss a strike. The meeting decided to go out on strike on Friday, December 4.

In the FSM Executive Committee, the majority were for launching a mass sit-in. There was also a proposal for leading off with a general student strike and reserving the sit-in weapon; but the understanding was that many of the graduate activists would be responsible for preparing the strike for Friday while the sit-in went ahead.

On Wednesday, December 2, the FSM leaflet was tersely headed *"Showdown"* and reported an ultimatum:

> We have asked the administration* to grant these demands by noon today:
> 1. The arbitrary and vengeful charges against our leaders and our organizations must be dropped.
> 2. There must be no new punishments for protesting administration policies.
> 3. Immediate and substantial improvements in the regulations must be made . .
> *The Chancellor has taken his direct action. Now we must take ours.*
> We have published our platform, asked for public discussion, petitioned, sent delegations, demonstrated, held a moral protest. Yesterday we demanded, and now we await a reply. If no satisfactory reply is given by noon, we will begin massive direct action to force the administration to heed us .. .
> *Except to threaten and harm us, the machine of the administration ignores us.* We will stop the machine;
> Come to the noon rally (Joan Baez will be there). Bring books, food and sleeping bags.

Joan Baez was at the noon rally, and so was a record-breaking crowd of about 6000. Mario Savio told the assembled crowd:

---

* In a letter formally sent to President Kerr the day before, December 1. It said, *inter alia:* "We are hereby making a final attempt to restore our political freedom without the use of mass direct action." Kerr simply filed the letter (according to Strong).

> We have an autocracy which runs this university. It's managed. We were told the following: "If President Kerr actually tried to get something more liberal out of the Regents . . . . why didn't he make some public statement to that effect?" And the answer we received from a well-meaning liberal was the following: he said, "Would you ever imagine the manager of a firm making a statement publicly in opposition to his Board of Directors?" That's the answer.
>
> I beg you to consider: if this is a firm, and if the Board of Regents are the Board of Directors, and if President Kerr in fact is the manager, then ... the faculty are a bunch of employees and we're the raw material. But we're a bunch of raw material that don't mean . . . to be made into any product, don't mean to end up being bought by some clients of the university . . . We're human beings.
>
> And that brings me to the second mode of civil disobedience. There's a time when the operation of the machine becomes so odious, makes you so sick at heart, that you can't take part, you can't even tacitly take part. And you've got to put your bodies upon the gears and upon the wheels, upon the levers, upon all the apparatus, and you've got to make it stop. And you've got to indicate to the people who run it, to the people who own it, that unless you're free, the machine will be prevented from working at all.

He introduced Joan Baez, who sang a song; asked the students to go in with love in their hearts, not anger; and finished with "Blowin' in the Wind." *(How many roads must a man walk down / Before you can call him a man? . . . )* Savio said: "Now no more talking. We're going to march in singing 'We Shall Overcome.' Slowly, there are a lot of us. Up here to the left—I didn't mean to pun."

With Joan Baez leading while they sang, about 1000 to 1500 entered the building. The offices suspended business and employees were sent home. The gage was thrown.

At 7 P.M. the guards locked all the doors on at least a thousand. Meanwhile Sproul Hall was temporarily organized as the "Free University of California." Gigantic letters F-S-M covered three upper-floor windows. The N. *Y. Times* described it:

> There was an air of festivity accompanying the beginning of the sit-in. . . . Beneath a table a young mother sat with her baby taking milk from a bottle. Nearby, oblivious to the songs and the high noise level, a young girl sat reading a language lesson. Free Speech Movement functionaries in armbands directed traffic. A class in Spanish was organized on the first floor, but it became a songfest. (Dec. 3.)

The fourth floor was set aside as a quiet study hall. Classes were held in several other parts of the building, generally taught by graduate students, on standard academic subjects as well as more fanciful topics. A press room was set up, and a food distribution center. Films were shown on the second floor, including old Chaplin and Laurel & Hardy classics. A Chanukah service was held in the main lobby, at which the story of the Maccabees was summarized with FSM overtones and the first song was "Hineh matov" *(How good is it for brothers to sit together).* Smaller discussion groups everywhere; Joan Baez strumming and singing; on the second floor, money—collecting and passing out sandwiches and drinks. In the basement, old civil defense food-drums were used as podiums for lectures on civil disobedience.

Outside the locked front door until a late hour, knots of students and *voyeurs* congregated on the steps: messages to people in and out of the building passing through the door crack; police guards standing by impassively; Professor Feuer industriously taking notes, peering through the glass at the Free University class advertised in the lobby, "The Nature of God and the Logarithmic Spiral."

Inside, complete order and self-discipline were maintained without incident. Explicit instructions were that no offices be opened, and this was obeyed. When the campus police chief reported that the office of President-emeritus Robert G. Sproul had been broken into and the files opened and scattered, Kerr included this charge in his public statement of December 3; but on Friday, Sproul's secretary explained that nothing of the sort had happened: Sproul's office *always* looked like that![*]

There was a deceptive air of organization about the whole thing, deceptive because it was mostly self-organized, not prepared in advance by an efficient apparatus. FSM leaders inside Sproul kept in touch with "Command Central" outside through walkie-talkies, and improvised as they went along.

At midnight the students settled down for the night. Then at 2:30 in the small hours, the lights came on again: the sit-inners struggled out of

---

* Another common derogation of the sit-in was the charge that it comprised a large proportion of non-students. This was proved untrue, but the facts never caught up with the erroneous statements spread throughout the nation's press. One of the best publicized figures was ascribed to a police official before the arrests were even completed, and the official repudiated the quotation the next day. The university gave out a set of figures in which, *mirabile dictu,* the number of Teaching Assistants (who are all graduate students) was left out of the number of "Students" and lumped into one statistic with "Unidentified Persons" among others! An FSM committee on Wednesday afternoon found that, of 637 demonstrators polled, 597 were students, 10 were university employees, and two were students' wives—leaving 28 (under 4.5 %) from outside the university community. No accurate figures are available on how many of the non-students were recent alumni, who still think of themselves as part of the university community. (Another survey showed 21 alumni out of 598 interviewed.)

sleep to hear FSM monitors circulating through the halls with electric megaphones giving instructions to prepare for arrest.

## *26. The Governor Calls the Cops*

The man who turned the university over to the police for the biggest mass arrest in California's history, in student history, and perhaps in national history, was the "liberal image" himself, Governor Brown.

Kerr had advised against it. His own predilection was for letting the students sit a while—perhaps even until they petered out in sheer exhaustion. His model apparently was the tactic which had been employed by the University of Chicago administration against a sit-down in the chancellor's office: they waited out nine days, then threatened police action, and the demonstrators finally quit quietly. The nation hardly even heard of it. Kerr was well aware of this episode; on October 2 (before the pact) he .had told a press conference: "This is a nationwide thing. I have just talked to Chancellor George Beadle of the University of Chicago; he recently had a nine-day sit-down in his own office."

This policy could have simply meant temporarily closing down the administration building to the public, operating a skeleton staff in the offices, and shifting as much of the work as possible to other centers. The calculation behind this strategy would go as follows: It would be a great inconvenience, but how many sit-inners would still be in after a week? How many after two weeks? At the end of two weeks the campus would be exactly two days away from the beginning of the Christmas holidays. When school resumed on January 4, the finals would be around the comer ... It would certainly not be business-as-usual, but then a determined mass sit-in was not exactly routine either.

It is true that there was some thinking (in the conversation stage) among FSM leaders about what to do in the event of a *sitzkrieg:* the problem would be how to escalate, by (for example) extending the sit-in to the Student Union building across the plaza. But even assuming that this attempt could be made, the administration's strategy need not only depend on waiting for the demonstrators to quit. At some point in the next few days, depending on the campus climate and the swing of opinion, it could still decide on some form of selective police action, perhaps picking off a few leaders in the style to which it had already grown accustomed.

This calculation assumes a degree of strategic intelligence on the part of the Berkeley administration which was obviously far outside the ken of Chancellor Strong, but not necessarily beyond the imagination of the more deviously schooled Kerr. In leading with the sit-in weapon, the FSM had staked almost its whole wad, excepting only a thin line of graduates who were still outside in anticipation of the Friday strike. It is hard to say what the combination of sit-in plus strike might have meant by Friday. In any case, a waiting game by the administration might have seen the FSM in trouble, with a possible larger-scale repetition of the fiasco of the abortive sit-in of November 23.

But just as the authorities had invariably come to their rescue in previous difficulties, so now the students were spared the burden of working out this strategy. Late that night, while Kerr was still advising holding fire, the Democratic governor ordered an iron-fisted, frontal, mass police assault.

There is no mystery about who had gotten to him. It was (according to the two papers that would know best, the Hearst *Examiner* and Knowland's *Tribune)* the office of the Alameda County district attorney, J. F. Coakley, a well-known far rightist and Goldwaterite, whose deputy Edwin Meese III phoned Brown at 10:30 P.M. from "on the scene":

> Meese, made an expert on the campus feud by special assignment, told the governor that temporizing would only make the eventual blowoff more dangerous, the district attorney [Coakley] said.
>
> Governor Brown said to go ahead—"There will be no anarchy, and that is what has developed at the University of California." (S.F. *Examiner,* Dec. 4.)

And so the liberal Democratic governor precipitately called the cops, taking the advice of a notorious Goldwaterite against the advice of the eminent liberal who was president of the university. It was not quite as bizarre as that: behind the nonentity Meese and even Coakley is the real political powerhouse in Alameda County, William Knowland, the ex-"Senator from Formosa" and recent Goldwater manager, whose publishing enterprise is the strident voice of the power structure in the East Bay. This was also, as we saw, the trigger which probably had precipitated the administration's September crackdown on "free speech" in the first place. Our cast of characters has now come full circle.

In all likelihood, the immediate motive for Brown was fear that unless he capitulated to the demand of the Knowlandites, they would smear him as condoning anarchy and Communist subversion, not to speak of (in Feuer's litany) "narcotics, sexual perversion, collegiate Castroism and campus Maoism." The "liberal" solution was, therefore: Beat the right wing to the punch; the lesser evil is to do *yourself* what the rightists would do anyway.

Governor Brown had another lesser evil to explain the day after: "It could have been far worse," he said. "We could have used tear gas." He added that felony charges for conspiracy could also have been brought against the sit-inners.

President Kerr likewise took a lesser evil into consideration: himself. In the opinion of many, a president of a great university whose campus had been taken over by an army of police against his wishes was honor bound to resign in protest; in fact, might have threatened to resign in order to stay Brown's hand. Kerr, on the contrary, publicly supported the action which he had privately opposed, and echoed Brown's cry of "Anarchy!"—while hinting that he was not responsible for the decision itself. *(When he saw that he could prevail nothing, but that rather a tumult was made, he took water, and washed his hands before the multitude . . . )*

It should not be thought that Brown always looses police on students. Sometimes he makes commencement speeches. Like this one:

> Far from discouraging your students' social and public interests, I propose that you positively exploit them. Here is an honorable source of college spirit; here is a worthy unifying and organizing principle for your whole campus life.
>
> I say: thank God for the spectacle of students picketing—even when they are picketing me at Sacramento and I think they are wrong—for students protesting and freedom-riding, for students listening to society's dissidents, for students going out into the fields with. our migratory workers, and marching off to jail with our segregated Negroes. At last we're getting somewhere. The colleges have become boot camps for citizenship—and citizen-leaders are marching out of them.
>
> For a while, it will be hard on us as administrators. Some students are going to be wrong, and some people will want to deny them the right to make mistakes. Administrators will have to wade through the angry letters and colleges will lose some donations. We Governors will have to face indignant caravans and elected officials bent on dictating to state college faculties.
>
> But let us stand up for our students and be proud of them. If America is still on the way up, it will welcome this new, impatient, critical crop of young gadflies. It will be fearful only of the complacent and passive.

That was read off a typed manuscript in June 1961 at the University of Santa Clara, where there was no Free Speech Movement.

Nor should it be thought that Brown is always so vindictive against derogation of Law and Order. Earlier in 1964 at the Democratic Party convention, as head of the California delegation he had faced the choice of recognizing the Freedom Democratic Party of Mississippi or the regular Democrats. He chose to whip the delegation into line to support the representatives of the system that condoned physical terror, church-burning and outright murder. But the non-violent student sit-in could not be permitted to go on for even 24 hours: it was "anarchy."

## *27. The Occupation by the Police*

The police showed up in the middle of the night, according to a pattern more popular in certain other countries. The announcement was made to the students by Chancellor Strong, "pale and slightly trembling from fatigue [according to the Berkeley *Gazette*], his eyes even more cavernous than usual."

All through the preceding day, Strong had remained holed up in his Dwinelle Hall office, from eight in the morning till eleven at night, even for dinner. At eleven Vice-President Bolton had come over with a message from Kerr indicating no immediate action against the sit-inners. But, by coincidence, just at this juncture Bolton was reached with a phone call informing him that Governor Brown had ordered mass arrests. The Chancellor went home for a while and returned to campus about half-past two, to act as herald for the police operation. Arriving at police headquarters in Sproul basement, he was handed a draft statement to read to the sit-inners, and revised it; he was handed a police bull-horn to talk through; and he made his way to the elevator flanked by officials and cops. It was about 3:15.

The statement he read on each floor was an order to disperse, ending with "Please go." (Once he added an abrupt "Now go! Get!" as momentarily the martinet showed under the mortarboard.) About 200 did leave the building before the police reached them, leaving about 800.

The ex-scholar's role was to make way for the Secular Arm. As he moved from floor to floor with the performance, a police lieutenant followed his route with a formal riot warning. Outside, there mobilized city policemen, county sheriff's deputies, and state Highway Patrolmen, some with crash helmets and baseball-bat-size "riot sticks."

At about 3:30 they' began making arrests, working down from the fourth floor. Booking desks were set up in the hall, and paddy wagons were backed up to the south end of the building. Most of the students went limp on arrest. At first the arrests were slow, but after the arrival of a contingent of Oakland police (whose reputation has already been mentioned), under chiefs named Toothman and Gain, the conduct of the operation changed.

Male students were generally dragged and bumped down the stairs, arms twisted, strong-armed, or kicked. Female students were dragged into the elevator and bundled down with less overt violence until they reach the basement. Stairwell windows, through which newsmen watched this at first, were covered with old newspapers. A number of policemen hid their badges to prevent identification.

Even members of the Faculty Committee on Student Conduct were barred from entering the building as observers, as were attorneys for the students. A few students, particularly recognized FSM leaders, were deliberately roughed up. A reporter present wrote down some typical remarks by Oakland policemen:*

"Hey, don't drag 'em down so fast—they ride on their heels. Take 'em down a little slower—they bounce more that way."

"We should do like' they do in them foreign countries: beat 'em senseless first, then throw 'em in the bus."

---

* Joel L. Pimsleur, associate editor of the S.F. *Chronicle's* Sunday supplement, in an article published in the Columbia *Daily Spectator* for Dec. 18, 1964. (Pimsleur is a former editor of the *Spectator.)* Other sources on police behavior are the report of the Berkeley-Albany ACLU, and a confidential summary prepared for the defendants by their attorneys; plus an abundance of press photos showing obvious brutal handling. The most sweeping denial of police brutality coming from anyone not in uniform was written by Prof. Lewis Feuer, who was not in the building.

"Yea, they're just a bunch of jerks—we oughtta show 'em."

"Don't worry, wait till we get 'em on the stairs."

When students began arriving for classes at 8, the sit-inners set up loudspeaker microphones on a second-floor balcony overlooking the plaza and for hours kept the crowds below informed of what was happening inside. In between reports, another microphone was used on the steps just below for addresses and information from the ground-level forces.

Climbing ropes dangled from both ends of the balcony. A few students climbed up to be arrested inside: some others climbed out on special missions, including the head of the graduate students, Steve Weissman, who was going to lead the strike while nearly all of the Steering Committee were in jail.

Suddenly the police on the second floor made a quick raid and managed to seize lack Weinberg and one of the microphones. A hundred of the students then packed in around the window near the microphones to protect them. There was a second attempt: a police captain ordered his troops to "kick your way through" the seated demonstrators. The S. F. *Chronicle* reported:

> Phalanxes of trained riot cops dived into the huddled students—seeking out the FSM leaders first their boots landing heavily on heads, arms, shoulders and legs. On at least two occasions over-zealous cops plunged into the middle of a pack of students only to be pulled back by their own colleagues. (Dec. 6.)

They did not get the microphone. After stomping over the bodies of girls and men indiscriminately, they withdrew in defeat. The balcony loudspeakers kept going till about 10:30 A.M., by which time the systematic arrests had penetrated to the windows. The last student dragged away barely had time to disengage the microphone and toss it down to the people below.

The last of the arrests was made at 3:30 P.m., twelve hours after they had begun. Law and Order now reigned in Sproul Hall; it was as silent as the grave.

As the police vans and buses hauled the batches of demonstrators away, the jails filled up in Berkeley and Oakland, and some were temporarily held at a National Guard Armory. Almost all of them ended up at the county's Santa Rita Prison Farm, henceforth known as the "Santa Rita campus" of the university. (During the war Santa Rita had been a concentration camp for Japanese-Americans.)

Before the arrests were completed, a committee of three eminent professors had collected '$8500 in non-refundable bail-bond money, mainly from other members of the faculty. Hundreds of cars were mobilized by word-of-mouth across the campus to go out to Santa Rita to be ready to bring the demonstrators back as soon as they were released on bail; the caravan of autos parked outside the prison gates stretched for two miles; friends, relatives, classmates and faculty members waited through the night in the chill air. Many of these were students who had felt, for one reason or another, that they could not participate in the sit-in, and who now were glad of the opportunity to demonstrate their identification with the 800.

When it was all over, a Berkeley policeman named William Radcliffe reminisced to a reporter:

> "They were singing and laughing, but I think they really were scared," he said. "You could feel some of the boys trembling as we carried them out. I don't think they were as brave as they acted." (Oakland *Tribune,* Dec. 3.)

Of course they were not as brave as they acted. Nobody is. But they acted—singing and laughing and scared and brave.

## *28. The Student Strike Starts*

We now have to return to the morning of the arrests. When the police operation in Sproul Hall was less than three hours old, the strike that had originally been called for Friday had already been moved up and was being organized, as a general strike of students and faculty. It was announced to the campus over the loudspeakers at Sproul Hall and by pickets at the main entrances.

It started "cold" before 6 A.M., but, before long, picket lines were formed at the roads leading to the Student Union cafeterias, with the aim of stopping food deliveries. Before nine, ten to fifteen trucks had turned away: the drivers refused to cross the picket line. (Teamsters Union Local 291 said that individual drivers could decide to observe the student picket lines if they wished, even though it was not a bona-fide labor dispute.) On the construction site for a new building, carpenters (whose union had picketed the Regents on November 20 in protest against their buying policy) honored the picket lines and did not return to work after lunch.

By the time the student population started streaming in through the gates toward 8, the strike committee and Emergency Steering Committee were in effective operation. This was almost a wholly new second echelon of leadership, since the entire Steering Committee save two were with the sitinners. The responsibility swung sharply toward the graduate students, who carried the ball for the next day and a half in one of the most complex jobs of organization that the FSM had yet undertaken.

"Picket Central" was set up around "Wheeler Oak," inside Sather Gate: a dispatch blackboard listed the various picket lines and the person in charge; around the base of the oak, students feverishly lettered strike placards. Mimeographed "Instructions to Pickets" were eventually handed out ("The purpose of lines is to inform and persuade, not to harass," etc.). A communications network was set up consisting of students with walkie-talkies, with relays stationed on top of the higher buildings like Barrows Hall.

At the Bancroft entrance, a widening circle of pickets went round on the very sidewalk where the line of demarcation between the university strip and the city strip had once been an issue. Police standing by grinned as the picket captain was heard trying to establish contact on his walkie-talkie with the words, "Command Central, calling Command Central, come in." Through the morning the picket lines were built up at the entrances to the various main buildings as at the lesser gates of the campus.

Even though the strike had started absolutely cold and unpublicized, with the mass of arriving students bewildered first by the police occupation of Sproul Hall and then by the strange idea of a strike, it started snowballing as the campus began to take in what was happening. The magazine of the Goldwaterite students, *Man and State,* later explained it this way: "No matter how disliked the action of the FSM, there was only one question now—self-defense of the university community. Faculty members who had denounced FSM supported it; many students who thought FSM was a bore, instinctively reacted to defend their friends."

A rally had been scheduled for Sproul Hall Plaza at noon as usual, but well before then the crowd of students standing in the plaza in front of the police-commandeered building had grown huge. As described, loudspeakers had been going on the steps for some time anyway, and after eleven this operation began to turn into a mass rally.

Not far away, at the Bancroft entrance to the campus, a loudspeaker had been set up too, informing arrivals of the strike and of what was happening behind the police lines which they could see on their right; behind those lines, the mass arrests were steadily going on. Around half-past eleven, a flying wedge of police commandos descended on this loudspeaker apparatus and captured it. The students on Sproul steps crowded around the loudspeaker there, now the only FSM amplifier operating on campus, to save it from a similar fate.

With crowds thickening and tension growing, the rally was formally started before noon struck. I took the microphone first pending the arrival of others, but was fated to get out only a couple of sentences that day. For on the 'stroke of twelve, loudspeakers on the other side of the plaza began blaring: it was an attempt at a "loyalist" rally organized by the president of the ASUC. There were a few minutes of amplified confusion as the FSM chairman pleaded with the newcomers to desist. (The "loyalists" soon retired to the Lower Plaza, where 500, in the N.Y. *Times'* estimate, listened to their arguments against the strike, while five to six thousand swelled the FSM rally.)

On the heels of this incident, another and uglier onslaught was then staged before the throng.

A line of policemen appeared on the left end of the steps and tried to slice through the press of people standing there, obviously aiming at the right end of the steps where the speakers and speaker-equipment were concentrated. Now this episode received little mention at the time or later, since it led to nothing, as we shall see; but I am convinced that it was of the greatest educational importance that day in driving home, before an audience of thousands, a vivid realization of the amazing thing that had happened to the campus.

Imagine it: Before the thousands in the plaza there was a genuine stage—the top of the broad steps, with the columned portico of the administration building ("Banker's Doric" in architecture) as the backdrop. Behind that backdrop, they knew, hundreds of police were still dragging students down the stairs to the waiting vans.

The stage directions now read that on the far right of the steps is the nerve center of the rally, the knot of people around the microphone and loudspeaker. *Enter left a* skirmish file of policemen, in their appropriate costumes, who proceed to spread themselves across the footlights from left to right like a chorus line making its entrance.

They are acting out the charade: *Cop Cossacks Hurl Themselves on Peaceful Students Engaged in Nothing More Criminal than Exercising Their Free Speech.* And they hurl themselves indeed, just as the script says, with their billy-clubs waving in the air, their shoulders bulling through. The platoon leader is half way across *(center stage)* when he is stopped by the stiffening resistance of the students, who pack in so tightly that he cannot get through. There takes place for a minute or two a veritable tug of war, pushing and hauling back and forth. The sun spotlights the action like a big Klieg.

There is dialogue in this scene, but it is not audible to the gallery. The people confronting the policemen simply stood their ground and asked them to leave the rally alone. Two or three yards away from me, the face of the leading policeman (who was a U.C. Police Department man and *not* a Cossack or even an Oaklander) registered sheer bewilderment and uncertainty.

Now the end of this act was either an anti-climax or a smash-finale, depending on how you look at it. After some dialogue, the students managed to elicit from the police the statement that all they wanted to do was clear the top of the steps, that is, the area a few feet in front of the doors. They were not after the loudspeaker equipment at all, they said.

This was the kicker: *it had never occurred to the authorities to speak to the students themselves about moving down a few feet,* before unleashing their raiding squad. Instead, even in this dynamite-laden atmosphere, they had simply attacked with brute force, like an occupation army in enemy country.

It was a parable, though not of "Cossacks" after all.

Even while the tug of war was going on, a squad of students was feverishly disengaging the amplifier equipment, and in a matter of minutes had hustled it away. It reappeared in the middle of the plaza, with a chair as podium, and with a packed crowd of students in a complete circle around it to defend it from any direction.

The rally went on. Before it was over, an emergency meeting of the faculty was in progress on the other side of Sather Gate, in Wheeler Hall.

## *29. The Faculty and the Strike*

The emergency faculty meeting had been organized during the morning—by a number of professors. It could not be an official meeting of the Academic Senate, whose wheels worked too ponderously such wonders to perform; but since its attendance—about 900, not counting the audience—was over twice as much as the usual Academic Senate meeting, there was no question of its representative character.

This was the only recourse for the faculty to make its voice heard. "All day department chairmen try to contact administration, to no avail," the *Graduate Political Scientists' Report* mentions; "apparently, Administration has orders not to talk to faculty members." Nor to talk to the students, nor even to the press. (That day, even the "loyalists" of the ASUC started demanding from Kerr that he address a university meeting the next day and answer questions from the audience. A joint editorial of the *Daily Cal* with the UCLA and Davis papers also demanded this "last straw afloat for a sinking campus.") Apparently the only section of the university community that could commune with the administration at this point was the Police Department.

The emergency meeting opened soon after 1 P.m. under the chairmanship of Professor Glazer. There was no question about which way sentiment went. The chairman of the campus AAUP (American Association of University Professors) chapter read a unanimous resolution of its executive board, adopted the day before: it condemned the use of outside police on the campus, asked for a complete amnesty, and called for the replacement of Chancellor Strong. The reading was greeted with prolonged applause, though no vote was taken.

Overwhelmingly adopted by voice vote, with perhaps 10-15 per cent dissenting, were motions presented by the chairman of the History Department, Henry May. They proposed that the "new liberalized rules" for political activity be put into effect immediately, "pending their improvement," that "all pending campus action against students" be dropped, and that an Academic Senate committee be set up as a final court to hear appeals from students on penalties for political activity. Added also were demands that the Regents retract the decision "that the university could prosecute students for advocating illegal off-campus action," and "that no student be prosecuted by the university for participating in any off-campus activity." A telegram to Governor Brown signed by 361 faculty members said they "strongly condemn" the sending of the Highway Patrol onto the campus and the exclusion of faculty members from entering Sproul Hall, and asked for "prompt release of the arrested students."

The meeting was naturally a great lift for the striking students. This was the first time the faculty had spoken *up* strongly, and it occurred precisely at the point where the students were engaged in their strongest action—exactly contrary to the predictions of the moderates that any strong action by the students must surely alienate the faculty.

Professor May and others had even urged at the meeting that classes be temporarily dismissed so that faculty members could devote their energies toward resolving the crisis. The strike was legitimized. The S.F. *Chronicle* (non-Hearst), in an editorial against "anarchy on the U.C. campus," raged at the faculty: "Their championship of students who have clearly defied university regulations and violated the law, plus their implied denunciation of the university official responsible for campus discipline, adds a highly disturbing element to a situation of great gravity."

The strike had begun in the early hours of that morning from a flat-footed standing start, but it had been picking up momentum. By its first afternoon it was at least 60 per cent effective. The greater impact came the next day, Friday, December 4.

For one thing it is significant that no important anti-strike movement could be developed among the students. Two "anti" groups emerged, "Students for Law and Order" and "Students for Cal," but both attracted little support, even from among students who did *not* support the strike.*

---

* Not necessarily connected with these groups were individual students who carried their opposition to the point of hooliganism and violence. These were few, but there were times when knots of Law-and-Order advocates surrounded girl students at tables and harassed them with obscenity and anti-Semitic remarks; or shouldered their way into picket lines in order to provoke violence; or cursed and threatened even professors who supported the majority

(continued...)

This is a very significant fact, under-appreciated by people who think that the figures of for-and-against exhaust the statistics of the situation. In a dynamic conflict, there is not merely a majority and a minority: the opposition is not a homogeneous whole. A section may be neutralized, dropping opposition altogether, without coming over to the active side. Another section, while remaining in opposition, may be so infected by uncertainty—so tacitly impressed by the appeal of the position which it formally opposes—that its opposition is enervated in practice. Just as a given force exercises a leverage proportional to its distance from the fulcrum, so a fighting force exercises a leverage in conflict which is proportional not simply to its numbers but also to the strength of its convictions and the firmness of its followers. This truth is anathema to many academic minds, but that does not stop it from operating in Academe in the same way as in the rest of the world.

The striking students received encouragement from some other quarters. The head of the state Building Service Union, which had a local among university employees and a long education in the shabby labor policies of the administration, now issued a ringing statement of support to the students, later also endorsed by the San Francisco Labor Council. Support was also announced by the three left-liberal assemblymen, John Burton, Willie Brown, and William Stanton, who spoke at the noon rally on Friday. Telegrams of support poured in by the hundreds from campuses throughout the country. Davis students picketed the governor in Sacramento.

All over the campus, students were wearing IBM cards like name tags, except that these IBM cards were punched with holes spelling STRIKE or FSM. Others, wearing patches over their hearts made of black paper with a large white V, were arrested sit-inners who had graduated *cum laude*

---

(...continued)
faculty tendency. These were kept down to isolated incidents by the remarkable self-discipline of the FSM students.

from the "Santa Rita campus." A committee of the FSM announced that university work would be continued during the strike by the "Free University of California," with classes off-campus taught by striking Teaching Assistants.

How effective was the strike?

There is no other aspect of the whole battle of Berkeley which was so systematically falsified by the press. Reporters in the field who turned in the restrained estimate that the strike was "moderately successful" were told by their editors that this statement was unacceptable. The prefabricated headlines reading "Strike a Failure" were intended to be self-fulfilling prophecies by discouraging the students, rather than news reports. This news management was not always coordinated: thus, on Saturday the Oakland *Tribune* said that only a small minority had struck, but an inside-page photo came through showing the huge Life Sciences lecture auditorium "almost empty during student unrest." (N.Y. *Times* reports were generally an exception to the press picture.)

The question was complicated by two other considerations. Effective when? Thursday morning or Monday afternoon? During Thursday morning the strike was just getting under way. On the other hand, on Monday (as we shall see) the administration itself called off classes in the morning; and that afternoon, after the events to be described, the strike was probably at its peak, when it ended.

Also, the effectiveness of the strike is not the same question as "How many students struck?" A trade union measures the effectiveness of a strike by how much production has been cut: if a union can idle a department full of scabs by choking off the supply of material, then this strategic capacity increases the effectiveness of the walk out beyond the number of strikers. Likewise, if a professor called off classes, then it became both impossible and irrelevant to find out how many students would have come. Furthermore, a large part of the actual teaching of undergraduates was done in class sections by Teaching Assistants, who were students too. One TA striker, therefore, equaled in effectiveness many undergraduates: hence the strategic strength of the Graduate

Coordinating Committee, affiliated with FSM but operating independently, which had projected the strike originally.

A majority of the department heads took the attitude that classes could be called off for the duration of the strike at the discretion of the individual instructor, and few made menacing noises about retaliatory penalties. Two departments canceled classes. Philosophy Professor John Searle expressed the feeling of many others when he said: "For me to teach would be a betrayal of those students who cannot be present."

During that weekend (December 5-6) an FSM telephone survey of 5000 students randomly selected showed 55 per cent of the students pro-FSM and willing to strike. (This figure undoubtedly went up on Monday after the Greek Theater drama.) Presumably, then, on the average those classes that *were* held would be less than half full.

TA's were not only strategic in the strike; they were also necessarily the best and most advanced students, the cream of the crop. A majority of the TA's went on strike; in the humanities and social sciences, 90 per cent. The FSM's over-all report was that 900 out of 1200 struck, but this was only a guess. As this suggests, there were wide variations in the effectiveness of the strike from department to department. The strike was weakest in Engineering and Business Administration, as almost anyone would have predicted. Perhaps fewer would have expected the strike to be as successful as it was in departments like Mathematics, Biochemistry, Zoology, Astronomy, Physics.*

---

* Another insight into these variations comes from a "Report on Berkeley" by Bea Rechnitz, published in the Los Angeles *Free Press* (Jan. 1, 1965.). During the December 5-6 weekend of the strike, an FSM telephone campaign made thousands of phone calls to listings in the Student Directory, which includes department, year, and address. The author listened as a student volunteer made call after call: and with this information, the student's response could almost be foreseen.

A Business Administration major with a fraternity address: "Drop Dead!"

(continued...)

Another indicator was the library. "Normally packed, [it] was only about one-quarter filled," reported an item in the S.F. *Chronicle* about the same Friday when the strike was supposed to have flopped, "and the Reserve Book Room, ordinarily a Mecca for undergraduates, had only ten or fifteen students in mid-afternoon." And besides, the FSM decided *not* to strike the library, so that there was no picket line trying to keep students out.

Even where students were not themselves striking, they would not necessarily have been willing to scab on TA's as distinct from going to classes themselves. "In one graduate department of over 200 enrollment, only one student answered in a straw poll that he would consider replacing a Teaching Assistant who had been fired or had resigned." *(Graduate Political Scientists' Report.)*

The FSM's over-all estimates were that the strike was about 60-70 per cent effective on Friday, and 81 per cent on Monday afternoon.* A wag has suggested that by Monday some of the anti's were so busy denouncing the

---

(...continued)

A Physics major with a dormitory address: "Well, I just really don't know. I can't really say for sure that I understand what the FSM is trying to do. But I'll give it some more thought and might join in. A Physics major with a dormitory address: "Well, I just really don't know. I can't really say for sure that I understand what the FSM is trying to do. But I'll give it some more thought and might join in.

An English major with an apartment address: "Don't say another word, pal, I'm with you. Where can I pick up a picket sign Monday morning?"

A foreign student living at International House: "I understand. But please realize my situation here at the university."

A mother taking the message for her son: "1 can't understand why you students are making such a big fuss. My son just loves Cal."

A graduate student in Architecture living in the [high income] Berkeley Hills: "I haven't been to classes for two months, anyway. I just got back this weekend from skiing in Colorado."

* The figure for Monday was established by a "task force" of 72 students mobilized for the job, who checked 90% of the classrooms; they also ascertained that 59% of all classes were canceled.

strike that they did not have time to attend classes. Others who did not think of themselves as strikers were no doubt so bemused, bewildered and bedeviled that going to class might have seemed irrelevant.

The right-wing student magazine *Man and State* summed up the result as follows:

> The strike was a success. Many teamsters refused to cross the lines; eighty professors canceled classes; attendance at classes severely dropped. The majority of the Teaching Assistants joined the strike. Student opinion solidified behind FSM...

The gears, wheels and levers of the Multiversity apparatus had been effectively checked—by the strike. As the *FSM Newsletter* put it:

> The sit-in was less of a threat to Kerr than the strike. He knew he could break the sit-in through mass arrests, but the strike was impossible to stop. (No. 5, December 10, 1964.)

The Oakland *Tribune* wrote: "The Berkeley campus uprising recalls the numerous student anti-war strikes which plagued the campuses . . . in the mid-1930's." It recalls them but there is an enormous difference. The anti-war strikes of 1934-36 were demonstration strikes of one hour—at the best, that is, when they were not converted into innocuous "peace assemblies"—and they demanded nothing of the administrations themselves. The Berkeley strike of December 3-7, 1964, lasting through three full school days, was undoubtedly the longest and most massive student strike in this country, and it demanded nothing less than a backdown by the administration of the largest campus of the largest state university in the country.

It was instrumental in winning a great deal for the students, and there were no reprisals. It was probably the mightiest and most successful single effort of any kind ever made by an American student body in conflict with authority.

## *30. The Administration Plans a Coup*

During the weekend, three forces mobilized to get the upper hand on Monday in order to take hold of the situation. One was the FSM exerting all resources to maximize the strike, thus providing the motivation for the other two.

The second was a wing of the faculty, about 200 strong, caucusing in anticipation of the Academic Senate meeting due Tuesday. Its aim was to establish a set of proposals which would implement the Emergency Faculty Meeting of December 3, by putting forward a reasonable pro-"free-speech" platform on the regulation of campus political activity. Not all of these faculty members, by far, regarded themselves as friends of the FSM; but the FSM came to regard "the 200" as friends of "free speech." This assembly met Sunday evening and worked up a draft to present to the Academic Senate on December 8. If adopted, this platform meant a hard blow against the administration.*

The third side of this triangle, the administration, had to make a move too. On Friday it almost seemed as if Kerr was going to try to ride out the storm simply by lashing himself to the mast: the press announced that he was going to Chicago "on business"—an incredible move by a president whose university was in convulsion. The FSM, being composed of scholars, compared it to Louis XVI's flight to Varennes during the French Revolution.

"But Kerr did not go to Chicago after all; he remained behind in the Tuileries to work out ways of stopping the revolution," added the FSM historian.

* There is only one difference of substance between this draft and the motions adopted by the Academic Senate on December 8: Point 1 of the draft also asked that the university refrain from pressing charges against the arrested sit-inners.

Over the weekend' the administration worked out a new tactic. An *ad hoc* Council of Department Chairmen, headed by Professor Robert Scalapino, had come into existence on Thursday, in response to the obvious power-vacuum in administration. This group now came together with Kerr on proposals embodying one concession: a university amnesty.* The draft was approved by Governor Brown and by a hastily assembled, informal Regents meeting held near the San Francisco Airport. It would be presented with fanfare at a special university convocation at the Greek Theater on Monday. Kerr's aim was to undercut "the 200," pre-empt the field at the Academic Senate, and rally all waverers to support it as a Generous Compromise which could be rejected only by intransigent disrupters and malevolent Maoists.

This much was already known to the students the same Sunday, through the FSM "intelligence service." This term is something of an FSM joke: it refers to the constant flow of unsolicited reports into FSM Central on what was going on, anywhere, that could be of interest. To invent an illustration (since we cannot give real ones) : a waiter who might be serving a couple of administrators in a restaurant would hear parts of their conversation and phone in . . .

An FSM leaflet was prepared for distribution on Monday morning, setting forth Kerr's scheme. It is of exceptional interest, first because it

---

** According to Strong (who was present at the meeting of the chairmen with Kerr on Friday evening), the chairman also proposed a second concession: not only a university amnesty but also "so far as the university could intervene, the withdrawal of charges against the students arrested for packing Sproul Hall. The president then called the attention of the delegation to the Regents' approval of the recommendation that disciplinary action be instituted against students in violation of university rules subsequent to September 30.... He made clear that the Regents and the general public and the Legislature rightfully expected the university to exercise its authority in requiring observance of its rules." On this ground—i.e., Kerr's justification of the "Thanksgiving letters"—the second concession was dropped from the package.

explains part of this story; second, because it is a remarkable contribution to one of the obscurest comers of sociology—the sociology of the academic establishment. Here is most of it.

It begins with a reference to the caucus of "the 200," and comments pessimistically:

> But prospects for their success are dim. For years President Kerr has effectively controlled the Academic Senate by a hand-picked group of faculty, like Professors Scalapino and Lipset, whose personal ambitions and professional concerns make their interests those of the administration rather than of the faculty. In the past, backstage manipulation has prevented an organized opposition from forming. By Friday, it was clear that on the issues of free speech and free political expression, the tide had turned. Kerr immediately began to act. Realizing that his earlier repressive stance was no longer tenable, and desiring to maintain his position as the absolute power on campus (i.e., to keep the Academic Senate from re-emerging as an independent force) he developed an ingenious plan. With the aid of Professor Scalapino, and in consultation with Governor Brown—the man who called out the cops—he set out to undercut the Academic Senate. Their plan was to come out with a proposal strong enough to take the wind out of the FSM, weak enough to be acceptable to the Regents, and to come out with it quickly enough to pre-empt the contemplated actions of the Academic Senate.
>
> Furthermore, Kerr found it necessary to give his proposal some semblance of legitimacy; so the proposal comes from a group which he knew he could persuade

to produce the proposal he wanted—the Departmental Chairmen. They are sincere and honest men, deeply concerned with the issues, yet Kerr was able to persuade them that these slight gains are the most that could be expected. The university was in danger of losing funds provided by the state legislature

Many of Ken's closest associates are departmental chairmen, and in most departments the chairmen are essentially faculty administrators. These men are closest in spirit and outlook to the administration. They live in the world of grants and funds rather than the world of academic or political freedom. They are the members of the faculty most sensitive to Kerr's threat that unless the controversy is resolved in the manner he proposes, the state legislature will withhold university funds. Kerr did not tell them that State Senator George Miller, chairman of the State Finance Committee and the ranking member of the Senate Education Committee, has said that legislative appropriations will be kept "entirely separate from political occurrences on and off the campus," and that he resents the implications to the contrary which have been made by Kerr.

The final step in Kerr's plan is to have all classes canceled from 9 A.M. to 12 noon so that the effectiveness of the FSM strike will be unassessable. Then from 11:00 to 12:00 he and Scalapino will appear before the campus community, present their proposals in the name of their so-called faculty committee, and urge all students to return to classes.

[There follows a passage about possible formulations of Kerr's proposals, not yet definitely reported by the "intelligence service" when the leaflet was put out.] Then:

> Some time after this leaflet has been written, the final form of the department chairmen's proposal will be drafted. Between 8 A.M. and 9 A.M. today [Monday] copies of the proposal will be picked up by department chairmen; between 9 and 10 the chairmen will try to sell it to the faculty; between 10 and 11 the faculty will try to sell it to the grads and TA's; and between 11 and 12 Kerr and Scalapino will try and sell it to the students.. At noon, the FSM will respond.
>
> The issues have not changed since the start of the semester. They are threefold:
>
> (1) Administrative policies must not affect the *content* of speech or tend to impose prior restraints on speech;
>
> (2) Administrative regulations must impose no unnecessary restrictions upon the *form* of speech;
>
> (3) The students should have a voice in the enactment and interpretation of the regulations affecting them.

More emphasis needs to be put on the fact that two different sets of motivations came together in this plan, the department chairmen's and Kerr's. The FSM statement should be read as describing Kerr's.

As planned, classes were called off from 9 to 12, and departmental meetings were held to pre-sell the new proposal. Its text turned out to be as follows:

> (1) The university community shall be governed by orderly and lawful procedures in the settlement of issues and the full and free pursuit of educational activities on this campus shall be maintained.

(2) The university community shall abide by the new and liberalized political action rules and await the report of the Senate Committee on Academic Freedom.

(3) The Department Chairmen believe that the acts of civil disobedience on December 2 and 3 were unwarranted and that they obstruct rational and fair consideration of the grievances brought forward by the students.

(4) The cases of all students arrested in conjunction with the sit-in in Sproul Hall on December 2 and 3 are now before the courts. The university will accept the court's judgment in these cases as the full discipline for those offences. In the light of the cases now and prospectively before the courts, the university will not prosecute charges against any students for actions prior to December 2 and 3,but the university will invoke disciplinary actions for any violations henceforth.

(5) All classes shall be conducted as scheduled.

The FSM had expected something more appealing; this was almost nothing under the circumstances. The only concession was in Point 4, quashing the charges instituted by Strong's Thanksgiving letters. It is true that thus the administration admitted that the sit-in and the strike had achieved their original objective, but in a peculiar way: the special singling out of the four leaders for punishment was superseded, they explained, by the fact that all 800 would now be punished by the courts. As long as hundreds were to be hurt, they would not bother with the four. They could not be accused of straining the quality of mercy.

It was not much noticed at the time, or since, that the language of the last sentence of Point 4 was ambiguous. The promise to "not prosecute charges against any students" was limited, in strikingly precise language, to "actions prior to December 2 and 3," whereas the threat to invoke discipline "henceforth" applied from December 7 on. The wording clearly left the door open to a crackdown on strikers, in particular on striking TA's, even though it was the understanding of the department chairmen that they were proposing a general university amnesty. The wording also left the door open to penalities (e.g., dissolution) against clubs, as distinct from individual students. (Both of these doors were specifically closed. the next day by the Academic Senate motions.)

On the "free speech" issues, the proposal showed Kerr simply standing pat.

That morning, at many a department meeting, the proposal was roughly handled and widely condemned in the discussion. But at 11, when the proposal was to be formally presented to the university community in the Greek Theater, there was not going to be any discussion. The ASUC had asked Kerr before the weekend to speak to the students *and answer questions.* Kerr chose a format to speak *at* the students.

## *31. Classic Drama in the Greek Theater*

The performance in the Greek Theater did not go off as planned.

The same morning, there was a mass arraignment of 781 defendants arrested in the sit-in. Since there was no courtroom in California big enough to hold them, the Berkeley Community Theater was rented for the occasion. Shortly before 10:30, the students filed out, formed a line four abreast, and paraded to the Greek Theater.

By that time, the great bowl was rapidly filling up, with half the forward section reserved for the faculty. By 11, even the hillside slopes above the top seats were thickly covered. A large number of pro-FSMers had come from the central campus in parade lines instead of arriving early, and now jammed the side entrances barely in sight of the stage. There were 15,000-18,000 ready to listen.

As the crowd was waiting, Mario Savio entered front and received an ovation from about half the assembly. He had been backstage requesting permission to make a response at the meeting; Kerr and Scalapino had turned it down. Also denied was permission to make an announcement at the end of the meeting that the FSM would discuss the new proposal at its noon rally. An ASUC request for a speaker had been turned down too.

Now a knot of reporters gathered around Savio, and he gave them a scoop: "I will make an announcement when the meeting is over." A reporter asked: "Whether you are given permission or not?"—"Correct," replied the FSM leader, going on to say, in reply to another question, that he would ask all, including the chairmen, to come to the noon rally, "Dr. Kerr too if he wants to."*

Several dozen department chairmen filled the seats on the stage. Professor Scalapino opened the proceedings with a speech, studded with eternal verities about education and freedom, in the course of which he paid his respects to the FSM leaders:

> There are a small number of individuals, I regret to say, who are interested in fomenting a crisis merely for the sake of crisis—in the hope that continuing chaos will bring about a total revolution and their own particular concept of utopia.

After this scholarly analysis, Scalapino presented the five points of the new proposal, and introduced Kerr.

"Today this university, this great campus, faces its future," Kerr's speech began, and continued in a similar Commencement Address tone. It ended with a plush passage invoking "the powers of persuasion ... decent means . . . constructive acts . . . opposition to passion . . . reasoned argument .. . enlightenment . . ." The best comment I heard later on the oratorical effort was this from a student: "*There* were 18,000

---

* This interview is reproduced from the tape recording made on the spot by KPFA. Not a single newspaper later printed the information that Savio had announced his intention to the press in advance.

people hoping against hope for a human word from their president on what had happened, and they get this rhetoric."

In between the elocution and the peroration, however, Kerr gave the following information: (1) He endorsed the chairmen's proposal and it was going into effect immediately. (2) Because of the court charges against the arrested students, "prior university charges are allowed to lapse." (3) The university would accept the ASUC's suggestion for a legal test of whatever new regulations were established for political activity. (4) The university was devoted to the 1st and 14th Amendments. (5) There were other problems too: "We must constantly seek added funds. We must face, I regret to say, external investigations of the recent conduct of this campus." It was a broad enough hint.

Scalapino then announced that the meeting stood adjourned. For the next scene we turn to the accurate account published in the N.Y. *Times:*

> As he turned away . Mr. Savio entered from the left side of the stage. He walked slowly toward the microphone, brushing past the faculty members. Mr. Savio was settling his hands on either side of the podium, taking in a breath before his remarks, when two campus policemen grabbed him. One put his arm around Mr. Savio's throat, forcing his head back; the other grabbed him in an arm
> lock.

As Savio went limp, he was dragged on his back to the dressing room backstage. Several thousands of students shouted toward the stage and surged forward to get closer.

Some department chairmen went backstage and tried to enter the locker dressing room. Someone shouted: "There's going to be a riot if he's not let out in one minute!" Sociology Professor John Leggett and Philosophy chairman Joseph Tussman argued forcefully with the police and with Scalapino. At the other end of the backstage area, Kerr stood in the doorway of another dressing room, dumbfounded by the scene. Speech Department chairman Beloof came up and shouted at him, "You have to let him speak!"* Kerr and Scalapino were finally persuaded; the latter returned to the microphone and announced to the accompaniment of a great cheer that Savio would be allowed to talk. The FSM leader, tousled and rumpled, made his brief announcement of the FSM meeting and invited the department chairmen to come. He added: "Please leave here. Clear this disastrous scene, and get down to discussing the issues."

Backstage, Kerr told reporters: "This is completely unexpected . . . It caught me completely by surprise . . . No, I didn't tell them to arrest him. I was quite surprised by the whole event." He later told a news conference "that the police had been summoned because it was understood that a move was to be made to take over the meeting." (N.Y. *Times,* Dec. 8.)

Another paper had him saying after the melee: "That was a hell of an ending." And this was *not* rhetoric.

The students streamed back to Sproul Hall Plaza, which filled up as solidly as had the Greek Theater, with 8000-10,000 people. Professor Beloof told the throng that, although he was one of the chairmen presumably sponsoring the convocation, he (and perhaps others) had never even been told that Savio had requested permission to make the announcement, and that he would have wanted permission granted. Professor Tussman told the students: "I think at this point the university is in your hands and we have to trust to your judgment as you consider what ought to be done . I leave the future of the university, which I assure you is now in your hands, with confidence that you care about the university, and that you will think about what you do, and do what you think is right."

Various FSM speakers explained the hollowness of the chairmen's proposal, and directed attention to the resolution of "the 200" coming up

---

* A sidelight on the Multiversity: Beloof has it that when he addressed Ken, he suddenly realized that this was the first time, in his sixteen years on the Berkeley campus, that he had ever spoken to the president of the university....

before the Academic Senate the next day. It was announced that the strike would continue for the rest of this day only, so that Tuesday would be a calm setting for the Academic Senate's deliberations. The Department Chairmen had originally planned to devote the afternoon to meetings of Department representatives with students, but by this time even the chairmen had forgotten the plan that fizzled.

## *32. The ESM at the Peak*

"The university is in your hands," the Philosophy chairman had told the students after the Greek Theater when he was given the floor by the same FSM that had been scouted as a handful of malcontents not long before. By sheer coincidence, a student vote was going on that same day—a scheduled election for seven representative positions on the ASUC Senate.

Slate, the student "party," was running seven candidates on a platform of support to the FSM as well as other issues. This was as close as the students were going to get to registering themselves on one side of the fence or the other in a choice between militantly pro-FSM representatives or pro-"loyalist" representatives.

They were voting, moreover, right in the midst of the FSM's most militant action. The one-third of the campus traditionally most favorable to Slate, the graduate students, were excluded from this vote, as we know; only undergraduates voted. The turnout was double its usual size: 5276 voters.

The result, announced the next day, was a massive victory for every one of the seven pro-FSM candidates, with some of them receiving nearly as much as the *total* vote cast in previous ASUC elections.

It was a sweeping repudiation of the "loyalist" leadership of the ASUC, whose "sandbox politics" had been startlingly exhibited just the evening before the vote was announced. That day, with the tumultuous events of the Greek Theater and its aftermath convulsing the campus, an emergency meeting of the ASUC Senate had been called: it had to be canceled because a majority of the Senate failed to attend.

After the result was known, the ASUC president, Charles Powell, sadly opined: "Over-all, we've missed the boat. We have in many ways been inadequate in dealing with the freespeech problem." This was something like the conclusion which Barry Goldwater announced *after* his defeat in 1964, that he had been the wrong candidate for the GOP . . . The same day, the head of "Students for Law and Order" said he "attributed the vast support the FSM appears to have at the present moment among the student body to a `power vacuum' ..."

There is undoubted difficulty for outsiders in grasping why the drama at the Greek Theater helped to swing student sentiment toward FSM, partly because the initial writing of magazine articles out of Berkeley to national magazines was so largely monopolized by a small group of die-hard enemies of the student movement (Feuer, Lipset, Glazer). Lipset & Seabury wrote, for example, that Berkeley needed a faculty which "understands how a few extremists can make the large majority of moderates do its bidding," in the best literary style of J. Edgar Hoover; and indeed many faculty members would be grateful if these two distinguished scholars would someday explain how the "few extremists" were able to pull this off right under their very nose. At the Greek Theater it all happened on a literal stage *(center front)* before the eyes of 18,000—announced in advance quite unconspiratorially.

The FSM's "secret weapon" on this day was basically the same as it had been right along: Kerr and the administration, including their brain trusters and advisers. Here are five considerations:

(1) By the time Scalapino adjourned the meeting, the "swing" part of the audience could not but have felt that the whole thing was anticlimactic. An impressive setting had been created, the university assembled in all its numbers in an unprecedented convocation, over fifty chairmen mustered on the stage to flank Kerr in all their eminence—and then the man simply had nothing to *say* to them that reached out. Kerr was not talking with them; he was reading them an administrative press release. In fact, he was acting out what the "extremists" had said was the trouble with the Multiversity; he was doing an excellent impersonation of the Captain of the Bureaucracy.

(2) That was the form. We have already pointed out that the content was slight, and it sounded even slighter than it was. This was another reason for letdown.

(3) The whole setup had been engineered to keep the students at arm's length. The ASUC and the *Daily Cal* editor, "loyalist" as they were, had pleaded with Kerr to hold an explanatory meeting at which students could at least ask questions. All the panoply and pomp of the Greek Theater *mise en scene* was designed to prevent any human contact between the students and the administration. But it was really too late for the administration to pretend to ignore the fact that there were thousands of students who could not be ignored. The refusal to let the FSM announcement be made was an apt symbol, only spotlighted when the administration argued that even the ASUC had been ignored too.

(4) The students were fighting for something they summarized as "free speech," and the administration had been maintaining stoutly that there was no issue about free speech. The forces of Law and Order that day gave the students a symbol of this disagreement too: the first move of the cop who pounced on the FSM leader was to choke his threatened words off with an arm about his throat *literally*. The "swing" opinions might have been able to take this if they had been convinced that this was necessary police protection against a "takeover" of the meeting. But the claim that it was a "takeover" faded before a fact: the fact that a few minutes later the administration *did* allow Savio to make the announcement they had refused. The "takeover" charge might have stuck only if the administration people had acted as if they believed it themselves.

(5) Lastly, there was a dramatic impact which could only be felt on the spot. This was the lightning transition from light-fingered prose to the heavy hand of the cop. One moment, Kerr's soothing phrases—about "the powers of persuasion against the use of force," "opposition to passion and hate," "decent means to decent ends"—were lolling on the breeze; and the next minute, the armed men of the state had darted out from behind the scenery to show what the "powers of persuasion" concealed and what the "passion and hate" were opposed to. Coming in

quick succession like that, the two pictures blurred together; and there was the face of the establishment.

It was part of the intensive education which the campus was undergoing: modern education, with visual aids.

## *33. The Story of a Rumor*

Most of these developments pointed toward the Academic Senate meeting to be held Tuesday, December 8, at 3:10.

The day before, after the Greek Theater events, the motions on "free speech" drafted by "the 200" had been substantially adopted as its own by the Academic Senate's Committee on Academic Freedom, which had been charged with bringing in a report on the subject. The original scheme of Kerr and his advisers to pre-empt the field with the chairmen's proposal was dead as a doornail, badly mauled by the departmental discussion meetings of Monday morning and then killed off in the Greek Theater.*

That evening in part, and then like wildfire the next morning, a startling rumor ran from end to end of the campus: Kerr had agreed to, or at least accepted, the motions of "the 200"! This rumor, if true, sounded like complete capitulation, for the FSM had been making clear for days that the motions of "the 200" would be accepted as tantamount to the full program of the movement. Mario Savio had declared that if the Regents accepted the motions, the FSM would become primarily a defense organization for the arrested students. Now if Kerr accepted them too ...

---

* The scheme was not the only casualty in that amphitheater. There had been a persistent report that Strong was slated to go as chancellor, and that morning it was the unanimous view that Robert Scalapino was scheduled for the post. After the fiasco, another department chairman is supposed to have called out, unacademically: "There goes the chancellorship, Bob!" If it isn't true, it should be.

It was too good to be true; but the very existence of this rumor, as well as the story behind it, was an important and unacknowledged conditioning influence on the subsequent action of the Academic Senate. The story behind it is still not entirely clear, but an informed version of it which is probably 95 per cent accurate goes as follows:

After the Greek Theater disaster, Kerr was approached by some of "the 200" in the hope of now getting him to agree to the motions (taking advantage, I presume, of the shattering of his own strategy). Such was his mood that in the course of the discussion, Kerr indicated that with some reservations he could accept general agreement with the "major policy content," including the content of Point 3 which barred university restriction of the content of speech or advocacy on campus as sweepingly as the FSM had always demanded. He did not express acceptance of Point 4, which transferred important disciplinary powers back from the administration to the Academic Senate.

However, Kerr was under the impression that he was engaged in *negotiations* with the faculty members, and that they were aiming to come out with an agreement which would present a jointly watered-down version of the motions to the Academic Senate. (A dark angel now whispers in my left ear: Kerr was assuming that after the Senate had passed the watered-down version beclouded by his reservations, and after this sticky moment had passed, who would stop him from "reinterpreting" the motions to death and "implementing" them in his own way? Yet who knows what Kerr felt like then?)

But the faculty members had no intention or even means of making a deal. Kerr had expressed a (partial) agreement with (part of) the motions, and that was a gain. This was the factual .basis of the rumor, it would seem. On the other hand, the account goes on to say that when Kerr saw that the motions were going to the Senate unchanged, he "blew his top," and was dissuaded from appearing at the Senate discussion himself only by the consideration that things would be much worse if the position was adopted against his personal opposition.

## *34. The Victory at the Academic Senate*

The Academic Senate assembled after 3, with by far the largest attendance in its history, about twice as high as usual. Outside Wheeler Hall, thousands of students listened to the debate, piped to them from loudspeakers installed on the steps, silent except for occasional stormy applause.

The motions for free political activity were presented by the chairman of the Committee on Academic Freedom, Professor Garbarino. (For the complete text, see page 175.) The onslaught was led by Professor Lewis Feuer, but it took the form of a hamstringing amendment rather than a frontal attack. Where Point 3 barred university restriction of "the content of speech or advocacy," the Feuer amendment made it: "the content of speech or advocacy on this campus provided that it is directed to no immediate act of force or violence ..."

One of the surprising things about the Academic Senate meeting was that no one presented the position which the administration and Regents had been counterposing to the FSM's for almost two months: viz., the restriction of on campus advocacy to "lawful off-campus action, not unlawful off-campus action." It was not brought up, as a motion or in discussion, even by the same faculty members who had supported its similars in the late CCPA. Feuer himself had been a defender of the administration's viewpoint on this formulation, but chose to make the fight instead on a proviso which had not previously been proposed.

Nor did Feuer overtly direct his amendment against any political activity actually mounted on campus, explaining it rather in terms of hypothetical future contingencies. It was only later that the amendment's seconder, Professor Glazer, admitted under some bombardment that he included a civil rights sit-in as an act of "force."* This indicated that the

---

* This admission came in the course of a debate with me on January 9, 1965, under challenge to answer a question from the floor. Feuer, who was present, did not dissociate himself from Glazer's reply. (For text of this debate, see

(continued...)

amendment would have given the administration the right to crack down on (for example) such actions by CORE. This meaning of the amendment was not intimated at the Academic Senate discussion.

The Feuer amendment was defeated 737-284, and the motions were adopted as presented by a vote of 824-115. Outside, the students cheered in the gathering dusk.

As Professor Tussman later summarized it: "Anything that is illegal in the community at large is still illegal on the campus. The question is: Should the university impose more restrictions on the students in the area of political activity than exists in the community at large? The Senate said: No."

The next action of the Academic Senate was to set up an Emergency Executive Committee to deal with "problems arising out of the present crisis." (The election to this committee a few days later returned a majority of "moderates," i.e. not members of "the 200.") The stand of the faculty was made so clear that the administration and its supporters have been constrained to make a type of attack on it which is unusual in academic circles, impugning the intellectual integrity of the overwhelming majority of the Academic Senate. In an interview on January 5, Kerr explained to the press, "I don't think the faculty ever went for the FSM argument, but they had their own grievances," viz., the Berkeley campus was being "challenged for supremacy" by other university campuses, and "this trauma" led the Berkeley professors into this action "against the state-wide administration." (I heard one of Berkeley's outstanding professors meditatively call this statement "infamous.")

Lipset & Seabury were by no means as vulgar: they merely wrote that "While many voted on principle, others voted for it as a strike settlement by the weaker party." This was also the theme of speeches at the

---

(...continued)
*New Politics, Vol.* 4, No. 1.)

Academic Senate debate: "Don't yield to the mob," "Don't vote with a gun at your temple," etc.

There is undoubtedly an element of truth in the latter point, for some; but there is a more accurate way of looking at this truth. What had happened by December 8 is that a large part of the faculty had gone through a process of education.

In the trade-union analogy suggested by Lipset, sweatshop employers who are forced to settle with the union also often rail bitterly at "the gun to the temple" and coercion; but they too are being educated—educated to the notion that they have to take the needs and interests of their workers into account, that these are not merely "hands." By December 8, many faculty members had been educated to the truth that the needs and demands of the students had to be taken into account, even if this modified their own more conservative notions of how the university should be run. A professor might well be in disagreement with the "free speech" demands of the FSM, and yet, while maintaining his own opinion as before, come around to the view, however reluctantly, that everything did *not* depend on his own opinion alone.

These faculty members had been educated to this conclusion by their students, and in a somewhat more concentrated way than is usual in academic institutions. The education was carried on in action, and there is a prejudice among academics against considering that action is educational—in fact, this view of the educational nature of action had been overtly attacked by Kerr in September ("What's so intellectual about collecting money?" etc. )

The education had been carried on through the sit-ins and the strike among other things. These conveyed the information to the pupils (the faculty and administration) that the students were quite serious in refusing to be docile "hands"—or IBM-punched Unit-Hours of Instruction. The administration, it turned out, could absorb this information only under the added stimulus of being rapped on the knuckles.

There is another angle of approach to this question, made in the *FSM Newsletter, No. 5:*

> Some of the professors who spoke against the resolutions claimed that they were offered for reasons of expediency rather than principle. They said the Senate was being pressured by "the mob."
>
> It would be ludicrous to deny that pressure has been exerted in the past few months. On our side, there have been the demonstrations of October 1 and 2, the Sproul Hall sit-ins, and Monday's mass rally. On the administration's side, there have been threats of expulsion, an army of policemen, and the spreading of false rumors that the legislature would cut off funds.
>
> The net result of these two sets of countervailing pressures was to create a situation in which the Academic Senate was able to make its decisions freely for the first time. The tremendous power wielded by the administration and the Regents had been canceled out by the mass action of the students.

One test of this truth is as follows: the same administration supporters who volubly deplore the pressure of the students' action on their decisions have never been known to denounce the regular, institutionalized pressures by which the administration habitually controlled the Academic Senate. Nor did they protest the type of pressure represented by the threat that rich donors would cut off contributions unless matters were settled to their satisfaction.

## *35. End of the Beginning*

Those who had been attacking the FSM as "intransigent," "can't be satisfied," etc., must have been amazed at the transport of joy and satisfaction with which the entire movement greeted the decision of the Academic Senate as the means of settling and ending the conflict. The next day's noon rally in Sproul Hall Plaza was a lighthearted victory celebration, spiced also by the fact that the Academic Senate's action had coincided with Mario Savio's twenty-second birthday.

An FSM leaflet was headed, "Happiness Is an Academic Senate Meeting," and said in part:

> With deep gratitude the Free Speech Movement greets the action of the faculty. The passing of the proposals of the Academic Freedom Committee is an unprecedented victory for both students and faculty. For months the FSM has fought to bring the issues to public discussion and to rouse the faculty to take action. Our efforts have finally succeeded, and our protest has been vindicated.

To the general public, who had been fed for months on the slanted accounts in the press, the action of the faculty must have been confusing and upsetting. If the disturbances had been due to a handful of red troublemakers, forlorn crackpots, and lumpen-beatniks, who wanted nothing but a Caracas-style university, then how on earth could one of the most eminent faculties in the country vote so overwhelmingly to vindicate their demands? How could one understand the S.F. Ex*aminer's* headline: "Academic Senate Asks 'TOTAL U.C. FREEDOM'"?

The discrepancy was amusingly illustrated the same day by S. I. Hayakawa, the semanticist teaching at San Francisco State College, who chose exactly December 8 to make a speech explaining that the FSM was "no longer interested in free speech" but only in humiliating the administration, in "marching the streets bearing placards," and in painless martyrdom. "Whatever concessions have been made, none has satisfied the student," Hayakawa told his audience, unaware that the same day the FSM was expressing happy acceptance of the faculty position as a solution to the long fight.

The students had the wry satisfaction of seeing the 180degree flipflop performed the next day by the editorialist of the *S.F. Chronicle,* who up to this point had been heaping vituperation and abuse on the students and their demands, suggesting their expulsion and insisting that no issues of "free speech" were involved. There was no more of this in the editorial on December 9; rather an earnest request that the authorities designate "adequate university sites" for students' speech and advocacy, and that only the civil authorities enforce disciplinary action at these sites.

Organized in part by a group of professors, a stream of supporting resolutions and statements poured in from various parts of the state and nation, backing up the stand taken by the Academic Senate.

But the trouble was not yet over.

Chancellor Strong, who had been hospitalized for an internal ailment on December 6, returned to work on the 12th, and launched a guerrilla harassment of the students. The next day a meeting of 768 defendants with their attorneys,. scheduled for days to be held in Wheeler Hall, was canceled by the chancellor's intervention late the same afternoon; the students barely had time to move the meeting to the Berkeley Community Theater. On the 14th, a benefit concert for the defendants, which had been advertised for Wheeler Hall on the basis of an informal notification of the dean's office, was canceled when the dean was asked for formal permission the same day and refused it. At the last minute, the concert had to be moved to a hall in Berkeley. The grounds, a ban on collecting any funds or admissions at such an affair on campus, also caused the transference to San Francisco of a proposed lecture appearance by author James Baldwin, on behalf of the FSM defense fund.

Finally, on December 15 of that week, a non-fund-raising meeting by the FSM was also pushed off-campus. James Farmer, national director of CORE, had come to Berkeley to speak in support of the students. Many faculty members put heavy pressure on the FSM to move the meeting to the city strip of the Bancroft sidewalk—off university property—in order not to offend the administration. It was ironic: in its long days of conflict, the FSM had held its rallies on Sprout steps with impunity; now, after its great victory, it was told that a similar rally would be a provocation, because the Regents were meeting in a few days.

The FSM yielded to this pressure reluctantly. James Farmer stood on a chair placed on the city strip, as he spoke to a crowd extending far into the plaza. He was introduced by Professor Jacobus ten Broek, who, being blind, had to rest his Braille notes on the head of a caryatid student.

The hope that the Regents would accept the December 8 position of the Academic Senate was doomed to disappointment. At their meeting on December 17-18, they summarily rejected the proposal that disciplinary powers be transferred back to the faculty,* declaring this non-negotiable in the old highhanded style. But they temporized with the "free speech" provisions, by setting up "a comprehensive review of university policies" on "maximum freedom on campus consistent with individual and group responsibility," and by making a deep bow to the First and Fourteenth Amendments. On the other hand, Strong's advice to inaugurate an ironfisted policy looking to summary expulsions was not adopted either.

This modest proposal by the chancellor was detailed in his confidential report to the Regents dated December 16—a document which makes clear that the ex-liberal professor of philosophy saw in the 'student movement nothing but a conspiracy to disrupt the university which need only be met by draconic discipline and police methods. But Strong's report was also an overt attack on Kerr for "vacillation, concessions, compromises and retreats," for by-passing the chancellor, for "a too political rather than a moral approach," and other sins. With this, Strong was through; but the actual process of his removal was devious.

The Regents' original plan had been to take the sting out of Strong by reducing. his role to that of "chairman of a board" while Martin Meyerson, dean of Environmental Design, became vice-chancellor and

* The Academic Senate had once controlled student discipline. It had yielded this power of its own volition (the faculty didn't want to be bothered)—de *facto* in 1921 and completely in 1938.

de facto executive officer. Now they seized on a relatively minor error in a public statement which Strong released on December 31, to inform him that he was fired. Chairman Ed Carter took the opportunity to tell him that he rated only a "C average" as administrator and that he had lost the confidence and support of the faculty. But it was agreed that a public dismissal would appear to be a victory for the FSM, and this must not be. Various stories were tried on for size, and it was finally decided to announce that he was taking a leave of absence to recover his health. This was made official at a Regents meeting on January 2 and Meyerson was proclaimed acting chancellor.*

Thus, when the students returned to campus from the year-end vacation, wondering whether they had to prepare for the final exams or for a different kind of test, the news of Strong's removal brought an immediate lightening of the tension. Formally, the proviso about "lawful action" and double punishment still stood; but in practice it was expected that there would be a large number of detailed changes in the regulations, as well as a new and wholesome respect by the administration for the temper of the students.

The acting chancellor announced that he had voted with the majority of the Academic Senate on December 8. The day after he took office, a number of campus regulations on student activity were eased: the noxious 72-hour-notification rule was reduced to 48 hours; Sproul Hall steps were made legally available for student meetings, with loudspeakers provided by the university; areas were designated for club tables, and the former ban on fund-raising, recruiting, etc., was as if it had never been.

On Monday, January 4, the Free Speech Movement held its first legal rally on the steps of Sproul Hall at noon, while perfectly legal "table-manners" diligently fund-raised, solicited and recruited near Ludwig's Fountain in the middle of the plaza. Several thousand students turned their attention to the oncoming finals, which had to be conquered too.

---

* This is a summary of the account given by Strong in his second confidential report to the Regents, dated January 3, entitled "Swan Song: Memoranda for the Record." (Full text in S.F. Examiner, March 13, 1965.)

But over 700 of the students whose mettle had helped to bring about this peaceful scene were still before the courts, threatened with vengeance for their success.

The "revolution" was over for the time being. There was a not wholly easy peace. The new administration walked softly and visibly jumped at a sharp word, involuntarily looking over the shoulder to see if there were any sit-inners left in the . corridors of Sproul Hall.

The students wondered: *Is this all we can do? Has anything changed fundamentally after all?*

## 36. Before the Second Round

The new "Era of Good Feeling" lasted for two months after the beginning of the year, long enough to show the positive consequences of the students' *de facto* victory, a victory in which the faculty also had its share. The feeling of community, the warmth of morale had never been so high; there was a new spirit of respect and trust on both sides of the classrooms and lecture halls.

The new provisional rules issued by Acting Chancellor Meyerson admitted, at least in practice, virtually all of the main free speech goals for which the students had been fighting. There was a change for the better even on minor gripes which had not figured prominently in the fracas, such as the right of off-campus clubs to schedule a series of connected meetings rather than singles only.

Early in January, a report to the Academic Senate by three .constitutional-law experts on the faculty of the law school clearly counseled against any regulation of the content of speech on campus, as "unnecessary, as well as Constitutionally unwise," thus reinforcing the December 8 stand of the faculty with eminent authority. On January 12, Meyerson announced the appointment of Sociology Professor Neil Smelser as his special assistant in matters of student political activity; this cut out of the circuit the vice-chancellor in charge of student affairs, Alex Sherriffs, a man widely regarded as specially hostile to the students' aspirations. On January 21, a large number of professors, eventually mounting to 255, put their names to a remarkably forceful document presented to the court arguing for the dismissal of the charges against the arrested sit-inners: *A Suggestion for Dismissal,* from which we have quoted more than once. This was a larger number of faculty members than attended many ordinary Academic Senate meetings.

The students' victory, far from disrupting the university, was making for an unprecedented solidarity.

One other moot question was settled for good. From the beginning the FSM had insisted that as soon as its basic aim of insuring free speech and free political activity on campus was secured, it would dissolve. Its enemies, on the other hand, lost no occasion to charge that any concession or victory would be used by the FSM leaders only to escalate their demands; that they were unappeasable, intransigent, interested only in utilizing fair-seeming issues to raise impossible demands. In point of fact, during January the FSM went on the shelf without a murmur from any quarter, so thoroughly that it could not even be wholly resuscitated in March when the opening of the Second Round demanded it. Remaining in operation was only the self-organized committee of the sit-in defendants.

But while the FSM as such faded away, in strict accord with its claim to have been a temporary response to an immediate crisis, student organization on campus was now significantly advanced beyond the ante-bellum picture. The Graduate Coordinating Committee remained as a militant organization defending the interests of the graduate students, and campaigned for the admittance of this one-third of the student body to the ASUC. In elections held by the ASUC in February and early March, this proposal was endorsed first by the graduate students themselves and then by an undergraduate vote. The entrance of the grads, everyone knew, would tend to transform the ASUC into a more militant and meaningful body.

The most important addition to student organization, however, was the new trade-union organization of the teaching assistants and other university-employed graduates (research assistants, readers, etc.). One of the most interesting effects of the FSM fight on students' thinking, and one of the least noticed, was the transformation of their attitudes on the labor movement and labor unions. Before, even many students who considered themselves liberals or radicals had been imbued with the stereotyped images —of Big Labor as nothing more than an integral part of the Establishment, which they got from the daily press and (in somewhat more sophisticated form) from their professors—images which identified the labor movement merely with union bureaucrats indistinguishable from corporate executives. One of the educational by-products of the semester of rebellion was a revaluation of trade-unionism on very practical grounds.

For one thing, the students had found themselves driven back on the typical trade-union weapon, the strike, to win their own objectives. They had found themselves lined up side by side with the workers' trade unions on the campus, such as the Building Service Employees and the Carpenters, who had long been harassed by the same administration, and they had appreciated this help. Off the campus, the main public support they had gotten in the non-academic community came from important sections of the labor movement, especially the San Francisco Labor Council (George Johns) and the Building Service union (George Hardy); from the state leaders of the Auto Workers (Paul Schrade) and the Amalgamated Clothing Workers (Leonard Levy); and from the local, state and national organizations of the American Federation of Teachers. Above all, facing the threat of possible reprisals by the administration, they rediscovered for themselves what trade unionism was all about. The way was somewhat eased by the fact that the American Federation of Teachers had already established a small local on the campus, representing faculty members and professional librarians. The teaching assistants thereupon, by December, formed another local of the AFT, and soon counted over 400 members.

On its side, the faculty-library local of the Teachers Union, beginning with two or three dozen members, came out of the semester's turmoil with better than a tripling of its membership and a considerably more militant and active leadership. There were other changes in the picture of faculty organization, as there had been changes in student organization. We have already mentioned that the Academic Senate acquired an Emergency Executive Committee of its own, a structural change which tended to make it somewhat less a creature of the administration. "The 200" remained on as a loosely coordinated group among the faculty, representing the spirit of the December 8 resolution. In opposition, a rival faction called the "Faculty Forum" was set up by Professors Lipset, Malia and others: this can briefly be described as the pro-Kerr group. (Professor Malia, a specialist in Russian history, described it reminiscently as "the Center or Marsh.") On the other side of the "Marsh," a 'very small right wing of the faculty, distinguished by its sympathy for the iron-fisted line of ex-Chancellor Strong as against Kerr, undertook no overt organization. It represented a handful of professors, as against two to three hundred for each of the larger faculty groups.

This burgeoning of self-organization among the students and the faculty (who together, after all, *are* the university) reflected the new moods of self-confidence and initiative that came in the wake of the victory. Both the new organizations growing and the new spirits blowing through the campus added up to one big difference: the whole university structure could no longer be as easily manipulated from above, that is, from the office of the president. Kerr's maneuvering space was sensibly curtailed by this big fact alone, to which must be added the consequences of his sharply diminished prestige, after his public performances in December.

Furthermore, he was falling between two stools: to *his* right, among a minority group of the Regents as well as in important power centers in the state, he was being sharply downgraded, as The Man Who Had Failed to Control the Animals. His liberal disinclination to resort to all-out terror had not won the gratitude of the movement which he had tried unsuccessfully to smash by more subtle means; but it had won the contempt of the more iron-gutted rightists who blamed the victory of the students on his vacillation and halfheartedness. He was in a perfectly classic squeeze; and no one who has read Kerr's books can doubt that he had the historical perspective to understand what was happening to him.

For the faculty and students, the continued development of the situation as they saw it was creative and exhilarating in its promise; but for President Kerr it bade fair to be fatal. The one thing he could not do was sit still; he had to make his move. When the opportunity to do so came, his execution was perhaps the most brilliant single operation in this story.

## *37. The "Restoration" Coup*

To restore the Berkeley campus to anything resembling a normal first-rate American university will be immensely difficult. It will require a high and rare level of administrative leadership and intelligence.

So wrote Prof. Lipset in his *Reporter* article in January; but by the time the words were on the newsstands it was clear that the Berkeley campus had not only been "restored" but was better than ever, *for the faculty and students.*

The immensely difficult problem was of a different Restoration, viz., of the previous "level of administrative leadership" from the top floor of University Hall. The opportunity opened up on March 3.

A young man named John Thomson, inspired by sensational newspaper stories about all those lumpen-beatniks, anarchists, and rioters at Berkeley, arrived from New York to "make the scene." As a total stranger to the university community, he stationed himself on the steps of the student union building at Bancroft and Telegraph, and held up a small sign with his own prescription for the world's ills. It read: FUCK. A passing student made a good-humored inquiry about the part of speech intended, and Thomson clarified his manifesto by adding an exclamation mark. Thus the campus got the Word which shook it to its foundations. Thomson got the word from a campus policeman and landed in a Berkeley jail.

The next noon, a handful of students and non-students used the loudspeakers on Sproul Hall steps to denounce Thomson's arrest. Since they used the "obscene" word, nine were subsequently arrested. Three of these were U.C. students. One of them, Arthur Goldberg, a Slate leader, had been prominent in the leadership of the FSM in the October days; in November he had been the "moderate" dropped from the Steering Committee for a while. His notorious opposition to the militancy of the FSM leadership, combined with his reputed admiration for Peking, had earned him the sobriquet of the "Marshmallow Maoist" in FSM circles.

Since another of the students had been arrested after challenging the police by reading passages from *Lady Chatterley's Lover* using the Word, and since English Department chairman Mark Schorer had written the introduction to the Grove Press edition of Lawrence's novel, Prof. Schorer showed up the following noon on Sproul steps to give the Wordmongers a lecture on the difference between serious literature and nosethumbing. He drew the distinction between using language in a book, where it is read voluntarily and privately in a given context, and "flaunting" it in public with the obvious intent only of baiting those who object to its use:

> ... if this language appears in a book, one can choose to read it or not to read it. This seems to me quite different from having that language or a single word from that language thrust upon one's attention in a public place. I do think that the whole business in unworthy of serious students and that it is going to make it more difficult for the faculty to protect what *are* your serious interests than would otherwise be the case.... I insist that there is a difference between reading and social conduct. One is a matter of private edification or indulgence; the other can easily become a public nuisance. There is a crucial difference between choosing to read what may be distasteful to others and imposing what is distasteful *on* others.

The Wordmongers generally argued that they were engaged in the socially significant task of exposing hypocrisy; presumably if the Word became generally accepted, hypocrisy would suffer a blow. It was easy enough to point out to them that this was the method of curing a fever by freezing the patient. There would be underground terms for sex as long as the underlying attitudes persisted. To try to change the psychological substratum by flaunting the Word made no more sense than trying to cure race prejudice by forcing racial intermarriage.

Where their case made its appeal was in its *tu quoque* argument against excesses of hypocritical indignation. However sophomoric the Wordmongers were in their approach to a real problem, they were largely sincere in their belief that something should be done to *separate* sexual terms from "dirty" connotations—just the reverse of what their philistine detractors ascribed to them. The administration had never taken much action against the real smutty stuff which gets winked at on every college campus. Just before this, a campus group had carried on a suggestive "Pussy Galore" campaign offensive to many for its simple vulgarity; nothing happened. Just a few yards from where the students were arrested, the ASUC bookstore prominently displayed and sold the usual raft of bare-breasted magazines; "unredeemed by any social significance," in a manner which imposed them on the perhaps unwilling passer-by. A letter to the *Daily Cal* told of a recent frat smoker, probably attended by administration officials as well, at which the Word had been flaunted. There was the usual problem of sniggering jokes in the campus humor magazine.

The opposition of faculty members like Schorer and the cold response of student public opinion to the martyrdom of the arrested students had their effect. Nothing dampened the Wordmongers' ardor like being treated merely as silly kids. The whole thing was a trivial incident involving a handful of students. The S.F. *Chronicle* noted that "The crowd of 750 students outside the Student Union cheered and applauded Schorer as he denounced the entire concept of the rally," and booed a student who tried to counter Schorer's argument.

Here is an observation from a little later in the affair: The Wordmonger group had called a rally in the Lower Plaza to explain their side. The *Daily Cal* reported that 50 came to listen at noon, which is an indicative enough figure; but when I got there at 12:45—usually the high point of a noon rally the scene was nothing short of amazing for this campus. There was the handful around the platform speaker, looking toward the plaza; and around the far end of thee plaza were the lunchers at the Bear's Lair tables; *and in between on the plaza there was absolutely nobody! I* have never seen a noontime audience of *zero* on the plaza before or since. This was a massive demonstration-in-reverse, by precisely the same students who had rallied to FSM meetings at the toughest times.

By the beginning of the following week it looked as if the momentary stir was over. Then on Tuesday, March 9, the real crisis was precipitated —by the president of the university. At a late afternoon press conference, Kerr, with Acting Chancellor Meyerson following in tow, announced their resignations.

It was certainly one of the most fantastic resignations ever submitted by a respectable university leader. Not at this press conference and not later did Kerr ever give a reason for his act; he allowed anyone to infer whatever he liked. It came out of the blue sky not only to the university community but also to a "dumbfounded" Governor Brown and to at least most of the Regents themselves. It was never even clear whether Kerr had actually resigned or was merely announcing that he would submit his resignation to the next Regents meeting. When Kerr later, in effect, apologized to the Regents for the peculiar act of announcing his resignation to a few reporters instead of to the Board, few people believed that this bizarre proceeding was without careful calculation by a man not notoriously given to boyish impulses.

The motivation which the community was allowed to believe, from various articles in the press, was that Kerr was resigning due to pressure from some Regents to expel the Wordmongers summarily. One story (in the S.F. *Chronicle,* which was pro-Kerr) said that this pressure came from only a minority of the Regents; this meant there was nothing new, and the need for the startling resignation remained unexplained. Another story (in the S.F. *Examiner)* said that a majority of the Regents had swung to the hard line—a version which appeared only momentarily and became even harder to believe as the affair unrolled. Writing in the N.Y. *Times* of March 14, education editor F. M. Hechinger was among those who rejected as unlikely the theory that Kerr resigned because of this kind of right-wing pressure. Elinor Langer, writing in *Science* for April, said: "Why Kerr resigned, taking Meyerson with him, is a question that would require the skills of an army of mind readers and detectives to answer fully." Nevertheless Hechinger speculated that Kerr's "administrative patience broke," and Langer guessed it was "pique and exhaustion."

The difficulty exists only for those who, for whatever reason, reject out of hand the obvious explanation which fits the picture.

Kerr's resignation was a power-play designed to restore the dominant role of the presidency among the countervailing pressures of faculty, students, Regents, community, and state legislature. One thing is certain: this is what it did substantially accomplish; and any claim that the result was merely accidental represents a gross underestimation of Kerr's ability in the one field on which he prides himself as a skilled professional performer with few peers in the country.

If a hard-line anti-Kerr majority had really captured the Regents, his resignation would only have made it easy for them to put their own man in. Kerr's coup effectually forestalled precisely such a possible future crystallization; it broke up the rightists' opposition before any of them were ready to move.

The dilemma before the faculty was acted out when the various groups met on March 11 to draw up resolutions for an emergency Academic Senate meeting the next day. The Kerr faction (Faculty Forum) drafted a resolution of fulsome praise for the president and a humble plea that he vouchsafe once more the light of his countenance to the university. The representatives of "the 200" wanted a resolution which warned against "efforts from any quarter to exaggerate and exploit this incident," cool toward Kerr and warmer toward Meyerson. The compromise between the two groups, adopted by the Academic Senate, did include a call for withdrawal of the resignations and a wish "to persuade Dr. Kerr and Dr. Meyerson to continue in office." The publicity, however, merely showed the faculty in overwhelming majority pleading with Kerr to come back.

To the students, the obvious pitch was: Would you be happier if Frank Murphy, or Richard Nixon, or *(gulp)* Max Rafferty came in as president? Even though an attempt to whip up a pro-Kerr demonstration of students outside the Academic Senate (to "Bark for Clark") fell like a lead balloon, still, consternation and dismay at the new crisis filled the student body, and disoriented many.

In the intellectual community, without his actually having to say so himself, Kerr was often taken as standing manfully for all the liberal virtues by objecting to summary expulsion of the "obscenity kids." This helped to refurbish his now rather dimmed aura of liberalism, about which he is sensitive. If worst came to worst and the resignation became real, he would be out, not as the man who had vainly tried to break the FSM, but as the man who had sacrificed his post to defend the students. Then there was always the Secretaryship of Labor to look forward to.

After the faculty, students, Regents, and public had united in coaxing him back to the presidency, who would be in a good position to object as he step-by-step restored the ante-bellum campus, and cautiously weeded out the "troublemakers"? It couldn't miss.

## *38. The FSM in Crisis*

Kerr's adroit power-play put the FSM before a dilemma that a far more experienced leadership would have been hard put to resolve.

From the beginning of the new crisis, the FSM separated itself decisively from the Wordmongers. An immediate statement issued by the FSM Steering Committee and the Graduate Coordinating Committee began:

> We are shocked by the resignations of President Kerr and Chancellor Meyerson. In the past months, the campus has quieted, and students, faculty, and local administration have been actively working on educational reform. Though there has been insufficient consultation of the student body at large, prospects for the future, and for the changes the university so desperately needs, have never been brighter.

The two student groups stated their position forthrightly:

> Only in the recent controversy over "obscene" words can students be said not to have acted responsibly. The FSM did not initiate or support this controversy. We regret both that the students involved acted in an unfortunate manner and that the police and some administrators chose to escalate the issue and endanger campus peace rather than permit student interest in the subject to wane. The problem is now in the courts, where it belongs. Any disciplinary action by the university will be directly contrary to the principles we supported last semester.

In a further statement, the FSM added: "Although the FSM holds the recent four-letter-word rallies to have been irresponsible, it upholds the rights of all students and faculty members to due process both on and off the campus."

This stand by the FSM did not prevent the press and others from doing their best to smear the FSM and the whole student movement with the opprobrium they were busily attaching to the "obscenity" row, now escalated into a life-or-death matter for the university by the Kerr-Meyerson resignations. While reporting the FSM statement at length, the S.F. *Examiner* omitted any reference to the central paragraph criticizing the Wordmongers, so that its readers were not confused when defenders of morality like the rightist state superintendent of schools, Max Rafferty, coarsely vilified both Free Speech Movement and "Filthy Speech Movement" as "slobs."

The dilemma before the FSM was this: it had to choose between turning its back on all the rights which should be enjoyed even by students who were wrong; or else, by standing up for the legitimate rights of the same students whose irresponsibility it had criticized, facilitating the aim of its enemies in smearing it with the "obscenity" issue. The FSM chose integrity and the latter course.

The administration took two steps to dig this trap deeper, though only the second of these worked. The first was to impose an arbitrary ban on the campus sale of a new magazine started by the Arthur Goldberg crowd, titled *Spider,* combining low-grade collegiate sex chatter with a rather witless form of pro-Soviet politics and dull literary efforts. Its crime was none of these, however, but rather its defense of the Wordmongers. Meyerson refused to give a reason for the ban, stating boldly that he had the power to be arbitrary. Since the banned magazine was being simultaneously sold a few yards away in the ASUC bookstore, and since the whole episode began to suggest to Meyerson admirers that he was filling Edward Strong's shoes too quickly, the chancellor backwatered and lifted the ban by the end of March.

The major provocation came in the latter part of April, when, following hearings by a specially appointed committee, but while the court trial of the "obscenity" defendants had barely opened, Meyerson announced draconic punishments for four students involved. Goldberg was expelled outright, and the other three (one of whom had not been arrested) were suspended. The penalties were so unexpectedly harsh that even the marsh-dwellers of the Faculty Forum were momentarily moved to protest them as unfair. Comparison was invited with the easy complacency with which university presidents customarily dealt with serious offenders in panty raids, even where real destruction of property or threats to physical safety were involved.

The immediate consequence was a crisis in the FSM. On the one hand, on grounds both of due process and the fairness of the penalties, anger built up against the new chancellor who was expending the credit he had gained in the "honeymoon" period by his hard-nosed implementation of Kerr's Restoration course. Goldberg was being victimized, not because he was a Wordmonger, but as a sacrificial goat in the administration plan to show the students who was boss.

On the other hand, every realistic student knew that, by this time, the "obscenity" issue and the Kerr coup had sown so much confusion and demoralization among the student body that a successful mass struggle under these circumstances was out of the question. The irrepressible dynamism which the civil-rights issue had given to the student struggle in the fall had now been turned into a minus-quantity, by the unplanned co-operation between the crusaders under the Banner With a Strange Device and the skillful general of the Restoration.

It was only because of this crisis that a new steering committee of the FSM was reconstituted at all, but the reorganization did not stick. Chaotic meetings took place but it is impossible to say now what, if any, decisions were made. For one thing, as we shall discuss later, most of the members of the fall Steering Committee had disappeared from the arena and the replacements were raw. At first (April 23) Mario Savio talked to a rally in terms of a threat of some kind of direct action; but he thought better of it over the weekend, when a number of confused FSM meetings took place;' and on Monday noon, unexpectedly announced to a rally that he was withdrawing from campus activity. The motivation he gave was disinclination to dominate the movement; but a widespread opinion was that, exhausted from the months-long struggle he was in no position to face the overwhelming problems of the new crisis under far less favorable conditions.

All plans for student resistance for that semester came effectively to an end, and the student activists' thoughts turned to longer-range preparation for a more drawn-out battle with an administration which might try to take further steps to turn the clock back. By the end of

April, a new organization, called the Free Student Union, was in the process of formation as *a* permanent membership movement, with its eyes fixed—beyond the oncoming finals and the intervening summer period—on September 1965 as the possible date of the next test.

## *39. Regents versus the University*

Although the "obscenity" issue dominated the spring semester, it was fortunately not the only issue. In current student parlance, this issue turned everybody off. What turned them on, to at least a small degree, were two or three others which the administration and the Regents did not fail to provide.

First came the efforts of the university administrations on the Berkeley and Riverside campuses to throttle student government resolutions in support of the Negro struggle in Selma, Alabama. Police brutality against the Selma marchers outraged the nation at about the same time that the good burghers of California were being outraged by disturbing words. When the Berkeley ASUC, not dominated by FSM, sought to pass a resolution of support to the Selma victims, Chancellor Meyerson threatened to junk the whole ASUC setup rather than permit it—this in enforcement of the Kerr Directives against the taking of stands on off-campus issues. At the Riverside campus a similar action by the Associated Students brought an iron-fisted demand by the chancellor that the student government rescind their support to Selma or face being disbanded. The student president resigned in protest.

The Byrne Commission report (about which more later) commented on this as follows:

> There were no vigils, no picketing, no sit-ins at Riverside, and, therefore, no newspaper headlines to disturb the public. But student "government" was exposed, in a dignified way, as an ineffectual instrument of student opinion.... We fail to see how the university

> itself is involved in off-campus issues so long as the ASUC Senate announces the vote results and the announcement makes it clear that the body which took the vote was not the university itself. Nor can we see any legitimate complaint of the student body involved. If the students do not want their representatives to vote on off campus issues, they can forbid this in the ASUC constitution. Whether or not the student Senate is authorized to take such votes, we think is a matter the students should decide.

There was a second way in which "student `government' was exposed, in a dignified way, as an ineffectual instrument of student opinion" at Berkeley. We have mentioned that both graduate and undergraduate students had voted, at the initiative of the ASUC, to reinclude the graduates in the student government structure. Kerr, who had jockeyed the graduates out of the ASUC in the first place, was not going to let this happen. At the next meeting of the Regents on March 25-26, Kerr recommended to the board that it annul the campus vote. The pretext was an alleged 1933 policy of the Regents requiring that half of the students must vote on, and two-thirds must vote in favor of, any compulsory fee. The graduate vote had been 1876 to 1193.

It turned out that Kerr's pretext was not even based on fact, let alone equity, and in April the Regents had to modify their opposition so as to leave the door open to later determination of the question. One of the most notable passages in the Byrne Commission report stressed that in this graduate-affiliation maneuver one could "see in microcosm" the attitudes and problems which had caused the events of the fall to escalate to a crisis. This criticism pointed out: The precedents alleged were not available to the university community; there was in fact no established policy at all; "subsequent investigations showed that the election precedents were mixed, therefore not giving support for the action taken." Kerr waited until *after* the graduates had won three times (in the

ASUC Senate, and two student votes) before fishing the alleged 32-year-old precedent out of the archives.

That a good deal less than half the graduate students had voted represented nothing unusual in student government affairs. Nor were the students specially delinquent. An ordinary attendance at Academic Senate meetings by the faculty was under 20 per cent; and even at the height of the fall semester's convulsions, about a third of the Academic Senate's members did not even show up in the hall on December 8!

> The decision was widely interpreted as an attempt of the administration and the Regents to interfere with the students' democratic decision out of fear of domination of the ASUC by a group of "radical" and therefore less "tractable" graduate students, thus adding to the students' mistrust of the administration and Regents. (Byrne Report.)

"Mistrust of the Regents" was reaching a new high. Recognizing this body as the anchor for reactionary policies *behind* Kerr, the FSM set out to bring its role out into the light. The state convention of the teachers' union (AFT) voted to back a citizens' inquiry into the Regents; the San Francisco Labor Council also called for investigation. An illuminating pamphlet published by the FSM, *The Regents by* Marvin Garson, brought together for the first time the astonishing facts about the overwhelmingly non-educational and big business character of the board's composition, so extreme as to indict its dictatorial control over a great university.

But under cover of the "obscenity" row, important elements in the Regents started a drive to turn the clock back at Berkeley. The push was launched in the Hearst and Knowland press, which published the hitherto-secret memoranda by ex-Chancellor Strong in favor of an ironhanded martinet's approach to campus discipline. This was thrown into the melee caused by Kerr's resignation in order to stampede the Regents to the right—to turn Kerr's controlled maneuver into a rout.

At the Regents' meetings, the whipped-up indignation over the Word covered an attempt to slip over a decree which would expel future teaching-assistant strikers. (Few things in the FSM struggle had enraged the big-business Regents as much as the idea that hired hands could strike and get away with it.)

An episode later in the semester gives an even better inkling of the caliber of some of these men.

At a June meeting of the Regents' educational policy committee, it was reported that Berkeley was going to experiment with a Special College Program for a small group of students, according to a plan drawn up by Professor Tussman. Edward Carter, big-business chairman of the Regents, thereupon wanted to know if it was true that this was going to be "a college in the history of Anarchy"—a danger suggested to him by anonymous faculty members who had gone clucking in alarm to him and other Regents, since four out of the five faculty members in the program were reputed to be supporters of the recent student fight.

Oil-man Regent Ed Pauley then declared: "I have heard that four of the five professors are, if not Marxists, then believers in Marxist theory. And if not that, they're not believers in our capitalist system." Before asking the legislature for university funds, he added, "I think I should at least have a letter from these men stating that they believe in the capitalist system."

The subsequent indignation concentrated on Pauley's public charge that four professors were "Marxists." Little attention was paid to the remarkable fact that a leading Regent, unreproved either by the Board or by the liberal educators in charge of the university, had asserted that a man who did not "believe in the capitalist system" could not teach at the university; and that, indeed, if there were such monsters on the university faculty, funds should be cut off from that contaminated institution. The spectacle of a great university entering the space age with troglodytes in command of its destinies was not, in truth, calculated to bolster students' faith in defenders of the capitalist system.

Out of this right-wing push on the Regents, and through the so-called Meyer committee which the Regents had set up in December, came a detailed plan ("Meyer Report") which would have laid the basis for wiping out every juridical basis for academic freedom and student rights on the university campuses. One of its shotgun provisions required students "to observe generally acceptable standards of conduct," and then made them subject to university discipline "whether or not violations occur on campus." It banned student-government stands on off-campus issues even if the student governments were made voluntary, thereby undercutting Kerr's established excuse for straitjacketing the ASUC.

Despite the fact that virtually the whole campus, from right to left, whispered, grumbled, or roared their dissent (in accordance with their several natures), there seemed to be a good chance that the substance of this medieval document might have gone through—when there came one of those unexpected breaks that were so frequent in the fall and so few in the spring. Another committee of the Regents, the Forbes committee which had been charged with an overall inquiry into the underlying causes of the FSM crisis, had set up an independent investigating commission under the Los Angeles lawyer, Jerome C. Byrne. Byrne, with a budget of $75,000, had assembled a professional staff of experts on education and management, who carried on a three-month survey-in-depth. The Byrne Commission report, dated May 7, came as a veritable bombshell. It was, in the words of the *S.F. Chronicle,* a "searing indictment of [the Regents] and the university administration ... a striking rebuke both to present university policy and to the Regents' view of their own responsibilities. Equally remarkable was the report's relatively mild censure of the students." (See excerpts from this report in the second part of this book.) There was an initial attempt to suppress its publication, but, with Byrne insisting, the Regents finally allowed it to be distributed (mimeographed). The Los Angeles *Times* was the only place where its text was made available to the general public, outside of an

FSM pamphlet reprint; no university paper or publication gave its full contents to the campus community.

The deck of cards flew up in the air again—for example, the Meyer report was postponed—and the spring semester ended on a hopefully indecisive note.

Yet, for all of the setbacks that the student movement had suffered in this second round, one thing was still true: the *de facto* freedom of speech and political activity on the Berkeley campus which had been won in the fall remained untouched in practice. The Restoration had not yet been achieved. The sort-of-revolution on the Berkeley campus had not been defeated. In all probability, there was still a fight ahead.

## *40. Why?*

Why did the student revolt break out? Why was it able to sweep such a large part of the campus? Why did it happen at Berkeley rather than elsewhere?

Virtually every magazine article that has appeared on the subject has repeated one all-purpose analysis, which lies right at hand and has the added virtue of pointing to an instant solution. A convenient summary of this analysis and its accompanying packaged remedy can be read in the following passage:

> . some of the unrest among students is traceable to a feeling that the university is a huge corporate enterprise run by remote administrators and geared to the mass production of research and of candidates for degrees. The present situation has produced tremendous soul-searching on the whole issue of impersonality and inaccessibility. Efforts at all levels should be intensified to improve the relations between the three segments of the university community: students, faculty, and administration. The Council especially urges that faculty

> members and administrators take a greater personal interest in students. Discussions with individual students should be encouraged concerning both personal and university problems. Furthermore, there is need to give continuing thought and attention to improving the educational environment of both undergraduate and graduate students.

About all that is missing in this summary is a reference to Alienation.

Now the Council which made this report on December 17 was the Academic Council of the state-wide University of California, and the report was then presented by President Kerr to the Regents. The next sentence after the passage quoted said: "President Kerr himself has been a leader in this search for ways to improve the university for students."

This makes the analysis official and unanimous. It is the same as saying that John Doe caught a cold because cold "germs" got into his system. This is undoubtedly a better explanation than possession by evil spirits, but it leaves something to be desired nowadays. Since there are cold viruses in the air and in the respiratory tract all the time, the fact is not an explanation of any given cold.

Likewise, there is little that is really new in the feeling of the student that the mass university of today is an overpowering, over-towering, impersonal, alien machine in which he is nothing but a cog going through pre-programed motions the "IBM" syndrome. Nor is it a new complaint that teaching, especially undergraduate teaching, is sacrificed to research and the publication rat race, at least at most of the major universities. Nor is Berkeley the first place where students have felt a lack of close personal relations with professors.

It is perfectly true that the mass universities have become finger than ever, but the alienation of a bewildered student in a campus of 5000 can be as thoroughgoing as in a Knowledge Factory of 25,000. One can be as completely lost in a forest of only a hundred square miles as in the High Sierra.

The correspondingly superficial remedy is the "warm bosom" solution, or "chuck 'em under the chin." Just as there is truth in the analysis, so there is virtue in the remedy, and enough of the remedial syrup can conceivably be poured to soothe the inflammations for a while. But it does not attack the roots of the problem.

There is an exact counterpart to this soothing-syrup approach: the "human-relations engineering" theory of how to counteract the alienation of the worker in the factory, with solutions ranging from elaborate paternalisms to Muzak music over the public-address system. The personnel manager is taught how to be "human" in relations with the "hands," as the university administrator is urged to encourage "greater personal interest" in the thousands of "head" of students.

It is true that there was a wing of FSM activists who emphasized the issue of educational reform at the university, and some who even looked on this question as the dynamic of the movement. While it is widely and warmly agreed that the result of this new interest in university betterment was valuable, it was a by-product of the movement, not its spur. This was quickly shown by the end of the semester: when the FSM became quiescent, an effort was made to fill the vacuum with a University Reform Movement, whose sponsors even talked naively about using the sit-in tactic (that cure-all) as a means of bringing about basic changes in the system of study. This illusion evaporated in a jiffy, and the new "movement" became merely one useful interest-group among many.

The results of the two Somers surveys likewise tend to show that dissatisfaction with the quality of education given by the university played no major role in motivating the fight, although the surveys do not exclude the hypothesis that such latent dissatisfaction contributed a background conditioning influence. In this connection, let us cite Professor Somers' own summary of his findings:

> We found sympathy for the demonstrators to be widespread and dispersed throughout the campus even to the extent of one third of the students approving the

> tactics that demonstrators had used. This support was clearly concentrated among students in certain fields—the social sciences, humanities, and physical-science—but as strong among freshmen as among graduate students, and not related to the number of semesters a student had been on this campus. Nor is support particularly related to feelings of dissatisfaction with the educational functions of the university. On the contrary, we found a remarkable amount of satisfaction with courses, professors, and so on, and appreciation of the efforts made by the administration to provide top-quality education for students here. Thus the prevailing explanation in terms of characteristics peculiar to the "Multiversity" seems to have no support. Rather, it appears that students resent being deprived of their rights to political activity, being excluded from full political citizenship, and this sentiment is especially strong among those who are emotionally involved in the civil-rights movement. Thus the material we collected suggests that the mainsprings of the rebellion are an optimistic idealism about the type of society which can be shaped by the new generation, and an unwillingness to allow the paternalism endemic to college campuses to extend its coverage to the activities necessary for the furtherance of those ideals.

The students' alienation from the university establishment was a function of their social and political involvement, not the other way around. Their discontent with the micro-society of the campus was an extension of their disillusionment with the values of the macro-society outside.

There was "something wrong" in the Multiversity. There was "something wrong" also, they felt, about the Great Society in which the

Multiversity was embedded, with its fraudulent non-war on poverty, its fraudulent crypto-war in Vietnam, and its fraudulent civil-rights laws in Washington to mention only three strings whose plucking evoked a sympathetic tone from thousands of students who followed the FSM. Most of these thousands did not claim to know what was wrong, let alone what to do about it: they had no "program." They wanted to "do something about it." (Significantly Berkeley is also the campus with most volunteers to the Peace Corps.)

But the social malaise was still there, and no "personal relations" with professors would help. In fact, beyond a certain point closer personal acquaintance with most professors only deepened the problem, for the student was likely to find the professor insensitive, timid or cynical about the social or political ideals which he, the student, took seriously.

To put it moderately, there are few professors on the Berkeley campus who are likely to provide inspiration or encouraging understanding to a student beginning to feel a radical estrangement from the values of the American Way of Life; much fewer if we omit young professors scarcely more integrated on campus than the students themselves, and still fewer if we consider only the eminent "name" professors who had arrived in the Establishment.

Now this meaning of the students' "alienation" does not leap to the eye of the journalist who visits Berkeley for two days to do an "on the spot" quickie piece and accumulates some fast quotes in interviews. Yet, if it is easy to overlook it, it is also tempting to overstate it in reactive emphasis. For these thousands of students are *not* finished radicals in any real political sense. At the same time, to an unexpected extent, it will be found that they do not think of themselves as "liberals"—that is, as mere liberals. Liberalism is too thoroughly integrated with the Establishment; they know there is "something wrong" with liberalism too.

The large majority of FSM activists would call themselves radicals, if forced to choose a label after strenuous objection to "labeling," but it is most commonly an amorphous kind of radicalism.*

Since the element of positive program is weak, since the estrangement from the Great Society has not yet led to a clear idea of an alternative society, the pent-up energy of dissent tends to burst out in forms that have two leading characteristics. One: concentration on concrete issues ("issue politics," in the jargon of the campus activists); and two: greater certainty on what one is against than on what one is for (what we can call "anti" politics). This is one of the natural forms of a radicalization that is in its first stages.

Hence the situation that the reservoir of radical *energies is* greater than the stream of radical beliefs.

---

* The *Graduate-Political Scientists' Report* plays down the radicalism of the bulk of FSM activists as a concession to respectability but its version will not withstand analysis. Asking "Are the [sit-in] demonstrators 'a bunch of radicals'?" it answers with the following statistics: "Only 4.5% of [them] belonged to 'radical' groups (DuBois Club, Young Socialist Alliance, Young People's Socialist League, Independent Socialist Club). The others covered the full range of the political spectrum: 18.2%, liberal groups like Young Democrats; 25.6%, civil-rights organizations like NAACP and CORE; 1.2%, conservative groups; 7.3%, religious organizations. Furthermore, 57% of the students belonged to no political organizations at all."

It is quite true that most of the FSM radicals do not belong to any of the groups representing known radical ideologies, but that does not settle the matter. Campus CORE (but not NAACP) consists largely of radicals, not liberals; so do Slate and SNCC; there is even many a Young Democrat who conceives himself as a radical working within the liberal establishment; etc. The following statistics presented by the *G. P. S. Report* are also of interest: "Are they 'hard core demonstrators'? ... the large majority (61.2%) of those arrested had never participated in any previous demonstration; 22% had participated in only one previous demonstration; 7.0% had taken part in two; and 9.2% in three or more demonstrations ... Furthermore, the vast majority of these protestors had never been arrested before on any charge prior to the Sproul Hall sit-in. Almost all previous arrests were for earlier civil rights demonstrations."

The civil-rights issue is, of course, made-to-order for the release of such radical energies, since its elemental appeal to the sense of justice is so powerful in itself that it does not require a more explicit political program—at least at the beginning. Very soon, of course, the civil-rights fight brings the neophyte nose-up against such programmatic problems as attitude toward the Democratic Party apparatus—typified by the decision of a section of the civil-rights leadership in the 1964 election campaign to declare a moratorium on militant actions in order not to embarrass Lyndon Johnson's Great Society. In the Bay Area this typical dilemma was dramatized around Mayor John F. Shelley of San Francisco, the liberal Democrat who was elected with the eager support of student civil-rights militants, many of whom were later hauled to jail by Shelley's police for civil-rights demonstrations.

A filtering process takes place among the civil-rights enthusiasts, and a section of them (on campus, a large section) pragmatically choose to hold to their anti-establishmentarian militancy rather than yield to the housebreaking influence of the liberal politicians who advise them to be "realistic" and "practical," i.e., to stop bucking the machine.

The choice is not necessarily made as the end-conclusion of a thought-through political analysis, and therefore the militant who makes the choice tends to think of it as being merely a "moral choice." And it *is* a moral choice, of course; but all moral choices in politics are also political choices; and even if the politics of the choice is not consciously evaluated, it is still implicitly there. At this point it is radical politics in an "issue" and "anti" form, even though the immediate demands may be positive enough.

The problem is more acute in the field of foreign policy and war—for instance the war in Vietnam—for here the issue is largely intractable to treatment by mere "issue politics." The civil-rights activist can attack injustice in Mississippi or in Oakland directly and in the life; but he has no handle at hand by which to intervene as meaningfully to determine whether Washington will or will not help to precipitate a nuclear war on this planet. On the one hand, the narrow "issue" approach may lead to concentration on a single aspect, like official lying about the situation in Vietnam—for this can be handled most easily within the non-programmatic "moral choice" field of vision. On the other hand, the simple "anti" approach tends to blur the distinction between two quite different groups of people who are against Washington's war in Vietnam: those who oppose U.S. policy because they oppose all dictatorship and colonialism in Vietnam, and those who oppose U.S. policy because they are partisans of the Communist side of that war.

## *41. The Non-I Radicals*

We are now discussing what was in fact the dominant tendency among the FSM activists and leadership and the decisive factor in making possible the Berkeley uprising. This is the amorphous radicalism which has been given various labels: the "new radicals," the "New Left," among others. I have referred to it as unprogrammatic but this is not strictly true. What is most characteristic of it is its conscious avoidance of any radical *ideology*. It is important to take a closer look at it.

These "new radicals" are non-ideological in the sense that they refuse to, or are disinclined to, generalize their ideas and positions. They fight shy of any systematization of their political and social views. They think of this approach as "pragmatic." They are inclined to substitute a moral approach—indeed, a dogmatic moral approach—for political and social analysis as much as possible. They like the description "existential" because it offers a non-political label. I once asked an active exemplar of this trend to define what he meant by calling himself a "radical." His answer was: "We take a position on a certain issue—say, civil rights. We have a particular position on another issue, say, Vietnam. And so on. I would define radicalism as the sum total of these positions." He was describing a kind of political induction. Obviously, this raises more questions than it answers.

First of all, why the extremely strong disinclination to generalize—that is, to move in the direction of a knit-together *theory* beyond issue-politics? At first blush, this is a strange development particularly for intellectuals, people who are involved ' in a whole period of life-training in the development and generalization of ideas. It is not that the non-ideological (for short, non-I) radicals question the need for generalization and theory in principle. I suggest that there are three powerful inhibitions at work.

(1) What they reject above all are "old" ideologies and radical theories, more than they reject ideology and theory itself. A new radical ideology could sweep them, but it is not even on the horizon. So to speak, there are "new radicals" but there is really no "new radicalism," in terms of program, theory or ideology.

This is above all a reaction against the failure of all previous wings of American radicalism to become mass movements. All the radical programs have "failed": there must be something wrong with them: we must do something new.

The operative word is *new*. The term "New Left" has a charisma unmatched by any other; and the vaguer it is, the more magical, since as soon as it takes on a specific content, the visage of some "old politics" is plain. The "old politics" has committed the sin of being unsuccessful: a very American sin.

A number of the non-I radicals on the Berkeley campus, and no doubt elsewhere, come from parents who went through the Communist movement; they associate "old politics" and "ideology" chiefly with the politics and ideology of the Communists. One way to reject Communist ideology without falling into the conformist rut of Establishment "anti-Communism" is to reject it not in the first place because it is Communist but because it is ideology.

(2) There is the fear that unity of action on issues would be impaired by ideological clarification. One of the distressful results of arriving at a more specific radical program is that different people are bound to disagree about what they specify.

There will be disputes, hostility, factions, splits, fragmentation —in short, disunity; and is this not part of the "old politics" that failed? Therefore it seems better to act most unitedly by remaining on the ground of "issue politics" only.

This consideration is a strong one up to a point, and indeed the FSM illustrated its limits to some extent. The FSM achieved a wide unity around an issue, but it did so only as an *ad hoc* fighting force temporarily united for that issue. It never considered itself a permanent organization or movement.

By January it took the course, envisioned from the beginning, of putting itself on the shelf. (The new organization which re-formed in April under the name of the Free Student Union is quite another story.)

The FSM was essentially a United Front plus some added representation, not a membership organization. Now United Fronts are indeed the "old" form through which different ideological radicalisms achieve unity on particular issues. The FSM was illustrating the "old" pattern—in a brand-new form, as history usually does.

The FSM quite consistently, and largely deliberately, declined to do very much about drawing broad societal conclusions from what it itself was doing. On campus the main job of expounding radical interpretations of the "free speech" fight was carried by the "old" radicals—mostly the Independent Socialist Club, in a number of interpretive meetings and a culminating "Conference on the Student Revolt" in January. A good part of the FSM leadership participated in such meetings, but it would have been unwise for the FSM to try to fill this role. It could play an action role, but not an ideological role.

(3) There is the pressure of the American political climate. In almost any other country of the world, a great many of the non-I radicals would be calling themselves socialists. But in the U.S., for most of the public, socialism (not to speak of Communism) is a "dirty word." Why get specific about "labels" which will only stand in the way?

. As a matter of fact, this notion of sneaking socialism past the American public by calling it something else is one of the oldest politics there is, as old as the socialist movement itself. There is a source of reluctance here to develop even *a new* radical ideology, since any new "ism" would hardly be more congenial to the current American temper than the old.

None of the characteristics of non-I radicalism that have been described is hard and fast; it is a process rather than a standpoint. It ranges from elements just beginning to doubt the immaculateness of the American conception all the way to people who are full-blown socialists in everything except "label."

Off at right angles to this line is another spectrum of students whose reaction against the American Establishment's party line has thrown them toward some degree of sympathy with the rival social system which disputes the world with Washington: the Communist power. It is a widely varied spectrum indeed, especially in the Bay Area, and over most of its range has little or no connection with the Communist Party. The spectrum begins with the student to whom the local Communists are simply "the enemy of the enemy," that is, other radicals opposed to the powers that be, and who literally refuses to think about the nature of Communist totalitarianism where it already has power, since such questions are divisive (dangerous thoughts). It ends with a thin scattering of the usual party-hack types who are apologists of terror against "free speech" in any country controlled by their friends.

Few of the present non-I radicals are aware that the Communist youth and student movement in its heyday was extremely skillful at setting up organizations which combined a, non-ideological and even non-political facade with the implicit Communist line *(vide* American Youth for Democracy and the later years of the American Student Union). There is a long history of Communists posing as non-ideological radicals. I mention this because, as one who went through a good deal of this history, I claim to know the difference. This element was very small in the Berkeley uprising.

The non-ideological radicalism which constitutes a sort of "New Left" on the campus *is* new. It is no one's invention and no one's patsy. It showed great strength and great weaknesses in the FSM fight, but both the strengths and the weaknesses were its very own.

## *42. "New Left" Balance Sheet*

The dominance of the new non-ideological radicals not only gave the tone of the Berkeley uprising but also accounts for its main strong points. Its advantages were at least these three, in ascending order of importance:

*(1) It made it very dii9acult to smear the FSM with the "Communist" label.* The point is not simply that the decisive FSM leadership and followers were *not* Communist in fact; innocence has not always stopped the ignorant or malicious from redbaiting or witchhunting. The point is that after a minimal amount of actual contact with the FSM, almost anyone close to the situation had to recognize that the "feel" was not only non-Communist but alien to any kind of Communist approach. Naturally this does not apply to those authorities on the Berkeley fight who became experts on the subject by reading the news dispatches 3000 miles away. It does apply particularly to the Berkeley faculty, and had its effect as time went on.

*(2) It accounts in part for the explosiveness of the student uprising.* This was the explosiveness of uncalculated indignation, not the slow boil of planned revolt. In many cases it was born of the first flash of discovery that the mantle of authority cloaked an unsuspected nakedness. The experienced radicals on campus did not consider this to be news; after one has become accustomed to taking a dim view of Important People, it is hard to experience a fresh movement of revulsion at every repetition of the lesson. There is first love; there is the first baptism of fire; there is the first time you realize your father has lied; and there is the first discovery of the chasm between the rhetoric of Ideals and the cynicism of Power among the pillars of society.

I talked with an FSM activist who was in the thick of the movement all through the fall semester. He was not only non-ideological but non-political, and had come in at first with the confident view that it was all merely a question of overcoming the administration's misunderstanding of what the students wanted, due to the fact that they had been antagonized by hasty clashes at the beginning. The process of rapid disillusionment was a personal shock, and the reaction was correspondingly violent. He read outright falsifications in the newspapers every day; he heard systematic distortions by the leaders of the university itself; he talked to faculty members who were bitter about what the administration was doing but declined to speak up for truth or justice; he was naively amazed at students who agreed that the administration was wrong but shrugged their shoulders and walked away from trouble. The real world did not seem to have much relationship to the ideals he had taken seriously. He had been sold ... This is the story in good part of the moral dynamism behind the impetuosity of the fight.

(3) Perhaps this is a continuation of point 2: *The FSM was able to do so much because they simply didn't know "it couldn't be done."* They were able to win so much because they didn't know it was "impossible." A certain amount of naivete and inexperience was as a shield and a buckler to them. After all, ideologies (by which I mean merely systems of ideas) are distillations from past experience, if they possess any validity at all; and past experience told the "old radicals" what powerful forces they faced. But lack of a radical ideology meant also lack of a systematic view of what basic social powers were at stake. It was only after it was all over that a leading Graduate Coordinating Committee student told me ruefully that he now realized the impossibility of revolution on one campus alone. If he had known more to begin with, he might have been able to do less: a plain case of "a little knowledge is a dangerous thing." Therefore the militant wing of the FSM comprised mainly non-I radicals, and to a lesser degree those who were moved not merely by a radical but by a revolutionary socialist ideology.

These advantages were decisive ones. President Kerr has testified that he was "taken by surprise"; so was the whole campus, including the students, many of whom were just as surprised at what they found themselves forced to do. The history of revolts and revolutions tells us that this pattern is not new: the explosive irruption of new strata of inexperienced but outraged masses, while ideologically more advanced movements stand flatfooted, is a frequent phenomenon in times of crisis.

Yet it always comes as something new, by its very nature; and of course these new and unawed forces are commonly non-ideological in motivation, being impelled not by theories but by intolerable conditions, not necessarily economic. In this generic sense, waves of "new radicals" are an old pattern.

The other thing that history tells us about such irruptions is their limitations, which tend to become more serious as the system recovers from the impact of the first massive assaults.

The first steps in the uprising are unitedly directed against the visible enemy, and the first demands are easy, being a direct response to the intolerable conditions. But beyond this elementary stage, the problems of perspective and program multiply, as more basic issues and powers are brought to the surface. Even to know now what the basic issues are, requires a broader and more general conception of what the fight is about—in effect, an ideology. The ruling authorities, who made decisions easier before by being flatly intransigent, now provide an enticing variety of compromises, halfway houses, promises—anything to get the headlong assault to pause, break up and mill in confusion. The non-ideological radical feels that the first pristine beauty and simplicity of the issues have faded, and moral indignation by itself does not seem to point to answers.

Even in the first stage, one of the most prominent characteristics of FSM functioning was the interminable, indecisive discussions of the leading committees at critical junctures. The picture of the FSM drawn by some in terms of sinister superefficiency and generalship so brilliant as to put the administration to rout, is one of the most ludicrous misrepresentations in this story. Time and again, the Executive Committee and Steering Committee of the movement discussed literally for days, coming finally either to no firm decision or to a decision which was negated the very next day by events, so that the actual policy was improvised. At such times the policy problems of the FSM were most often solved not by its councils but by some new "atrocity" by the administration. One of the main reasons for this often paralyzing disability was the fact that there were no fixed points in any discussion: everything was always "up for grabs." Every problem which any movement of opposition inevitably runs into had to be explored *ab ovo:* how long would it have taken Adam to learn to walk if he had had to figure out separately the proper function of every muscle, ligament, and nerve cell in the ambulatory process?

There was another problem before the non-I radicalism of the FSM, which became especially troublesome in the spring semester. This was a certain blurring of the difference between serious political and social opposition to the status quo (even if considered non-ideologically) and the nihilism of the disaffiliates.

The latter term requires an apology, but it is a significant phenomenon and needs a name. The best definition I know of is provided, by example, in the motto of Céline which is quoted admiringly in Henry Miller's "Red Notebook": *Je pisse sur tout d'un grand hauteur.* From a great height—that is, from above the real world, and outside it. The French have another word for something like it: *je m'en-fichisme;* which roughly means fuck-it-all-ism. Unlike the beats (one extreme variety of disaffiliation) the types under consideration do not "opt out of society" (the rat race) in consistent practice, only in attitudes.

*Je pisse sur tout* is a kind of social program, with a primitive ideology of its own, which provides a simulacrum of social radicalism, since among other things it rejects also the going social system and its authorities. But it is only a simulacrum, for it has no real social vision or even moral vision of its own. These types want to disaffiliate from society, not to transform it. They are basically hostile to the social radicals, since the latter *are* deeply concerned about and involved with society. They tend to be scornful of tactics and strategy in a social struggle, however militant, since such considerations make for further involvement; the alternative is simply to smash things up, or pull the linchpins. They propose their own version of "militant" tactics mainly to scandalize that Beast, the Public *(epater la bourgeoisie)* and not to win, for winning involves taking responsibility. Their salute is not the clenched fist but the thumb to nose. They actually achieve their personal program of disaffiliation from society only by opting out of the real world with marijuana or LSD, which is their personal "revolution."

To the historically-minded, this description may partially suggest the old Bakunin type of anarchist, but the nihilism we have here is non-ideological. What we have described applies to only a small fringe of the university community in Berkeley, but it shades into the non-ideological radical tendency on one side, and tends to have a certain coloring effect upon it. I think this was one factor, not in the FSM struggle of the fall, but in the "obscenity" row of the spring semester. . Finally, there was another limitation of non-I radicalism which was prominently manifested in the spring. It is the other side of the coin of the movement's explosiveness: lack of persistency.

The FSM itself, as an organization, was not expected to persist, as we have mentioned; we are speaking of the individual non-I activists of the FSM. When the outbreak of the Second Round called for the reorganization of the FSM, it became painfully plain that a strange thing had happened by the end of April: of the FSM Steering Committee that had led the fight during the fall, only two were still taking part in the renewed struggle. One was the DuBois Club representative—hardly non-ideological-and the other was Jack Weinberg. Virtually the entire stratum of non-I leaders of the FSM Steering Committee had, for one reason or another, retired from the arena, after one semester of eruption, with no adequate replacement leadership in sight. It would appear that the simple/moral drive to action is more ephemeral than the ideological, and it is not hard to understand why.

All of this makes a very mixed balance sheet. The conclusion may be that both ideological radicalism and the "new radicalism" have a great deal to learn from each other.

## *43. The "New Radicals" and the "Old Radicals"*

While the non-I radicals set the dominant tone of the FSM, their role cannot be fully understood except in relation to the programmatic radicals of the political clubs on campus which we have mentioned in the course of the story. One of the unique features of Berkeley student life is the "across-the-board" array of radical clubs representing a wide variety of left-wing viewpoints in a turbulent climate of political discussion and controversy. It is dubious whether there is any other campus in the country today that resembles it in this respect.

A membership count of these clubs would show perhaps 200-300 members in all, but their influence extends pretty strongly to another few hundred, and in more diluted form to perhaps a thousand; from this point it would shade off rapidly.

This is a small minority of the campus, but it accounts for an enormously disproportionate amount of the ideological life that goes on and an even greater proportion of the political life. Previous to the FSM, it gave its tone to much of the campus far out of line with its strength.

> Berkeley students have always made more use of their political rights to meet and speak freely on campus than American students elsewhere. Every sort of extreme-left group is represented—the DuBois Club (Communist), the Young Socialist Alliance (Trotskyist), the Independent Socialist Club (Revolutionary Marxist Socialist), and the Progressive Labor Council (Maoist) ... [Lipset & Seabury in the *Reporter.]*

Kerr put it this way in an interview:

> If anything in the United States today could be said to resemble the Paris left bank, it is the area around Telegraph Avenue just off campus . . . This disorganized, anarchist, "Left bank" crowd was able to strike a responsive chord among so many students this fall because . . . a new student generation ... is now with us.

## *Berkeley: The Student Revolt*

> The tone of a student generation is set by rather a small number of people .. .

"Berkeley," wrote *Look* magazine (February 23), "is the most 'politicalized' campus in America." There is naturally a constant air of political debate going on, not only in formally organized meetings but in the pages of the *Daily Cal,* in impromptu rallies, in bull sessions on the Terrace of the cafeteria. There is a market place of political ideas, with a direct counterposition of leftish liberalism (Young Democrats) to right-wing social-democrats (YPSL) to revolutionary democratic socialists (Independent Socialist Club), as well as to the pro-Soviet tendencies (DuBois Club, Trotskyists, et al.), and shades of less programmatic radicalism in such groups as Slate and Students for Democratic Society. Nor can the civil rights groups be left entirely out of this picture, for they owed part of their existence to the work of committed radicals. Independent Socialist influence was considerable in CORE, as was Slate and DuBois influence in the Ad Hoc Committee while that group existed.

It was the radical clubs, including the radical civil-rights groups like CORE and SNCC, which formed the skeleton about which the FSM fleshed itself. It is quite true that the leading committees of the FSM were to the left of the ranks throughout the fight. Most of the time this was due to the fact that no one but radicals (various kinds of radicals) were willing to take the risks and burdens of leading a militant struggle. Whenever the going got sticky, the groups further to the right—from the social-democrats and the Young Democrats to the Republicans—began to veer away, leaving the militants on a limb.

On the left the relationship between the "old radicals" and the new is symbiotic. In this exchange the former tend to be the reservoir of ideas for the latter. In point of fact, the nonideological radicals do have the benefits of ideology at their service.

There is another kind of "radical" whose role in the situation must be mentioned: the ex-radicals—of the faculty.* This is an aspect of the Berkeley story that is notorious in the FSM and never mentioned in outside accounts.

The fact is that the bitterest and most virulent enemies of the FSM among the faculty were not the conservatives or rightists, and not Kerr's admirers, but rather a hard core of ex-radicals who had made their own peace with the system. This was the pattern at the December 8 meeting of the Academic Senate, where every one of the speakers for the Feuer amendment, with one exception, belonged to this category: in particular, Feuer himself, Nathan Glazer, William Petersen. In the nation's periodical press, these three have also distinguished themselves by articles of vituperation against the FSM.

The dean of this group, and the author of the most violent abuse of the student movement (in a series of articles in the *New Leader,* which is more or less the organ of reformed ex-radicals), is Professor Lewis Feuer. Long a Communist fellow traveler, Feuer has been moving right quite rapidly, especially in the last few years. In the course of his savage fulminations against the FSM, Feuer put forward a theory in explanation of the Berkeley uprising which is interesting in what it reveals.

The theory itself is very simple: the students' motivation is the Generational Conflict—young vs. old, the sons rising against the fathers. What is interesting about this theory is not what it explains about the students, for it clearly can explain little about what happened. Students are *eo ipso* young, and the authorities they oppose are always an older generation, and so every student movement *must* have the aspect of a generational conflict. But the students of the Silent Generation of the fifties were also young, and so are the students on every other campus in the country however quiescent or rebellious. This is a theory which can never account for any differences among student reactions,

---

* I call them a kind of "radical" on the assumption the reader has heard the old story about the New York cop who is clubbing a demonstrator outside the Russian consulate. "But, officer, I'm an anti-Communist," expostulates the victim. "I don't care *what* kind of Communist you are!" says the cop—*Bash*!

since it is based on what is biologically common to all. The one thing Feuer's theory can never explain is why such an uprising should occur on one particular campus at a certain time.*

Yet there is a "generational conflict" behind Feuer's theory, though not so much the one he is concerned about. Conflict cuts both ways; and if there is not much evidence of any special student antagonism to the older generation as such (though plenty of evidence of distrust), one must look also at the other side of the antagonistic relationship. In Feuer's shrill diatribes against the students, some of which we have quoted, and many of which make even campus conservatives embarrassed, it is difficult to overlook the extreme emotional content. We have here a typical representative of the generation of ex-Communists who, having devoted a good part of their lives to the service of apologizing for totalitarians, are now lashing out in fury at the tragedy of their own pasts. The hatred they unleash against the radical students is a self-hatred in the first place projected against the new generation which (they think) mirrors their sad youth.

This sort of thing plays a distinctly negative role in the education of the non-I radicals, who do not see the political pathology of the case but take it as a bogeyman. ("This is what happens if you become too anti-Communist," or "This is what happens to `old radicals.' ")

"How do I know that won't happen to me?" mused one FSM leader in a bull session, as if he were talking of a disease. "You don't," I told him cheerfully. "Take the 800 [arrested sit-inners]. Ten years from now, most of them will be rising in the world and in income, living in the suburbs from Terra Linda to Atherton, raising two or three babies, voting Democratic, and wondering what on earth they were doing in Sproul Hall—trying to remember, and failing."

---

* Also, the Somers spring survey has some material tending to negate the relevance of "generational conflict" as a specific motivation.

He shuddered—a literal, physical shudder. "It won't happen to me; I'll remember."

Maybe; but while it is easy to remember that one had a feeling of moral indignation, it is harder to recall the feeling. If the FSM activists were really as non-ideological as they think they are, it would be even harder. But the fact is that they do have a sort of working ideology.

The central core of the working ideology of the typical radical activists is not defined by any one issue, but consists of a choice between two alternative modes of operation: *permeation* or *left opposition.* The former seeks to adapt to the ruling powers and infiltrate their centers of influence with the aim of (some day) getting to the very levers of decisionmaking—becoming a part of the Establishment in order to manipulate the reins to the left. The latter wish to stand outside the Establishment as an open opposition, achieving even short-term changes by the pressure of a bold alternative, while seeking roads to fundamental transformations.

What separates the style of the radical "New Left" from liberals who may agree on many given issues, is their rejection of the permeationist method. This was, of course, at bottom the basis for the bifurcation between FSM militants and moderates too; and the difference was dramatized as in a charade when, on the very same day (November 9), the militant leadership of the FSM went into illegal opposition with a civil-disobedience policy, while a wing of the moderates went to try to make a deal with President Kerr: a symbolic split. Many of the non-I radicals are fairly conscious of what their rejection of permeationism means—its relation, for example, to their rejection of any kind of support to the Democratic administration and their hostility to the Democratic Party as a trap for liberals. Instead of adapting to power, they talk in terms of organizing for struggle from below. This wing of Students for Democratic Society, for example, look to work among the urban poor and unemployed as their special kind of project. Leaving aside what results can be expected from this particular work, the effort exemplifies their chosen alternative. On campus, other non-I radicals, looking for a road to take that does not lead to integration with the Establishment, have been attracted to work among California's exploited farm laborers—literally at the grass roots. I cite these as examples of a groping in a certain direction, not as a program.

This also helps to explain what even some friends of the "New Left" radicals have complained about. Thus in a *Nation* article Jack Newfield writes a glowing account of "The Student Left: Revolt Without Dogma," and then chides:

> Immediate predecessors like Socialists Bayard Rustin and Michael Harrington are repudiated on the absurd ground that they have "sold out to the Establishment"—Rustin because he supported the 1964 moratorium on street demonstrations and the compromise offered the Mississippi Freedom Democratic Party at the 1964 Democratic Convention, and Harrington because he is a consultant to Sargent Shriver and Walter Reuther. The new radicals also reject the Rustin-Harrington theory that social change is achieved by an institutionalized coalition of church, labor, Negro and liberal groups reforming the Democratic Party. *(The Nation,* May 10, 1965.)

To the "New Left" radicals, the point is not that people like Rustin and Harrington have "sold out" in the usual venal sense, but that they have moved to attach themselves to the pillars of power, as advisers at the left ear of authority, while the "New Left" radicals are moving in the opposite direction. The crux is not the sincerity of any individuals but the permeationist theory which is stated in Newfield's last sentence. Probably few of the new radicals would give as theoretical a form to their alternative course as the permeationists give to theirs, but there is a basic ideological element there for all that. It is not surprising that so many observers were moved to comment on the "revolutionary" feel of the FSM uprising, for we are now discussing, as a matter of fact, what has been the historical line of demarcation between revolutionary and reform currents in social movements of dissent. In fact, the new radicals are in process of rediscovering another `old politics"—the politics of left opposition to the ongoing system in the name of a new social and moral vision.

No one can say whether this is a stream of thought and action that will deepen and extend, or whether it will dry to a trickle while new social movements arise elsewhere. It has already made a significant contribution in jolting the affluent complacency of middle-class, liberal America. It has been a catalyst—a trigger, an example—unleashing FSM-like actions and movements throughout the nation. No matter what happens now, whether there are advances or setbacks ahead for this unformed movement, it is laying a groundwork for the future freedom-fighters of the United States, by training and inspiring new cadres of idealistic youth with social goals so imbued with a new moral vision as to raise basic questions over the established order of society.

# *Voices from Berkeley*

## Documents of the Revolt

## • *The Academic Senate's Motions of December 8*

*These were the motions adopted at the climactic meeting of the Academic Senate (consisting of all faculty members from assistant professors up) following the sit-in and the strike. The motions were introduced by the Senate's Committee on Academic Freedom and adopted 824-115.*

1. That there shall be no university disciplinary measures against members or organizations of the university community for activities prior to December 8 connected with the current controversy over political speech and activity.

2. That the time, place, and manner of conducting political activity on campus should be subject to reasonable regulation, to prevent interference with the normal functions of the university; that the regulations now in effect for this purpose shall remain in effect provisionally, pending a future report of the Committee on Academic Freedom concerning the minimal regulations necessary.

3. That the content of speech or advocacy should not be restricted by the university. Off-campus student political activities shall not be subject to university regulation. On-campus advocacy or organization of such activities shall be subject only to such limitations as may be imposed under Section 2.

4. That future disciplinary measures in the area of political activity shall be determined by a committee appointed by, and responsible to, the Berkeley Division of the Academic Senate.

5. That the division urge the adoption of the foregoing policies, and call on all members of the university community to join with the faculty in its efforts to restore the university to its normal functions.

## • *Academic Freedom and Student Political Activity*

In January, 1965, a large group of faculty members, well over two hundred, submitted a long and carefully written statement to the court considering the cases of the sit-inners arrested in Sproul Hall on December 3, arguing for dismissal of the charges. Entitled "A Suggestion for Dismissal," *written collectively by a number of professors, it discussed the wider implications of the case as well as the legal aspects. This is one section.*

Academic freedom has its own distinctive and honorable tradition, at least as old and perhaps older than that which governs the general freedom of speech. But the importance of speech and discussion to the university is first and foremost instrumental: it is indispensable to learning and indispensable to teaching. The very activity of education, for student and teacher alike, is the free exercise of open minds. Whenever in the pursuit of knowledge speech is guarded and minds are sealed, the educational dialogue deteriorates into monologue, arguable hypotheses harden into dogma, and the will to stimulate active inquiry yields to the demand for passive acceptance.

What transpires in such an atmosphere does not deserve the name of learning, but of conditioning. Closed minds, on the part of students, can doubtless be indoctrinated; they may even be trained; but they cannot be taught. Closed minds, on the part of professors, can issue directives; they may even give lectures; but they cannot teach. And closed circuits of communication between students and teachers can never conduct the intellectual spark by which the minds of students and teachers alike are ignited.

Academic freedom then is not an end in itself. It is an indispensable means to the unique objective of the university: that of the cultivation of minds and the provocation of thought. "Academic freedom and tenure," as Alan Barth has written *in The Loyalty of Free Men,* "are not privileges extended to the teaching profession, but a form of insurance to society that the teaching profession will be able to discharge its function conscientiously." To this it may be added that freedom of speech and advocacy are not privileges extended to students, but equally a form of insurance to society that the next generation of citizens will be able to discharge their functions and conduct their affairs conscientiously, reasonably and responsibly.

It was this general conception of the purpose and spirit of academic freedom which Justice Frankfurter had in mind when he reminded us (*Wieman v. Updegrafl, 344 U.S. 183* [1952], at 195-197) that ". . . public opinion is the ultimate reliance of our society only if it be disciplined and responsible. It can be disciplined and responsible only if habits of open-mindedness and of critical inquiry are acquired in the formative years of our citizens.... It is the special task of teachers to foster those habits of open-mindedness and critical inquiry which alone make for responsible citizens, who, in turn, make possible an enlightened and effective public opinion." And he warned that ". . . unwarranted inhibition upon the free spirit of teachers . . . has an unmistakable tendency to chill that free play of the spirit which all teachers ought especially to cultivate and practice; it makes for caution and timidity in their associations by potential teachers."

Justice Frankfurter's reference to "potential teachers" points to a further aspect of academic freedom as it bears upon students. College students are not only citizens-in-training; they are also scholars-in-training. They are apprentice or junior members of the scholarly community, whose interest in open inquiry, speech and discussion is identical with that of their seniors. Of course not all will become teachers; but some of them will and any of them might. If they have learned their trade in a restrictive or fearful environment, they cannot be expected to practice it fearlessly and wisely when their turn comes to teach.

There is growing recognition today that students can no longer be treated as mere transients who "receive" an education from their teachers, but they must be accepted as a constituent part of the academic community. The rights and privileges of membership include not only the freedom to learn, to inquire, and to discuss, but the right to be treated with dignity and to be allowed to take a responsible part in the affairs of the community. The harassment, petty vindictiveness, and arbitrariness suffered by the students throughout the Fall semester of 1964 indicate the utter failure of the University Administration to understand how members of an ancient and proud community ought to treat one another....

If, in the present age, the boundaries of a campus symbolize a free community pledged to rational inquiry and not a closed community separated from the public world, there is pressing need to reaffirm the political rights, as well as the academic freedom of the members of the university. What is often denied them, not only outside the campus boundaries, but more recently inside, is the right to take their ideas seriously. Freedom to discuss and to inquire has been granted members of the academic community presumably in order to allow them to reflect, among other things, upon questions of human conduct, the dignity of the person, and the values of liberty, equality, and voluntary consent. But when students have sought to translate these ideas into campus practices and social realities, they have been hampered and discouraged by university restrictions severely infringing their rights as participating members of an academic community and as citizens of American society. Idle thought and idle talk make idle citizens.

It is no less true of freedom in the academy than of freedom in society that it requires regular and vigorous exercise if it is to survive and serve its ends. That exercise is found in continuous contest and criticism, the free competition of the academic market place. Students and faculty members who seek personal safety in the avoidance of all uncertain commitments and outrageous hypotheses do no service to the cause of higher education. In this connection, not the least of the constructive consequences which have followed upon the past semester of student activity at Berkeley has been the shock of recognition it has produced in the ranks of the faculty—the recognition, at last or once again, of the necessity to take their vocation seriously: to practice in the concrete what they have always preached in the abstract.

## • *An End to History by Mario Savio*

*Published in* Humanity, *December, 1964, a Berkeley magazine published by an inter-faith editorial board. The article is an edited version of a tape recording made by Mr. Savio during the Sproul Hall sit-in.*

Last summer I went to Mississippi to join the struggle there for civil rights. This fall I am engaged in another phase of the same struggle, this time in Berkeley. The two battlefields may seem quite different to some observers, but this is not the case. The same rights are at stake in both places—the right to participate as citizens in democratic society and the right to due process of law. Further, it is a struggle against the same enemy. In Mississippi an autocratic and powerful minority rules, through organized violence, to suppress the vast, virtually powerless, majority. In California, the privileged minority manipulates the University bureaucracy to suppress the students' political expression. That "respectable" bureaucracy masks the financial plutocrats; that impersonal bureaucracy is the efficient enemy in a "Brave New World."

In our free speech fight at the University of California, we have come up against what may emerge as the greatest problem of our nation—depersonalized, unresponsive bureaucracy. We have encountered the organized status quo in Mississippi, but it is the same in Berkeley. Here we find it impossible usually to meet with anyone but , secretaries. Beyond that, we find functionaries who cannot make policy but can only hide behind the rules. We have discovered total lack of response on the part of the policy makers. To grasp a situation which is truly Kafkaesque, it is necessary to understand the bureaucratic mentality. And we have learned quite a bit about it this fall, more outside the classroom than in.

As bureaucrat, an administrator believes that nothing new happens. He occupies an a-historical point of view. In September, to get the attention of this bureaucracy which had issued arbitrary edicts suppressing student political expression and refused to discuss its action, we held a sit-in on the campus. We sat around a police car and kept it immobilized for over thirty-two hours. At last, the administrative bureaucracy agreed to negotiate. But instead, on the following Monday, we discovered that a committee had been appointed, in accordance with usual regulations, to resolve the dispute. Our attempt to convince any of the administrators that an event had occurred, that something new had happened, failed. They saw this simply as something to be handled by normal University procedures.

The same is true of all bureaucracies. They begin as tools, means to certain legitimate goals, and they end up feeding their own existence. The conception that bureaucrats have is that history has in fact come to an end. No events can occur now that the second World War is over which can change American society substantially. We proceed by standard procedures as we are.

The most crucial problems facing the United States today are the problem of automation and the problem of racial injustice. Most people who will be put out of jobs by machines will not accept an end to events, this historical plateau, as the point beyond which no change occurs. Negroes will not accept an end to history here. All of us must refuse to accept history's final judgment that in America there is no place in society for people whose skins are dark. On campus, students are not about to accept it as fact that the University has ceased evolving and is in its final state of perfection, that students and faculty are respectively raw material and employees, or that the University is to be autocratically run by unresponsive bureaucrats.

Here is the real contradiction: the bureaucrats hold history as ended. As a result significant parts of the population both on campus and off are dispossessed, and these dispossessed are not about to accept this a-historical point of view. It is out of this that the conflict has occurred with the University bureaucracy and will continue to occur until that bureaucracy becomes responsive or until it is clear the University can not function.

The things we are asking for in our civil rights protests have a deceptively quaint ring. We are asking for the due process of law. We are asking for our actions to be judged by committees of our peers. We are asking that regulations ought to be considered as arrived at legitimately—only from the consensus of the governed. These phrases are all pretty old, but they are not being taken seriously in America today, nor are they being taken seriously on the Berkeley campus.

I have just come from a meeting with the Dean of Students. She notified us that she was aware of certain violations of University regulations by certain organizations. University friends of SNCC, which I represent, was one of these. We tried to draw from her some statement on these great principles: consent of the governed, jury of one's peers, due process. The best she could do was to evade or to present the administration party line. It is very hard to make any contact with the human being who is behind these organizations.

The university is the place where people begin seriously to question the conditions of their existence and raise the issue of whether they can be committed to the society they have been born into. After a long period of apathy during the fifties, students have begun not only to question but, having arrived at answers, to act on those answers. This is part of a growing understanding among many people in America that history has not ended, that a better society is possible, and that it is worth dying for.

This free speech fight points up a fascinating aspect of contemporary campus life. Students are permitted to talk all they want so long as their speech has no consequences.

One conception of the university, suggested by a classical Christian formulation, is that it be in the world but not of the world. The conception of Clark Kerr, by contrast, is that the university is part and parcel of this particular stage in the history of American society; it stands to serve the need of American industry; it is a factory that turns out a certain product needed by industry or government. Because speech does often have consequences which might alter this perversion of higher education, the university must put itself in a position of censorship. It can permit two kinds of speech: speech which encourages continuation of the status quo, and speech which advocates changes in it so radical as to be irrelevant in the foreseeable future. Someone may advocate radical change in all aspects of American society, and this I am sure he can do with impunity. But if someone advocates sit-ins to bring about changes in discriminatory hiring practices, this can not be permitted because it goes against the status quo of which the university is a part. And that is how the fight began here.

The Administration of the Berkeley campus has admitted that external, extra-legal groups have pressured the university not to permit students on campus to organize picket lines, not to permit on campus any speech with. consequences. And the bureaucracy went along. Speech with consequences, speech in the area of civil rights, speech which some might regard as illegal, must stop.

Many students here at the university, many people in society, are wandering aimlessly about. Strangers in their own lives, there is no place for them. They are people who have not learned to compromise, who for example have come to the university to learn to question, to grow, to learn—all the standard things that sound like cliches because no one takes them seriously. And they find at one point or other that for them to become part of society, to become lawyers, ministers, businessmen, people in government, that very often they must compromise those principles which were most dear to them. They must suppress the most creative impulses that they have; this is a prior condition for being part of the system. The university is well structured, well tooled, to turn out people with all the sharp edges worn off, the well-rounded person. The university is well equipped to produce that sort of person, and this means that the best among the people who enter must for four years wander aimlessly much of the time questioning why they are on campus at all, doubting whether there is any point in what they are doing, and looking toward a very bleak existence afterward in a game in which all of the rules have been made up, which one can not really amend.

It is a bleak scene, but it is all a lot of us have to look forward to. Society provides no challenge. American society in the standard conception it has of itself is simply no longer exciting. The most exciting things going on in America today are movements to change America. America is becoming evermore the utopia of sterilized, automated contentment. The "futures" and "careers" for which American students now prepare are for the most part intellectual and moral wastelands. This chrome-plated consumers' paradise would have us grow up to be well-behaved children. But an important minority of men and women coming to the front today have shown that they will die rather than be standardized, replaceable, and irrelevant.

## • *The Free Speech Movement and Civil Rights by Jack Weinberg*

*Published in the Campus CORE-lator for January, 1965, the magazine of Campus CORE, Berkeley. Jack Weinberg became a leading member of the FSM Steering Committee after being "the man in the police car" of October 1-2.*

### FSM AND THE CIVIL RIGHTS MOVEMENT

Over the past few years, there has been a change, both quantitative and qualitative in Bay Area student political activity. Until 1963, only a relatively small number of students had been actively involved in the civil rights movement. Furthermore, until that time, student political activity of all kinds was quite impotent in terms of any real effect it had on the general community. Organizations such as peace groups raised demands which were so momentous as to be totally unattainable. Civil rights groups, on the other hand, often raised demands which were attainable, but quite inconsequential; a job or a house for an individual Negro who had been discriminated against. In no way was student political activity a threat, or even a serious nuisance to large power interests. In early 1963, a new precedent in the Bay Area civil rights movement was established; civil rights organizations began demanding that large employers integrate their work forces on more than a mere token basis. Hundreds of jobs would be at stake in a single employment action. In the fall of 1963, a second important precedent was established. Starting with the demonstrations at Mel's Drive-in, large numbers of students became involved in the civil rights movement. And as they joined, the movement adopted more militant tactics. Thus with more significant issues at stake, and with more powerful weapons available, the civil rights movement became a threat, or at least a real nuisance to the power interests. Not only was the civil rights movement, "a bunch of punk kids," forcing employers to change their policies, but it was also beginning to upset some rather delicate political balances.

Attempts were made by the civil authorities and the power interests to contain the movement: harassing trials, biased news reporting, job intimidation, etc. But the attempts were unsuccessful, the movement grew, became more sophisticated, and began exploring other fronts on which it could attack the power structure. Throughout the summer of 1964, Berkeley Campus CORE maintained a hectic level of continuous and effective activity. The Ad Hoc Committee to End Discrimination planned and began executing a project against the Oakland *Tribune*. Since those who wished to contain the civil rights movement found no effective vehicles in the community, they began pressuring the university. Because a majority of participants were students, they maintained that the university was responsible. After initially resisting the pressure, the university finally succumbed, and promulgated restrictive regulations with the intent of undercutting the base of student support for the civil rights movement. The reactions to these regulations should have been predictable: immediate protest and a demand for their repeal. Since the civil rights movement was responsible for the pressures applied to the university which led to the suppression of free speech and free political expression, and since their interests were the ones most seriously threatened, the civil rights activists took the lead in protesting the suppression, many conclude that the FSM is an extension of the civil rights movement.

## THE FSM AS CAMPUS PROTEST

But if we view the FSM simply as an extension of the civil rights movement, we can not explain the overwhelming support it has received from students who have been indifferent to the civil rights movement and even from some who have been hostile to it. Civil rights activists, those whose interests are really at stake, make up a very small part of the ardent FSM supporters. The vast majority of the FSM supporters have never before had any desire to sit at tables, to hand out leaflets, or to publicly advocate anything. The Free Speech Movement has become an outlet for the feelings of hostility and alienation which so many students have toward the university. Early in the movement, one graduate student who was working all night for the FSM said, "I really don't give a damn about free speech. I'm just tired of being shat upon. If we don't win anything else, at least they'll have to respect us after this." Clearly, his was an overstatement. Free speech *has* been the issue, and virtually all the FSM supporters identify with the FSM demands. The roots, however, go much deeper. The free speech issue has been so readily accepted because it has become a vehicle enabling students to express their dissatisfaction with so much of university life, and with so many of the university's. institutions.

The phenomenon we describe is not at all unprecedented, even though the FSM may be an extreme example. There have been wildcat strikes which in many ways are quite similar to the Free Speech protest. The following pattern is typical: There is an industry in which the workers are discontented with their situation. The pay may or may not be low. There is hostility between the workers and the management, but it is hostility over a great number of practices and institutions, most of which are well established, and none of which have been adequate to launch a protest over the abstract issue. One of the greatest grievances is likely to be the attitude of the managers toward the workers. The union has proven itself incapable of dealing with the issue. Then one day a work practice is changed or a worker is penalized over a minor infraction. Fellow workers protest and are either ignored or reprimanded. A wildcat strike is called and the protest is on.

The same kind of force which creates a wildcat strike has created the FSM. Alienation and hostility exist, but are neither focused at specific grievances nor well articulated. There is a general feeling that the situation is hopeless, and probably inevitable. There is no obvious handle. No one knows where to begin organizing, what to attack first, how to attack. No one feels confident that an attack is justified, or even relevant. Suddenly there is an issue; everyone recognizes it; everyone grabs at it. A feeling of solidarity develops among the students, as among the workers.

The students at Cal have united. To discover the basic issues underlying their protest one must first listen to the speeches made by their leaders. Two of the most basic themes that began to emerge in the very first speeches of the protest and which have remained central throughout have been a condemnation of the University in its role as a knowledge factory and a demand that the voices of the students must be heard. These themes have been so well received because of the general feeling among the students that the University has made them anonymous; that they have very little control over their environment, over their future; that the University society is almost completely unresponsive to their individual needs. The students decry the lack of human contact, the lack of communication, the lack of dialogue that exists at the University. Many believe that much of their course work is irrelevant, that many of their most difficult assignments are merely tedious busy work with little or no educational value. All too often in his educational career, the student, in a pique of frustration, asks himself, "What's it all about?" In a flash of insight he sees the educational process as a gauntlet: undergraduate education appears to be a rite of endurance, a series of trials, which if successfully completed allows one to enter graduate school; and upon those who succeed in completing the entire rite of passage is bestowed the ceremonious title, Ph.D. For those who cop out along the way, the further one gets the better the job one can obtain, with preference given according to the major one has selected. All too often, the educational process appears to be a weeding-out process, regulated by the laws of supply and demand. The better one plays the game, the more he is rewarded.

To be sure, there are some excellent courses at Cal; some departments are better than others. Although a general education is difficult, if not impossible, to obtain, in many fields the student is able to obtain an adequate though specialized preparation for an academic career. Furthermore, successful completion of a Cal education is quite a good indication that the student will be agile and adaptable enough to adjust to a position in industry and to acquire rapidly the skills and traits that industry will demand of him.

When viewed from the campus, the Free Speech Movement is a revolution, or at least an open revolt. The students' basic demand is a demand to be heard, to be considered, to be taken into account when decisions concerning their education and their life in the university community are being made. When one reviews the history of the Free Speech Movement, one discovers that each new wave of student response to the movement followed directly on some action by the administration which neglected to take the students, as human beings, into account, and which openly reflected an attitude that the student body was a thing to be dealt with, to be manipulated. Unfortunately, it seems that at those rare times when the students are not treated as things, they are treated as children.

## THE IMPLICATIONS FOR AMERICAN SOCIETY

It is inadequate, as we have shown, to characterize the FSM as a purely on-campus phenomenon, as a protest stemming from a long overdue need for university reform, or as a response to a corrupt or insensitive administration. Invariably, when students become politically and socially active, one can find that at the root, they are responding to their society's most basic problems.

Let us first consider why students have become so active in the Northern civil rights movement. The problem with which the civil rights movement is trying to cope, the problem of the effect of our society on the Negro community, is exactly the problem of our entire society, magnified and distorted. Unemployment, underemployment, poor education, poor housing, intense social alienation: these and many more are the effects of our way of life on the Negro community, and these to one degree or another are the effects of our way of life on all of its members. When taking a moral stand, when doing what they can in the struggle for equality for all Americans, students invariably find that as they become more and more successful they come into conflict with almost all the established interest groups in the community. Students have turned to the civil rights movement because they have found it to be a front on which they can attack basic social problems, a front on which they can have some real impact. In the final analysis the FSM must be viewed in this same light.

The University of California is a microcosm in which all of the problems of our society are reflected. Not only did the pressure to crack down on free speech at Cal come from the outside power structure, but most of the failings of the University are either on-campus manifestations of broader American social problems, or are imposed upon the University by outside pressures. Departments at the University are appropriated funds roughly in proportion to the degree that the state's industry feels these departments are important. Research and study grants to both students and faculty are given on the same preferential basis. One of the greatest social ills of this nation is the absolute refusal by almost all of its members to examine seriously the presuppositions of the establishment. This illness becomes a crisis when the University, supposedly a center for analysis and criticism, refuses to examine these presuppositions. Throughout the society, the individual has lost more and more control over his environment. When he votes, he must choose between two candidates who agree on almost all basic questions. On his job, he has become more and more a cog in a machine, a part of a master plan in whose formulation he is not consulted, and over which he can. exert no influence for change. He finds it increasingly more difficult to find meaning in his job or in his life. He grows more cynical. The bureaucratization of the campus is just a reflection of the bureaucratization of American life.

As the main energies of our society are channeled into an effort to win the cold war, as all of our institutions become adjuncts of the military-industrial complex, as the managers of industry and the possessors of corporate wealth gain a greater and greater strangle hold on the lives of all Americans, one cannot expect the University to stay pure.

In our society, students are neither children nor adults. Clearly, they are not merely children; but to be an adult in our society one must both be out of school and self-supporting (for some reason, living on a grant or fellowship is not considered self-supporting). As a result, students are more or less outside of society, and in increasing numbers they do not desire to become a part of the society. From their peripheral social position they are able to maintain human values, values they know will be distorted or destroyed when they enter the compromising, practical, "adult" world.

It is their marginal social status which has allowed students to become active in the civil rights movement and which has allowed them to create the Free Speech Movement. The students, in their idealism, are confronted with a world which is a complete mess, a world which in their eyes preceding generations have botched up. They start as liberals, talking about society, criticizing it, going to lectures, donating money. But every year more and more students find they cannot stop there. They affirm themselves; they decide that even if they do not know how to save the world, even if they have no magic formula, they must let their voice be beard. They become activists, and a new generation, a generation of radicals, emerges.

## • *We Want a University*

*We here give most of a pamphlet published by the FSM during the controversy. The first part, not included here, comprised an article by Neal Blumenfeld, a Berkeley psychiatrist, who emphasized the moral element in the FSM struggle. The rest was collectively written, mainly by members of the FSM Steering Committee; the pamphlet was published unsigned.*

### THE MORAL IMPETUS

Our stand *has* been moral. We feel, that to a great extent, our movement has accomplished something which so many of the movements of the past few generations have failed to accomplish. We have tried, in the context of a mass movement, to act politically with moral justification. We have tried to be sensitive to each of our supporters and the individual morality he has brought to the movement. This is what has been unique about our movement.

Although our issue has been Free Speech, our theme has been solidarity. When individual members of our community have acted, we joined together as a community to jointly bear the responsibility for their actions. We have been able to revitalize one of the most distorted, misused, and important words of our century: comrade. The concept of living cannot be separated from the concept of other people. In our practical, fragmented society, too many of us have been alone. By being willing to stand up for others, and by knowing that others are willing to stand up for us, we have gained more than political power, we have gained personal strength. Each of us who has acted, now knows that he is a being willing to act.

No one can presume to explain why so many thousands have become part of the Free Speech Movement. All we can say is what each of us felt: something was wrong, something had to be done. It wasn't just that student political rights had been abridged; much more was wrong. Something had to be done about political rights, and in actively trying to cope with political rights we found ourselves confronting the entire Berkeley experience. The Berkeley campus has become a new place since the beginning of the semester. Many are trying to tell us that what we are trying to do may destroy the University. We are fully aware that we are doing something which has, implicitly, proportions so immense as to be frightening. We are frightened of our power as a movement; but it is a healthy fear. We must not allow our fear to lead us into believing that we are being destructive. We are beginning to *build* a great university. So long as the students stand united in firmness and dignity, and the faculty stands behind us, the University cannot be destroyed. As students, we have already demonstrated our strength and dedication; the faculty has yet to show it can do its share. Some faculty members have stated that if what they call "anarchy" continues, then they will leave the University to seek *employment* elsewhere. Such faculty members who would leave at this point would compromise themselves by an antiseptic solution to a problem of personal anguish, rather than stay and fight for a great university. There is reason to fear these professors, for *they* can destroy the University by deserting it.

And sadly there is reason to believe that even after all of the suffering which has occurred in our community, the overwhelming majority of faculty members have not been permanently changed, have not joined our community, have not really listened to our voices at this late date. For a moment on December 8, eight hundred and twenty-four professors gave us all a glimpse—a brief, glorious vision—of the University as a loving community. If only the Free Speech Movement could have ended that day! But already the professors have compromised away much for which they stood on that day. They have shamed themselves in view of the students and their colleagues all over the country. The ramparts of rationalization which our society's conditioning had erected about our professors' souls were breached by the relentless hammer-blows of conscience springing from thousands of students united in something called "FSM." But the searing light of their momentary courage became nakedness to them —too painful to endure. After December 8, most faculty members moved quickly to rebuild their justifications for years of barren compromise.

We challenge the faculty to be courageous. A university is a community of students and scholars: be equal to the position of dignity you should hold!! How long will you submit to the doorkeepers who have usurped your power? Is a university no more than a physical plant and an administration? The University cannot be destroyed unless its core is destroyed, and our movement is not weakening that core but strengthening it. Each time the FSM planned to act, it was warned that to act was to destroy. Each time, however, the campus community responded with new vigor. Too many people underestimate the resilience of a community fighting for a principle. Internally, the health of the University is improving. Communication, spirit, moral and intellectual curiosity, all have increased. The faculty has been forced to take the student body more seriously; it has begun to respect students. Furthermore, it has gained the opportunity to achieve a profound respect from the students. Those professors at Cal and other universities who love to teach, should be looking to Berkeley as the nation's greatest reservoir of students who embody the vital balance of moral integrity and high intellectual caliber. If the University community can maintain its courage, stand firmly together in the face of attacks from without, it will survive. Those who fearfully warn us that we are destroying the University are unwittingly weakening the FSM and the University. In the final analysis, only fear destroys.

### FREE SPEECH AND THE FACTORY

In our fight for Free Speech we said the "machine" must stop. We said that we must put our bodies on the line, on the machinery, in the wheels and gears, and that the "knowledge factory" must be brought to a halt. Now we must begin to clarify, for ourselves, what we mean by "factory."

We need to clarify this because the issues of Free Speech and the factory, of politics and education on the campus, are in danger of becoming separated. For example, the press has had the tendency to assert this separation when they insist that we return to our studies; that we are not in a center for political activity, but a center for education. Likewise, the faculty betrays the same tendency in its desire to settle the Free Speech issue as quickly and quietly as possible in order that we may return to the "normal conduct" of our "great University."

In contrast to this tendency to separate the issues, many thousands of *us,* the Free Speech Movement, have asserted that politics and education are inseparable, that the *political* issue of the First and Fourteenth Amendments and the *educational issue* cannot. be separated. In place of "great University," we have said "impersonal bureaucracy," "machine," or "knowledge factory." If we emerge as victors from our long and still hard-to-be-won battle for Free Speech, will we then be returning to *less* than a factory? *Is* this a great university? If we are to take *ourselves* seriously we must define precisely what we meant when we said "knowledge factory."

The best way to identify the parts of our Multiversity machinery is simply to observe it "stripped down" to the bare essentials. In the context of a dazzling circus of "bait," which obscures our vision of the machinery, we get a four-year-long series of sharp staccatos: eight semesters, forty courses, one hundred twenty or more "units," ten to fifteen impersonal lectures *per week,* one to three oversized discussion meetings per week led by poorly paid graduate student "teachers." Over a period of four years the student-cog receives close to forty bibliographies; evaluation amounts to little more than pushing the test button, which results in over one hundred regurgitations in four years; and the writing of twenty to thirty-five "papers" in four years in this context means that they are of necessity technically and substantially poor due to a lack of time for thought. The course-grade-unit structure, resting on the foundation of departmentalization, produces knowledge for the student-cog which has been exploded into thousands of bits and is force-fed, by the coercion of grades. We all know what happens when we really get "turned on" by a great idea, a great man, or a great book: we pursue that interest at the risk of flunking out. The pursuit of thought, a painful but highly exhilarating process, requires, above all, the element of time.

Human nerves and flesh are transmuted under the pressure and stress of the university routine. It is as though we have become raw material in the strictly inorganic sense. But the Free Speech Movement has given us an extraordinary taste of what it means to be part of something organic. Jumping off the conveyors, we have become a community of furiously talking, feeling, and thinking human beings. If we take seriously our common agreement that we stopped a "machine" how can we be accused of conspiring to destroy a "great university"? Where?

The history of rather volcanic emotions which led up to the eruption of the Free Speech Movement did not result from thin air. It came from within *us.* On November 29, a letter appeared in *The New York Times Magazine.* It is a beautiful and sad letter from a young girl, and describes well the "volcanic activity" in all of us.

> To the Editor:
>
> I'm a student in the oldest girls' school in the country. I love my school, but your recent article on homework

really hit home ("Hard Day's Night of Today's Students" by Eda I. LeShan). . . .

After dinner I work until midnight or 12:30. In the beginning, the first two weeks or so, I'm fine. Then I begin to wonder just what this is all about: Am I educating my

self? I have that one all answered in my mind. I'm educating myself the way THEY want. So I convince myself the real reason I'm doing all this is to prepare myself for what I really want. Only one problem. After four years of this come four years of college and two of graduate school for me. I know just where I'm going and just what I want, but I'm impatient.

Okay, I can wait. But meanwhile I'm wasting those years of preparation. I'm not learning what I want to learn. I don't care anymore whether 2X2=4 anymore. I don't care about the feudal system.. I want to know about life. I want to think and read. When? Over weekends when there are projects and lectures and compositions, plus catching up on sleep.

My life is a whirlpool. I'm caught up in it but I'm not conscious of it. I'm what YOU call living, but somehow I can't find life. Days go by in an instant. I feel nothing accomplished in that instant. So maybe I got an A on that composition I worked on for three hours, but when I get it back I find that A means nothing. It's a letter YOU use to keep me going.

Every day I come in well prepared. Yet I dread every class; my stomach tightens and I sit tense. I drink coffee morning, noon, and night. At night, after my homework I lie in bed and wonder if I've really done it all. Is there something I've forgotten?

> At the beginning of the year I'm fine. My friends know me by my smile. Going to start out bright this year. Not going to get bogged down this year. Weeks later I become introspective and moody again. I wonder what I'm doing here. I feel phony; I don't belong. All I want is time; time to sit down and read what I want to read, and think what I want to think.
>
> You wonder about juvenile delinquents. If I ever become one, I'll tell you why it will be so. I feel cramped. I feel like I'm in a coffin and can't move or breathe. There's no air or light. All I can see is blackness and I've got to burst. Sometimes I feel maybe something will come along. Something has to or I'm not worth anything. My life is worth nothing. It's enclosed in a few buildings on one campus; it goes no further. I've got to bust.
>
> NAME WITHHELD
>
> P.S. I wrote this last night at 12:15 and in the light of day I realize this will never *reach* you.

This letter is probably one of the most profoundly shared expressions of anguish in American life today. It is shared by millions of us.

## THE FACTORY AND THE SOCIETY

The emotions expressed in that letter reflect the problems of the society as expressed in the Multiversity as well as in a small prep school for girls in the East. The University has become grotesquely distorted into a "Multiversity"; a public utility serving the purely technical needs of a society. In Clark Kerr's words, it is a factory for the production of knowledge and technicians to service society's many bureaucracies.

Current federal and private support programs for the university have been compared to classic examples of imperialism and neocolonialism. The government has invested in underdeveloped, capital-starved institutions, and imposed a pattern of growth and development upon them which, if disrupted, would lead to economic breakdown and political chaos.

Research and training replace scholarship and learning. In this system even during the first two years, the student is pressured to specialize or endure huge, impersonal lecture courses. He loses contact with his professors as they turn more to research and publishing, and away from teaching. His professors lose contact with one another as they serve a discipline and turn away from dialogue. Forms and structures stifle humane learning.

The student is powerless even to affect those aspects of the university supposedly closest to him. His student "government" by political castrates is a fraud permitted to operate only within limits imposed autocratically by the administration. Thus it is constitutionally mandated to serve the status quo. Likewise, the student has no power over the social regulations which affect his privacy, and little influence in shaping the character of the dormitories in which he lives. The university assumes the role of the parent.

As a human being seeking to enrich himself, the student has no place in the Multiversity. Instead he becomes a mercenary, paid off in grades, status, and degrees, all of which can eventually be cashed in for hard currency on the job market. His education is not valued for its enlightenment and the freedom it should enable him to enjoy, but for the amount of money it will enable him to make. Credits for courses are subtly transformed into credit cards as the Multiversity inculcates the values of the acquisitive society.

It has been written that "The main concern of the university should not be with the publishing of books, getting money from legislators, lobbying for federal aid, wooing the rich, producing bombs and deadly bacteria." Nor should it be with passing along the morality of the middle class, nor the morality of the white man, nor even the morality of the potpourri we call "western society." Nor should it be with acting as a second household or church for the young man away from home, nor as a playground for twisters, neophyte drinkers, and pledge classes. Already the parallels between the habits of the university and the habits of the society are many; the parallels between our academic and financial systems of credit, between competition for grades and for chamber of commerce awards, between cheating and price rigging, and between statements of "Attendance is a privilege, not a right," and we reserve the right to refuse service to anyone.

In an article in *The New York Review of Books,* Paul Goodman poignantly comments upon the plight of the modern student:

> At present in the United States, students—middle-class youth—are the major exploited class. (Negroes, small farmers, the aged are rather outcast groups; their labor is not needed and they are not wanted.) The labor of intelligent youth *is* needed and they are accordingly subjected to tight scheduling, speed-up and other factory exploitative methods. Then it is not surprising if they organize their CIO. It is frivolous to tell them to go elsewhere if they don't like the rules; for they have no choice but to go to college, and one factory is like another.

In saying these things it is important to avoid a certain misunderstanding. By identifying the parts of the machinery in our factory, the way in which we have described them, and their blending into our society of institutionalized greed, might lead people to assume that we have a fundamental bias against institutions as such; that we wish to destroy the structure altogether, to establish politics on the campus, and lash out against the power structure for the purposes of expressing a kind of collective orgasm of seething resentment against the "power structure." When we assert that Free Speech and the factory, or politics and education, are bound up together, we are again pointing to the obvious. In a twentieth-century industrial state, ignorance will be the definition of slavery. If centers of education fail, they will be the producers of the twentieth-century slave. To put it in more traditionally American terms, popular government cannot survive without education for the people. The people are more and more in the schools. But the pressure of the logistics of mass popular education combined with excessive greed has resulted in the machinery of the educational process having displaced the freedom to learn. We must now begin the demand of the right to know; to know the realities of the present world-in-revolution, and to have an opportunity to learn how to think clearly in an extended manner about that world. It is ours to demand meaning; we must insist upon meaning!

## THE FREE UNIVERSITY OF CALIFORNIA

The question of how to break down the machinery and build "intellectual communities worthy of the hopes and responsibilities of our people," is one on the minds of many participants in the Free Speech Movement. No one supposes he has the answers, but they can come from the Berkeley community. Our task is to generate these answers and to discover how they can be implemented. The Free Speech Movement proposes that the Free University of California be formed. We are inviting prominent intellectual and political figures to address the University community. We would like to see seminars on the educational revolution and many other topics which are not considered in the University. In the near future we hope that discussions with students, faculty, and members of the community, will take place independent of the University community. Such discussions would deal with any topic in which a sufficient number of people are interested. We would like to establish the availability of a revolutionary experience in education. If we succeed, we will accomplish a feat more radical and significant than anything the Free Speech Movement has attempted. We will succeed in beginning to bring humanity back to campus.

## • *Are You All Right, Jack?*
## *(Graduate Coorinating Commitee)*

*This was a leaflet addressed to graduate students, by the Graduate Coordinating, Committee, an FSM affiliate. The trade union organization of graduate student teachers which was projected here was formed in December as an affiliate of the American Federation of Teachers.*

The events of October and November on the Berkeley Campus of the University of California have brought to the surface a chronic condition which is inherent in the nature r of the university's structure as it now exists: absolutist rule by 'the administration. Whatever the cause of such a development, the fact is that the. jurisdiction of the administration is unchallenged by any organized body. The only means of opposing a particular action of the university is through spontaneous organization of those who oppose that action; a consequence is that campus groups have difficulty surviving the crises from which they originate.

From these events has arisen the awareness that there is a need for a permanent body which will represent the interests of an important segment of the Berkeley campus community, the graduate students. Suddenly these ten thousand graduate students, who see their situation as solely their own problem, realize that their personal problems are to a large extent determined by a common situation and that therefore their common interests bind them to one another and make them an interest group. We have been intent on fulfilling our department requirements, trying to establish good relationships with our professors, learning our profession and producing publishable materials, but every action has had to be one that we fought on our own, and hence one which has put us in opposition to and in competition with our fellow graduate students. We must lay aside the distrust and suspicion that has developed out of our past situation and realize that despite our differences our similarities are much greater, and that the advantages in our uniting are much greater than in our remaining disorganized. Above all, disunited we remain without a voice, individuals alone, completely impotent in our situation, whereas unity will provide us with an organization which will express and effectuate both our individual and common interests and protect us from an arbitrary administration.

The GCC, a good beginning for an association of graduate students, will reconstitute itself to promote all graduate student concerns. It will be voluntary, democratic, a dues-collecting organization, organized departmentally and interdepartmentally with each department dealing with the matters which pertain to it. Issues arising in one department which bear upon graduate students generally, as a result of the fast bond between all departments through the GCC, will be taken up on behalf of all students.

The concerns of the GCC are our concerns. We will formulate these concerns according to our needs and will develop with our needs. We are concerned with TA, RA, Reader and Proctor salaries, medical benefits, tax exemptions, unemployment compensation and social security, fellowships and grants, bookstore discounts, and housing and parking facilities. Academic concerns include fair hiring practices for both faculty and graduate students, library improvement and privileges, the revision of courses under the quarter system, the transition from tutorial to automated instruction, the improvement of education generally, and long-range educational aims and policy. Stands will be taken on political and social issues affecting graduate students as members of both the University and the community at large, and graduate students will be defended by the GCC in court actions resulting from graduate students' political actions.

Within the GCC is being formed a Union of University-employed Graduate Students. Its concerns will include those of the GCC but through the union we will be able to enjoy a strength which we would not have if we were only a fraternity of graduate students. Given an administrative autocracy, it is necessary to establish an independent body fully able to represent the interests of its members. In trying to conceive of such a body which would not be, like the ASUC or the Academic Senate, under the continual pressure of the administration, the Board of Regents or the State Legislature, the idea of a union was born. Through possible affiliation with organized labor, the UGS can bring to bear the pressure, enjoin the co-operation, and command the sympathies of a large body of support from the outside community to counteract the pressures placed on the administration by self-interest groups, and balance the pressures placed on us by the administration.

It is necessary to organize ourselves to maximum strength in order to reform our conditions radically within the University and the purposes of education: in other words, to redefine the uses of the University. There is no concern of any graduate student, either academic or economic, social or political, which is not a concern with the purposes of education within a free society. Individually, we fight to maintain our integrity, and because we are only men standing alone, we slowly give way under the lasting, concerted pressure of the establishment. If we are not to move closer and closer toward the Multiversity, if we can still resist the tendency toward autocratic determination of education, we must act now. Time works for the establishment, which counts upon our losing momentum, dissipating our energy and weakening our commitment. The more responsibly we now act the more strongly we will all organize.

## • *The Mind of Clark Kerr by Hal Draper*

*This pamphlet was published by the campus Independent Socialist Club a few days after the police-car blockade of October 1-2. The subtitle was: "His View of the University Factory and the 'New Slavery'."*

With his book *The Uses of the University* (Harvard, 1963), Clark Kerr, President of the University of California, became the outstanding theoretician and proponent of a particular view of the university. It is true that his foreword claims that the views put forward do not constitute "approval" or "defense" but only "analysis" and "description." He is only "describing" the Wave of the Future (he uses this term), and all realistic people must bow and accept it, like it or not.

Kerr, like many others, has perhaps forgotten that the very phrase comes from the 1940 book by Anne Lindbergh, *The Wave of the Future,* which presented the thesis that fascism or some type of totalitarianism was inevitably coming. She did not argue that this fascism be approved but only that it must be accepted. This was the identical approach also of Burnham's *Managerial Revolution.*

The new type of "multiversity," Kerr writes later, "is an imperative rather than a reasoned choice." You cannot argue with an imperative. It is not Kerr's methodology to say, "This is what I think should be done." He represents himself simply as the interpreter of inexorable "reality." He is, so to speak, the Administrator of History, merely informing us how to act in conformity with its Rules.

What is beyond question is that Kerr does present a "vision of the end," and that he tells us it *must* be accepted, just like any other ruling of the Administration. What is his vision?

In the first place, Kerr presents the university as an institution which is, and will be, increasingly indistinguishable from any other business enterprise in our industrial society. The reader is likely to think, at first, that this is only a metaphor: "the university's invisible product, knowledge," or "the university is being called upon to produce knowledge as never before." But Kerr means it literally:

> The production, distribution, and consumption of "knowledge" in all its forms is said to account for 29 percent of gross national product . . . and "knowledge production" is growing at about twice the rate of the rest of the economy. ... What the railroads did for the second half of the last century and the automobile for the first half of this century may be done for the second half of this century by the knowledge industry: that is, to serve as the focal point for national growth.

Naturally, there is a kernel of truth in this language; but can Kerr mean literally that his "multiversity" must become increasingly like a factory and its professors reshaped as businessmen? Consider this:

> The university and segments of industry are becoming more alike. As the university becomes tied into the world of work, the professor—at least in the natural and some of the social sciences—takes on the characteristics of an entrepreneur.... The two worlds are merging physically and psychologically.

One might think that the writer of these lines would hardly have patience with a university president who sternly forbade members of this university community to "mount" activity on campus which eventuated in political and social action off campus—that is, a university president who issued a decree against the "merger." We shall resolve this contradiction later: but we must note that the book is chock-full of statements about the infeasibility of enforcing a boundary line between the university and the society with which it must merge.

### NO CLOISTER

The university, Kerr quotes, is "inside a general social fabric of a given era." He rejects with justified contempt the Cloister and Ivory Tower approach. He points out that American universities are more "intertwined with their surrounding societies" than the European:

> When "the borders of the campus are the boundaries of our state," the lines dividing what is internal from what is external become quite blurred; taking the campus to the state brings the state to the campus.

But do not think that Kerr is here thinking of (say) CORE picketing of the Bank of America, on the ground that if Finance takes its problems to the campus, then the campus will be moved (by inexorable History) to take up certain problems of Finance.

Indeed, Kerr even writes the following in this connection: "Today the campus is being drawn to the city hall and the state capitol as never before." This was true in the Bay Area especially in 1960: the campus was drawn to the San Francisco City Hall, and a platoon of police tried to liquidate History by washing students down the steps. But it is not likely that Kerr was thinking of *this* brilliant confirmation of his thesis, for his next sentences are these:

> The politicians need new ideas to meet the new problems; the agencies need expert advice on how to handle the old. The professor can supply both.

He is thinking, of course, of the role of the university in providing intellectual servicemen for the ruling powers—not students but professors, who are not barred from "mounting" *their* interventions into the political and social action of society.

> The campus and society are undergoing a somewhat reluctant and cautious merger, already well advanced. M.I.T. is at least as much related to industry and government as Iowa State ever was to agriculture.

### QUESTION OF CURRENCY

It is *a good* thing to be related to the industrial and grower interests and to the state in the notorious fashion of Iowa State and M.I.T., and Kerr reiterates and insists on the term "merger"

> The university is being called upon ... to respond to the expanding claims of national service; to merge its activity with industry as never before; to adapt to and rechannel new intellectual currents.

To become "a truly American university," what are the "new intellectual currents" which we must adapt to? It turns out, at bottom, to involve a large amount of currency, indeed, but less intellectuality. The new current, the "vast transformation," the Wave of the Future to which the university must adapt is the impact of the new mass of government money (federal grants) pouring out of Washington "beginning with World War II," under the stimulation of the Cold War, the space race, Sputnik, the concurrently stimulated concern with health programs, etc. And: "The multiversity has demonstrated how adaptive it can be to new opportunities for creativity; how responsive to money .. ."

STATIFICATION

Not just money: Big Money. Kerr has a very useful section, highly recommended for reading, on the essence of this "vast transformation." "The major universities were enlisted in national defense . . . as never before . . . `the government contract became a new type of federalism.'" He is illuminating on what we should call the *statification* of the university in the Cold War. "Currently, federal support has become a major factor in the total performance of many universities . . ." There has been "a hundredfold increase in twenty years" in higher education's revenue from government; and the two-thirds of this sum devoted to research projects in or affiliated to universities went to "relatively few" universities, accounting for 75 per cent of all university expenditures on research and 15 per cent of total university budgets.

These are stupendous figures, truly. This is what we get; what do we give away for it? Kerr draws the consequences which, remember, we must all accept as inevitable:

> The federal agencies will exercise increasingly specific controls and the universities dependent on this new standard of living will accept these controls. The universities themselves will have to exercise more stringent controls by centralizing authority, particularly

> through the audit process. In a few situations, self restraint has not been enough restraint; as one result, greater external restraint will be imposed in most situations.

THE LADY FROM KENT

Writing these lines took moral courage, for, as is obvious, this is precisely the charge which the Goldwaterites have thrown at federal money in education, against the indignant denial of the liberals. Kerr is saying that it is true and must be accepted, because, he says, the nation and the universities are "stronger" as a result. It is at this point that, to the distinguished audience listening to these lectures at Harvard, he made the following cogent point about the consequences of taking certain kinds of money, in the form of a limerick:

There was a young lady from Kent
Who said that she knew what it meant
When men took her to dine,
Gave her cocktails and wine;
She knew what it meant—but she went.

And he follows with this comment: "I am not so sure that the universities and their presidents always knew what it meant: but one thing is certain—they went."

Now in turn I am not sure whether I can plainly state, in a booklet intended as reading for the whole family, just what Kerr seems to be calling his fellow presidents; but at least one thing is clear. In all this Kerr himself is *not* striking the pose of the innocent maiden who is in danger of being bowled over by a fast line and losing Virtue unawares.

In fact, we had better drop this Kerr line of metaphor altogether, because the image which he does try to project is a different one. It is that of the tough-minded bureaucrat.

Please do not think this term is a cussword or a brickbat; you will be selling Kerr short. He likes it.

CAPTAIN BUREAUCRAT

Discussing the role of the university president today, as distinct from the old days of the campus autocrat, he writes:

> Instead of the not always so agreeable autocracy, there is now the usually benevolent bureaucracy, as in so much of the rest of the world. Instead of the Captain of Erudition or even David Riesman's "staff sergeant," there is the Captain of the Bureaucracy who is sometimes a galley slave on his own ship ...

And he is gratified that the "multiversity" has emerged from the phase of "intuitive imbalance" into that of "bureaucratic balance." Mainly he is intent on emphasizing that the Coming Men in the new university-factory are *not* the scholars (either humanist or scientist), *not* the teachers, *not* the faculty, but that its "practitioners" are "chiefly the administrators, who now number many of the faculty among them, and the leadership groups in society at large."

Administrators—and "leadership groups in society at large": it may be somewhat clearer now what Kerr means by "merging" the university with "society," i.e. with what part of "society." The multiversity, writes Kerr, is no longer to be thought of as an "organism," as Flexner did:

> It is more a mechanism—a series of processes producing a series of results—a mechanism held together by administrative rules and powered by money.

Now another difference between an organism and a mechanism is that a mechanism is always controlled by a superior power outside. This points up the inaccuracy of Kerr's constant use of the term "merger": a mechanism does not "merge" with its controller. The kind of "merger" that Ken is celebrating is the "merger" of a horse and rider.

### CHIP OR CHOP?

He quotes Nevins: the main strain for the growing multiversity is "not in finding the teachers, but expert administrators," and he propounds the theorem that the multiversity president is now "mostly a mediator." This brings us to Kerr's vision of himself, not as an individual but as the Multiversity President; and it is a poignant one. Especially if we read it right after the events of the Battle of Berkeley of October 1-2, 1964:

The mediator, whether in government or industry or labor relations or domestic quarrels, is always subject to some abuse. He wins few clear-cut victories; he must aim more at avoiding the worst than seizing the best. He must find satisfaction in being *equally* distasteful to each of his constituencies .. .

And so should the student constituency be harsh on him if it finds him distasteful in chopping a piece here and there off student rights? After all, they must think of how distasteful he is to some of the Regents who believe it is the will of inexorable History that all dissenters be thrown in the clink immediately; they must think of the abuse he invites when he explains (in effect) : *No, we can't do it that way; we have to be liberal*—and proceeds to chip (not chop) off a liberal piece. Isn't it realistic to understand that the difference between the "liberal" bureaucrat and the reactionary is the difference between Chip or Chop?

### THE CONTRADICTION

Does this make him seem two-faced? Kerr goes one better:

> It is sometimes said that the American multiversity president is a two-faced character. This is not so. . . . He is a many-faced character, in the sense that he must face in many directions at once while contriving to turn his back on no important group.

It will be readily agreed that this is a good trick if you can do it. It might even seem to explain the tricky course of the Berkeley campus administration in the days preceding the October 1 explosion, when it appeared to be adopting a different line every twenty-four hours to explain why student political activity had to be restricted. The deceptively easy conclusion is to equate Kerr's aspiration toward manyfacedness with what old-fashioned people called simple hypocrisy. But this is misleading because it finds the locus of the trouble in Kerr, and this is not the point.

The locus is elsewhere. It is in a contradiction which Kerr refuses to face in his writings and perhaps in his head.

We have pointed out that there seemed to be a wide gap between Kerr's published theory about the "merger" of the university and "society," and his moves toward restricting student involvement in political and social action off campus. On the one hand he tells us we must accept the integration of the university with the state and industry in this Cold War (in fact, with what has been called the Military-Industrial Complex) and must erase the boundary lines; on the other hand, he tries to muzzle and rein student activity on campus which tends to step beyond the boundary line—which, as his administration puts it, "mounts" political and social action off campus—while at the same time other "constituencies" in the university community are lauded for doing just that.

## ANOTHER FACTORY

This contradiction is not due to muddleheadedness. Behind it is a clear consistency, which appears as soon as we make explicit the assumption which permeates Kerr's book.

This is: The use of the university, or the role of the multiversity, is to have a relationship to the present power structure, in this businessman's society of ours, which is similar to that of any other industrial enterprise. There are railroads and steel mills and supermarkets and sausage factories—and there are also the Knowledge Factories, whose function is to service all the others and the State.

We are here to serve the Powers that rule society: this is the meaning of Kerr's reiterations that the university is merging with society. But now, suppose you have "nonconformists" and "extremists" who *also* want to move outside the obsolete boundary line, *but as dissident or radical critics and adversaries, not as intellectual flunkies?*

Obviously, this is not the same thing. The contradiction disappears. It is not "society" that the multiversity must merge with: it is the *"leadership groups in society,"* which, to the mind of the Captain of the Bureaucracy, are identical with "society." Kerr virtually says as much, in a revealing sneer at "nonconformists":

> A few of the "nonconformists" have another kind of revolt [than one against the faculty] in mind. They seek, instead, to turn the university, on the Latin American or Japanese models, into a fortress from which they can sally forth with impunity to make their attacks on society.

SOME SALLIES

A whole thesis on the Bureaucratic Mind could be derived from a dissection of this last sentence alone, but here we are interested only in one facet of the gem. As we know, it is honorific for the good professors of the University of California's Giannini Foundation and the Division of Agricultural Sciences to sally forth with their apologias for the growers' bracero program. And similar respectable activities are "mounted" not only with impunity but even with appropriate raises in salary and perquisites. But when CORE students sally forth to picket the Bank of America or, perhaps worse, Knowland's Oakland *Tribune,* this is an attack on

The Giannini financial empire of the Bank of America? Or Knowland? No: they are "attacks on *society.*"

This gives "society" a local habitation and a name. Now non-Latin-Americans and non-Japanese can understand how reprehensible are the students who wish to attack *society!* We can also understand the worth of Kerr's claim, in his foreword, that he is not "defending" any view but merely handing down the Rules of History.

There is more to Kerr's theory of "society." It is given in a passage in which he deprecates the "guild view" of the university which is held by some faculty members, because it "stands for self-determination and for resistance against the administration and the trustees." In opposition to this deplorable Resistance view, he advances *(fasten your seat belts)* nothing less than

> . the socialist view, for service to society which the administration and the trustees represent.

"We are all socialists now," said a Tory long ago. "We are socialists," say the Russian despots now, the Nasser bureaucrats, the Indian nationalists, and some other demagogues. It is interesting to see these varied characters reach for the word "socialist" when they need a good-looking label for their wares. But don't buy it. What Kerr is selling under the label is the old mildewed article: that "society" is represented by the capitalist Establishment, its bureaucrats, agents and brain trusters.

### OCCUPATIONAL HAZARD

It is true we have been told that the multiversity president I must be many-faced, but at this point we must ask whether there isn't a limit. A man who conscientiously tries to face in *this* "many directions at once" faces an occupational hazard: the risk of eventually forgetting where the boundary line is between a soft-soaping mediator and an academic confidence man. It is only a risk, to be sure, like silicosis for coalminers, but it is well to be forewarned.

*The Independent Socialist view is that students must not accept Kerr's vision of the university-factory, run by a Captain of the Bureaucracy as a parts-supply shop to the profit system and the Cold War complex. We do not think they will.*

### KERR'S *1984*

Behind Kerr's vision of the university-factory is a broadgauged world view, a view of a Brave New World (his term) or Orwellian *1984* toward which all this is headed. What we have discussed so far is, according to him, only the "managerial revolution" of society at large as applied to the campus world. There is a larger picture, of which we have examined only one corner.

Kerr described the coming New Order in 1960 in *Industrialism and Industrial Man.**

It is a remarkable work, which failed to get the attention it deserves.

The methodology we have already seen: Kerr is presenting the Wave of the Future, which must be accepted as the imperative of history. It is roughly a variant of Burnhamism, with "bureaucrats" and "managers" interchangeable. We have space here for only a summary of its leading ideas. While no element is new, the whole is presented with a frankness unusual nowadays:

(1) The New Order will result (is resulting) from the presently ongoing *convergence* of the two dominant systems: a capitalism which is becoming more and more authoritarian and bureaucratic, along the road *toward* Russian totalitarianism; and a Russian Communist system which has softened up and become somewhat milder; the two merging somewhere in between into an undifferentiated "Industrialism." The imperative is the force of industrialization; it is the road of progress.

(2) It is refreshing to note that Kerr wastes no space on ritualistic obeisances to democracy. There is no pretense, no lip-service. It simply is not in the picture. The reader must remember that this does not mean Kerr dislikes democracy, any more than Anne Lindbergh approved of

* Kerr is the chief author of this work, listed first, with joint authors J. T. Dunlop, Frederick Harbison and C. A. Myers (Harvard University Press). An Oxford paperback edition has appeared this year, with some parts shortened or condensed; a cursory examination indicates that some of the frank passages, but not all, have been left out. This discussion is based on the original work.

fascism, or Von Papen of Hitler. In the shadow of the New Order, you do not approve, you merely have to *accept.*

STATISM

(3) Statism: the leviathan State has taken over; it has expanded everywhere. It is "omnipresent." (There is no mention of TV eyes in the glades, but "Big Brother" is in the book.) The State will never "wither away" as Marx utopianly predicted, Kerr assures us.'

(4) Full-blown bureaucratic (or managerial) elitism: The progressive and socially decisive elements are only "the managers, private and public," with their technicians and professionals. "Turning Marx on his head, they are the `vanguard' of the future." Kerr bluntly defines the elements he is addressing: "In particular, we hope to speak to the intellectuals, the managers, the government officials and labor leaders [another species of bureaucrats, to Kerr] who today and tomorrow will run their countries . . ." There is no pretense of a role for "the people" other than as the working cattle who are to be herded by the manager-bureaucrats.

ROAD AHEAD

With this theoretical equipment, Kerr comes to the last chapter, "The Road Ahead," in which his perspective of "a new slavery" is sketched: Here is a quick run-down:

There is a convergence toward one-partyism in form or fact. "The age of ideology fades." "Industrial society must be administered; . . . The benevolent political bureaucracy and the benevolent economic oligarchy are matched with the tolerant mass." "Parliamentary life may appear increasingly decadent and political parties merely additional bureaucracies . . . Not only all dictatorships but also all democracies are `guided' [a term for authoritarian]." "The elites become less differentiated . . . all wear grey flannel suits." Professional managers run the economy: "Economic enterprise is always basically authoritarian under the necessity of getting things done . . . Authority must be concentrated . . ." The managers "will be bureaucratic managers, if private, and managerial bureaucrats, if public." "Class warfare will be forgotten and in its place will be the bureaucratic contest . . . memos will flow instead of blood." An individual will identify as "the member of a guild," not of a class or plant community. The individual will be neither an independent man nor a human ant, but something between. As a worker, "he will be subjected to great conformity," regimented by the productive process, and will accept this "as an immutable fact. The state, the manager, the occupational association are all disciplinary agents."

There will be a certain "freedom" in a certain sense (if not democracy). "Politically he can be given some influence. Society has achieved consensus and it is perhaps less necessary for Big Brother to exercise political control. Nor in this Brave New World need genetic and chemical means be employed to avoid revolt. There will not be any revolt, anyway, except little bureaucratic revolts than can be handled piecemeal." (Has anyone before actually written down such an orgiastic dream of the Bureaucrat's Paradise?)

## SCHIZOID SOCIETY

Where will the freedom lie? Maybe, muses Kerr, "in the leisure of individuals." "Along with the bureaucratic conservatism of economic and political life may well go a New Bohemianism in the other aspects of life and partly as a reaction to the confining nature of the productive side of society .. . The economic system may be highly ordered and the political system barren ideologically; but the social and recreational and cultural aspects of life diverse and changing . . . The new slavery to technology may bring a new dedication to diversity and individuality."

Hence his comforting conclusion, offering a glimmer of cheer: "The new slavery and the new freedom go hand in hand."

In this Kerrian picture, the alienation of man is raised to clinical heights: if this society "can be said to have a split personality, then the individual in this society will lead a split life too . . ." (Since ideology has faded, the only "ism" will be schizoidism.)

NO PROTEST?

There is a good deal more, but this sample will have to do. Now a natural question arises: Won't people fight *against* the coming of this monster-bureaucratic state, no matter how cogently it is alleged to be inevitable? Won't there be protest, opposition, struggle—from people who take seriously exhortations to stand up for democracy, given (say) at commencement exercises? What about all the people who are now supposed to be eager to defend the American Way of Life by sternly sacrificing to pay for H-bombs, Polaris missiles, and Livermore research programs?

Will there not be troublemakers who will say: *"Is it for this that we have to sacrifice? Is this why we have to fortify even the moon? Is this why we have to spend more for an Atlas missile than for all cancer research? Is it the right to this future that we are asked to defend by our statesmen, pundits, editors, and (on most occasions) even university presidents?"*

Nonsense, says Kerr. There will be no protest. That's *out.* (Can you now understand the *full* depths of the "disappointment" which he publicly professed to feel on October 2, after so many students ignored this rule of the Administrator of History?)

There will be no protest, Kerr wrote. From whom could it come? The intellectuals? Here is how he deals with them:

> The intellectuals (including the university students) are a particularly volatile element ... capable of extreme reactions to objective situations—more extreme than any group in society. They are by nature irresponsible, in the sense that they have no continuing commitment to any single institution or philosophical outlook and they are not fully answerable for consequences. They are, as a result, never fully trusted by anybody, including themselves.

In all likelihood, dear reader, you did not read this carefully enough. Did you notice that the entire tradition of humanistic and democratic educational philosophy has been contemptuously tossed into the famous garbage can of history? It teaches "irresponsibility"; you cannot trust people brought up that way...

TOOL OR DANGER

How does the Bureaucratic Manager or the Managerial Bureaucrat deal with these untrustworthy irresponsibles? Kerr is concerned about this problem because today we have a war of ideas, and ideas are spun by intellectuals:

> Consequently, it is important who best attracts or captures the intellectuals and who uses [sic] them most effectively, for they may be a tool as well as a source of danger.

There are the alternative roles of the intellectual in the Kerrian world: *tool* or *danger*. It is a notorious dichotomy, celebrated in the literature of totalitarianism. But we need not go abroad to translate it. If we apply the Kerr method of extrapolation, we get this: Everybody must be either on the FBI informer rolls or on the Subversive List. . . . Remember that you do not have to approve this; you are expected only to accept it.

Will there be protest from the ranks of the workers' movements? No, says Kerr: *vieux jeu.* In the New Order, labor is controlled in institutions hierarchically set up. "One of the central traits is the inevitable and eternal separation of industrial men into managers and the managed." Not only inevitable: *eternal!* There are few men since St. Peter who have thrust their Vision so far. . . .

But Kerr's confidence in his no-protest prediction derives from undeniable models:

> Today men know more about how to control protest, as well as how to suppress it in its more organized forms—the Soviet Union has industrialized and China is

> industrializing without organized strikes. A controlled labor movement has become more common.

It is no part of our present task to pause on the scandalous puerility of this view of the history of protest in Russia and China, where literal millions of human beings had to be destroyed in the process of "controlling protest." We wish only to remind that on October 2, 1964, there was an army of almost one thousand police called onto campus—to "control protest" by students—by the man who wrote these lines in cold blood.

### DETACHED?

Obviously we are, in these few pages, able only to exhibit Kerr's views, not refute them; we do not pretend otherwise. Many of the elements therein are rife in academic elitist circles in more or less attenuated form, more or less "underground," or else formulated in "minced" and allusive terms, instead of with Kerr's candor, which is the main contribution of his work.

But Kerr's candor is partly due to the device which we have already mentioned several times, and to which we must now return in a different way. This is his posture as the detached, uninvolved historian of the future, registering his vision of Eternity, and as far above approval-or-disapproval as the Recording Angel.

This posture is an intellectual imposture.

There is an extraordinarily serious question here of intellectual responsibility. *By adding a single sentence, Kerr's book would become the work of a proto-fascist ideologue.* But, of course, this he is not; he is a sort of liberal; he really does *not* approve, and so the single sentence is not there.

Yet he is not detached and uninvolved. There is another basis for judgment than approval-or-disapproval.

### POLITICAL ACT

By 1932 the pressure of (what we now know to be) the impending assumption of power by Hitler in Germany was enormous. The Nazis and their conscious tools were, as is well known, yelling at full cry that their victory was in the cards, that heads would roll, and that all realistic people must jump on their bandwagon. What now should we think of a professor, *not* a Nazi tool, who at this juncture announced that, in his utterly scientific opinion, the triumph of the Nazis was indeed written in the scrolls of history and must be accepted (not approved)?

This is itself a political act. It is also, of course, a selffulfilling prophecy. It is a blow struck to bring the event predicted. But is it not also a scientific opinion? No, it is not, because there is no historical "science" so reliable as to make an opinion on this subject more than an estimate of probability and tendency. We have a right to make a value judgment on political acts, even when they result from self-delusion (like most evil political acts, including those of the Nazis). There is no academic right to grease the road to fascism in the name of "scientific" detachment.

### THE JUGGERNAUT

Whenever the Juggernaut of Power starts rolling, there 'always are, and always will be, the servitors and retainers who will run before, crying: *It cometh! Bow down, bow down, before the God!* The men who perform this function have done more than made a choice of what to believe; they also have made a choice on how to act. We have the right to make a moral, as well as a social, judgment of the *act,* even apart from the accuracy of the announcement.

But there is a bit more involved in Kerr's book.

We present our views,. says the introduction, to aid understanding of this moment in history

> ... and possibly, as an assistance to some of those who would guide this moment to its next stage ...

With this statement the author strikes a different note. It is not detached and uninvolved; he is seeking to *assist* the transformation toward the New Slavery. Is it because he really does approve after all? No. Is it because he is simply in the intellectual habit of servicing whatever is in the works anyway, because he has no other mode of being than that of the bureaucratic assistant of whatever Power is rolling? It may be 3 slip, but only in the sense that underneath the cap and gown peers out the retainer's livery.

There is another passage that gives pause. It is not merely `he repeated statements, in the introduction, that he has :hanged his former views: "We unlearned many things . . ." `We changed our program . . . ' "Many of our original convictions turned into nothing but once-held prejudices." The last remark is followed by this meditation on the critical question of state control of labor:

> "Free trade unions" under some conditions become no more than Communist unions sabotaging efforts at economic development. Should they be that free? Completely free trade unions are sometimes not possible or desirable at I certain stages in the industrialization drive. . . . The "free worker," in our sense, cannot exist in some social systems; in others he might exist, but to his detriment. . . . The "heavy hand of the state" over trade unions and enterprises may be the only substitute, at times, for the "invisible hand" of market competition which we have so long preferred. And some generals, in some situations, may be by far the best leaders of an industrializing nation, all doctrine of civilian control of the military to the contrary.

## A MATTER OF INDIGNATION

Kerr is speaking here of changed views, not new cables from the Future on recent changes in the nature of Eternity. His changed views concern, in a word, *democracy*. He continues

> Thus we came to be much more conscious of the significance of time and place in the evaluation of some judgments, and of all slogans. [Slogans like democracy?] The whole world cannot be like the United States or the Soviet Union, or India, and one should not be morally indignant about it.

But may one be politically indignant about despotism at any time and place? or just indignant? Is this advice offered only to well-fed political scientists, or is it also relevant to the human beings who are starving and suffering under the despotisms which are declared inevitable? Or let us try this one on the platitude-machine: Since not everybody can be like Clark Kerr, why should Clark Kerr get morally indignant at the rebellious students who did not behave according to his lights?

## THE MORAL CHOICE

Now, perhaps this injunction against moral (or other) indignation at despotism and authoritarianism is also to be' regarded as a detached and uninvolved report on eternal verities. We do not think so. The issuance of this injunction, against moral indignation is itself a moral choice on Kerr's part. The Compleat Bureaucrat does not approve of moral indignation or of political protest and struggle, not because he is cruel and unfeeling, but simply because these phenomena do not file neatly; they cannot be efficiently punched onto IBM cards; they upset routine; they raise non-regulation questions; they cannot be budgeted for in advance; they are refractory to manipulation.

The Compleat Bureaucrat does not believe that protest and struggle really exist even when they explode under his nose: since all this has been ruled out by the historical imperative, he ascribes it to a "Maoist-Castroite" plot. He tries to meet it first by facing in many directions at once, and then, when this gyration naturally lands him on his face, by blowing the whistle for the cops.

Clark Kerr believes that the student's relationship to the Administration bureaucracy can be only that of a tool or a danger. This is also a self-fulfilling prophecy. A university president's very belief of this sort tends to *force* students into one or the other camp.

It is easy enough to become a tool. There are all kinds of tools, and they can come without head, teeth, or point. On the other hand, there is danger in becoming a danger. Which will it be?

Everyone must choose, and it is a matter of life or death: life as an independent human being, or death as a man.

## • *The Regents by Marvin Garson*

*This twenty-four-page annotated pamphlet was published by the FSM in January, 1965, as a preliminary research report on a continuing study of the nature and role of the Board of Regents, established by the state constitution to control the University of California. We give here two excerpts, from the beginning and end of the pamphlet.*

Edward Carter, Chairman of the Board of Regents, is president of Broadway-Hale Stores, the largest department store in the West. He is a director of Emporium Capwell, a Northern California chain controlled by Broadway-Hale.

Carter is a director of the Northrop Corporation, which produces military aircraft; Pacific Mutual Life Insurance Company, with assets of $692 million; Western Bancorporation, a bank holding company that owns majority interest in twenty-three full service commercial banks and has assets of $6.2 billion; the United California Bank (owned by Western Bancorporation), the fifth largest bank in California; Pacific Telephone and Telegraph; and the Southern California Edison Company. He is a trustee of the Irvine Foundation, which owns 51 per cent of the Irvine Ranch, which owns 20 per cent of Orange County (93,000 acres).

Jesse Tapp is Chairman of the Bank of America, the biggest bank in the United States.

Theodore Meyer is a member of Brobeck, Phleger and Harrison, one of California's top two law firms. He is also a director of Broadway-Hale Stores, along with Carter; and of the Newhall Land and Farming Company.

W. Thomas Davis is President of Blue Goose Growers and of its parent company, Western Fruit Growers Sales Corporation.

Dorothy Chandler is Vice-President and Director of the Times-Mirror Company. The company not only publishes the Los Angeles *Times,* but manages extensive real estate holdings in Los Angeles and owns majority or complete interest in the following companies: gist omitted here] ...

Donald McLaughlin is Chairman of the Homestake Mining Company, the nation's largest gold producer. Homestake mines other metals all over the West. Together with United Nuclear Corporation, (of which McLaughlin is a director) it has a contract with the Atomic Energy Commission to supply $135 million worth of uranium oxide.

McLaughlin is a director of the International Nickel Company of Canada, one of the most important mining companies in the world, with annual sales of $500 million. He is also a director of the Bunker Hill Company, an important lead and zinc producer; the Cerro Corporation and the San Luis Mining Company, which operate South American copper mines; Western Airlines; and the Wells Fargo Bank.

John Canaday is a Vice-President of Lockheed Aircraft.

He is also Vice-President of the California Manufacturing Association.

Catherine Hearst is the wife of Randolph A. Hearst, President of Hearst Publications and the Hearst Publishing Company.

Samuel Mosher is Chairman of the Signal Oil and Gas Company and owns 53 per cent of its voting stock. Signal is a major California producer. In addition it owns 33 per cent of the American Independent Oil Company (of which Mosher is Vice-President) which holds a 50 per cent interest in a 2600 square mile concession in the neutral zone between Kuwait and Saudi Arabia. Signal Oil and Gas of Venezuela owns 50 per cent of a 28,000 acre concession in Lake Maracaibo.

Signal also owns 48 per cent of American President Lines, and the entire stock of the Garrett Corporation,. an aerospace manufacturer with annual sales of $225 million.

Mosher is also Chairman of Flying Tiger Lines, a cargo operator.

Philip Boyd is a director of the Security First National Bank, along with Norman Chandler. He is also a director of the Citizen's National Trust and Savings Bank (Riverside) and is President of Deep Canyon Properties, a real estate concern.

Norton Simon is President of Hunt Foods and Industries, one of the two giant companies that dominate the California food processing industry. Simon is also a director of the McCall Corporation (publishing) ; the Northern Pacific Railway; and Wheeling Steel.

Edwin Pauley is Chairman of the Pauley Petroleum Company. The company holds a minor interest in the American Independent Oil Company (see Mosher), and has extensive operations in Mexico and the western United States. In addition, Pauley is a director of Western Airlines and of the First Western Bank and Trust Company (Los Angeles), which has assets of $680 million.

William Roth is a director of the following corporations: Matson Navigation, which operates Matson Lines; Crown Zellerbach, the largest paper producer in the United States; Pacific Intermountain Express, a trucking line; and United States Leasing Corporation, a financing company.

These thirteen "business regents," taken together, represent a big hunk of the California economy. We have here the Bank of America, three other big banks and a few smaller ones; two oil companies; three aircraft manufacturers; two shipping lines, two airlines, a trucking line and two railways; two giant utilities; several chain stores; two publishing empires; half of the food packing industry; and hundreds of thousands of acres of irrigated farmland.

There may be quite a bit more. The number of shares owned by individuals or family trusts is usually not a matter of public record. It is entirely possible that some of these Regents have share interests much more significant than the corporate positions we have listed. Limiting ourselves to the public record, we notice that many of their corporate positions serve to plug various Regents into a high-powered network of interlocking directorates stretching across California and much of the nation. Here are some examples:

Prentis C. Hale is Chairman of Broadway-Hale Stores, Regent Carter's major interest. Hale is at the same time a director of the Bank of America, Union Oil, Pacific Vegetable Oil, and the Di Giorgio Fruit Corporation. The bond between Broadway-Hale and the Di Giorgio interests is strengthened by the presence of Robert Di Giorgio on the board of Broadway Hale. Di Giorgio is, like Hale, also a director of Bank of America and of Union Oil; and like Carter, of Pacific Telephone and Telegraph.

Charles S. Hobbs, a vice-president and director of Broadway-Hale is also on the board of the United California Bank (along with Carter) and of Trans-World Airlines. Another Broadway-Hale director, Roy Shurtleff, is a director of Del Monte Properties.

The board meetings of Pacific Mutual Life which Carter attends are chaired by Asa V. Call, who is also on the board of Southern California Edison and Western Bancorporation (where he meets Carter again); and of North American Aviation and Standard Oil of California.

The board meetings of United California Bank and Western Bancorporation are chaired by Frank L. King, who is also a director of Pacific-Mutual Life and of the Times-Mirror Company (see Chandler).

The Chairman of Southern California Edison is W. C. Mullendore, who is also a director of North American Aviation. On the board of trustees of the Irvine Foundation, Carter serves along with Robert Gerdes, Executive Vice-president of Pacific Gas and Electricity.

This is just a sample. To trace all the threads would require more pages than there are in this pamphlet and more computer time than we can pay for. If we should take each corporation of which a Regent is a director and trace the connections of every other director, the threads would extend and double back, getting denser and denser until they formed a solid fabric which might well assume the shape of the state of California. When we deal with these thirteen Regents, then, we are dealing not with mere businessmen but with Business.

The other eleven people on the Board of Regents by no means represent a unified force capable of counterbalancing business domination. They are a mixed bag of lawyers, politicians, educational administrators, a labor leader. (None of them is an independent scholar or a working teacher, needless to say).

[Here follows a rundown of this latter group, consisting of: Governor Brown and Lieutenant-Governor Glenn .Anderson; Assembly Speaker Jesse Unruh; State Superintendent of Education Max Rafferty, an ultra-rightist; labor leader Cornelius Haggerty; William Forbes, an advertising executive; Frederick Dutton, a corporation lawyer and government official; Lawrence Kennedy, a corporation lawyer; William Coblentz, a lawyer; and Elinor Heller, Democratic Party career woman and widow of Edward Heller, director of Wells Fargo Bank and other big companies.]

## THE UNIVERSITY

The Regents maintain on principle that they are absolutely independent of the students and faculty. They claim full power to override the decisions of student or faculty governments, and even to establish and dissolve such governments at their discretion. . . .

The Regents also claim independence from the State and from political parties (although several Regents are political appointees, as we have seen). To whom then are they responsible? . . .

In fact, the Regents cannot help feeling responsible to the huge private corporations that dominate-indeed, constitute -the economy of the state of California. In their minds, this is not corruption or prostitution; they cannot see that things could or should be any other way. Big business they call "industry," and "industry" is society. Shouldn't the Board of Regents and their University be at the service of society?

The corporations do not merely buy the University's products and hire its graduates; they reproduce in the heart of the University itself their own bureaucratic power system, their own goals and values. (The idea is not original with us, for President Kerr has expounded it at great length.)

The University's power structure is explicitly modeled after that of the corporation. We have a Board with final and total authority; a President and Chancellors responsible only to it; and a mass of students and faculty with no rights except those they can extort by the threat of direct action.

It is not so obvious, however, that the corporations' goals and values also prevail within the University. Corporations are supposed to make money, while Universities are supposed to discover and disseminate truth. It is seldom that the two come into conflict so directly as in the censoring of the Berkeley report on agricultural labor. In day to day practice, money does not confront truth; it infiltrates, corrupts and subverts. "Let truth but take the field . . ."; but truth is often so discouraged that it does not even bother to take the field.

There are people in this University who want to use their skills and knowledge to benefit their society. There are people in city planning and architecture who want to preserve and develop real neighborhoods instead of designing empty and impressive civic centers; people in agriculture who worry about the lot of the laborers or the overuse of pesticides; people in the natural sciences who care about the uses of the discoveries they make; people in the humanities who think culture should be more widespread. Such people accept the prospect of a tough fight in the community outside; what demoralizes them so completely is the knowledge that they face an uphill battle within the University itself.

Even within an institution that is supposed to be passionately dedicated to truth, such people are considered renegades or eccentrics. The sympathetic say: "They'll learn"; and the unsympathetic say: "They'd better learn."

They know from the beginning that it would be ridiculous to expect help from the Administration and the Regents in a fight against money. What they have to learn is that even their colleagues will not back them up. More often than not, they learn to measure men by the length of their bibliographies or the amount of research money that goes through their hands.

Their own community becomes an unconscious parody of private industry.

If it were not so, the University would be a constant threat to the world from which the Regents come. That is why the Regents insist so strongly that it is *their* University.

## • *On Mounting Political Action by James Petras*

*James Petras, a graduate student in political science, teaching assistant and research fellow, was a member of the Emergency Steering Committee of the FSM during the strike. In this talk, given at the Conference on the Student Revolt held by the Independent Socialist Club on January 9, 1965, many notes are struck which were common in FSM discussions but rarely showed up in the published accounts. Following are excerpts taken from the tape as recorded by KPFA.*

The fact that we had to have an independent organization, the fact that we had to mobilize large numbers of students, the fact that this had to be independent of the two parties should give us something to think about, especially in the light of the success that we have had up to now. And I'd like to mention parenthetically the fact that the civil rights movement, which for the first time curtailed its demonstrations in many areas because of the last election, is now in disarray; that many of their projects are faltering; that they haven't initiated any large-scale projects precisely because for the first time they did subordinate themselves to the Democratic Party. Now you can read *The liberal democrat,* the liberal journal on the West Coast here, and find some second thoughts about the future of liberalism in the Democratic Party. You can draw a parallel: FSM, which refused to buckle before pressure from the liberal Democrats in the Democratic Party and carried out its struggle in terms of the goals it was committed to, and not *in* terms of the maneuverings of these people behind the scenes—the FSM has had a considerable measure of success.

Another important point about the impact of the Free Speech Movement: the state college teachers issued a declaration yesterday calling for slowdowns on campuses. You see, we've legitimized a whole series of actions that professors and other people never thought of doing before. Slowdowns in the classrooms! by god, that's almost as bad as what those greasy workers do in the factory! I think we've also stirred up some people on Eastern campuses.

I think this is really the long-range good that will come out of this movement, the extent to which it serves as a catalyst. A lot of people have said that a lot of things are wrong. It's a question of people getting into motion and acting and breaking rules, and standing up to authority and saying, "Look, we have a grievance; we want you to sit down and talk to us; don't just give us a lecture." The outstanding characteristic of the people I've worked with in the FSM leadership is that they don't have this awe and reverence of bureaucrats, full professors, professors emeritus, and what-have-you. I think this psychological change is part of the change that's going on in political and economic action. It is very important, because it sets a new tone and style for the politics we're engaged in.

Another factor: democratic politics used to mean involving large numbers of people; that is, if democracy means government by the people, for the people, and of the people, the *people* somehow are supposed to be involved. But it's become fashionable of late to talk about democratic politics in terms of elites, bargaining with each other, discussing with each other; and the masses are some sort of Id-out there-dangerous. "Don't let the masses get involved; they'll shake things up; they won't allow reasonable people to deal with the issues." This kind of authoritarianism, this elitism, has permeated not only the university, but also the minds of some liberals. It's precisely because the students were the real democrats and discussed the issues publicly with large numbers of people, that they were accused of "haranguing." You see, when you talk to a lot of people openly and tell them what the issues are, who their friends are and who their enemies, and you have a dialogue and criticism, that's *haranguing;* but when you sit down a few leaders behind closed doors, and take up the issues that *you* think the people should be interested in and you decide for them, that's called "responsible statesmanship."

It is true that Governor Brown sent the police into Sproul Hall as a result of pressure politics, but the fact of the matter is that Brown *himself* only represents one person in a political party. The Democratic Party is not just a free-floating organization; it has its own history, its ideology, and its process of socializing politicians; there are the goals it sets for its members, the kind of identity it creates for its leaders. Brown the governor was only acting out the whole experience of the Democratic Party which has been under the influence of agribusiness for a long time. And the fact that he hasn't responded this time to political pressures from our side—and there's been lots of pressures put on him, by massive student demonstrations, by lots of professors and other liberals, CDC people, labor—the fact that he doesn't respond to these people should lead us to question whether Brown is an independent agent or subject to pressures, and what pressure groups he listens to. I would say this: Brown is less responsible than the party which he is part of and leads. And if you're really looking for villains, if you're looking to place political responsibility and I think one of the good things about the FSM is that it has not been afraid to point the finger—then one must point to the Democratic Party. (And I'm not talking about Burton and Willy Brown, who, after everything is said and done, really don't represent much in the Democratic Party; it's good to have them on our side, except I wish they'd criticize Brown openly.)

I think the important thing is that the political parties in this state and country have really cut us off from the kind of political leadership which is necessary to carry this issue to the public. Someone like Brown who can sell his case to the working people, who don't know what the issues are—they're concerned about bread and butter issues—comes on and cries "Anarchy!" and that's the image people get from him and the press. If we had a labor movement or party which could articulate demands related to the working class and tie them with a defense of civil liberties, then I think we would have some power in the community. But Brown ties up his *anti*democratic stand, his use of police violence against students, with lib-lab demagogy.

There are two styles of politics we have seen in the course of this fight—two styles which clearly show the difference, not in generations (as some people have it) but in the whole view of what democratic politics is all about. One is *elite politics,* by people who function as follows: They consider themselves liberals and are for good things', but they believe in working by maneuvering behind the scenes; they think in terms of influencing the top people through personal channels, button holing the right people, etc. Their whole approach is: get next to the Important People. Therefore they are also always reluctant to criticize, since "we have to be united" even with people who are really opposing us. *They* want to negotiate ad infinitum, without involving people—because, of course, large numbers of people, once involved, may interfere with behind-the-scenes negotiations, may raise all kinds of sticky issues.

The FSM students have functioned in a totally different way. They have insisted on clarity in all issues, on honest presentation of the situation even when things haven't looked very good, on spelling out the meaning of the results whatever they may be, on telling us who are our friends and who our enemies, at least in their honest opinion; on trying to be responsible to constituents, even under very difficult circumstances; on facing criticism. I recall that at one point during the strike, seven different involved groups were drawing up a leaflet for the same action. Maybe that wasn't the efficient way to do it, but it indicates the popular nature of the participation in the strike

## • *From the "FSM Newsletter"*

*The following four items are taken from the five issues of the* FSM Newsletter *published during the fall semester. The first was published unsigned in No. 5, December 10. "Catch801" was written by Marvin Garson, a Cal alumnus '63; "Freedom Is a Big Deal" by Barbara Garson, an editor of the* Newsletter *and a graduate student in sociology; they appeared in No. 5 and No. 4 respectively. "How to Observe Law and Order" by Hal Draper was published in No. 2, October 20, under the title "UC's Real Politics."*

### DO NOT FOLD, BEND, MUTILATE OR SPINDLE

At the beginning, we did not realize the strength of the forces we were up against. We have learned that we must fight not only Dean Towle, Chancellor Strong, and President Kerr, but also the Board of Regents with their billions of dollars and Governor Brown with his army of cops.

But neither did they realize the forces they were up against. At the beginning, they thought they had only to fight a hundred or so "beatniks," "Maoists," and "Fidelistas." But they put eight hundred of the "hard core" in jail and found they still had to face thousands of other students and faculty members.

The source of their power is clear enough: the guns and the clubs of the Highway Patrol, the banks and corporations of the Regents. But what is the source of our power?

It is something we see everywhere on campus but find hard to define. Perhaps it was best expressed by the sign one boy pinned to his chest: "I am a UC student. Please don't bend, fold, spindle or mutilate me." The source of our strength is, very simply, the fact that we are human beings and so cannot forever be treated as raw materials—to be processed. Clark Kerr has declared, in his writings and by his conduct, that a university must be like any other factory—a place where workers who handle raw material are themselves handled like raw material by the administrators above them. Kerr is confident that in his utopia "there will not be any revolt, anyway, except little bureaucratic revolts that can be handled piecemeal."

As President of one of the greatest universities in the world, one which is considered to lie on the "cutting edge of progress," Kerr hopes to make UC a model to be proudly presented for the consideration of even higher authorities.

By our action, we have proved Kerr wrong in his claim that human beings can be handled like raw material without provoking revolt. We have smashed to bits his pretty little doll house. The next task will be to build in its stead a real house for real people.

## CATCH-801—Marvin Garson

Joseph Heller's authoritative work on constitutional law offers the following definition of Catch-22: "Catch-22 says they have a right to do anything we can't stop them from doing." This fundamental section has been construed by American law enforcement authorities to override any conflicting provisions in our Constitution.

Many students, inexperienced in the ways of the law, thought that they had been subjected to irregular and illegal procedures. One student, for instance, said to a sheriff's deputy, "You can't do this," even though the deputy had, in fact, just done it.

In the booking room at Oakland City Jail, a pay telephone hangs on the wall. Next to it is a very clear sign saying that prisoners have a right to two completed phone calls immediately after being booked. We were told we could make only one phone call. Those who protested were threatened with loss of their one phone call.

Our bond had already been posted, which set us free according to the law. Instead of telling us we were free, they took us to the Alameda County Prison Farm at Santa Rita. In another part of Santa Rita, fifty girls who wanted to telephone were told to wait in a cage. After a few hours, the wardens told them that they couldn't telephone; but if they handed in signed slips saying they had already telephoned, they would be let out of the cage.

Like the police, the University Administration has the right to do anything we can't stop them from doing. They tried to exercise that right in September by taking away our tables. We were entitled to those tables; even they admit it, now that it doesn't matter so much. They ordered the police to arrest one of our people sitting at a table; *but we stopped them from doing it.* On October 2, we first realized that Catch-22 is the fundamental law of California and the world, so we began to act accordingly to protect ourselves.

When the Regents met, they confirmed the principle by saying they had a right to do anything they wanted except take away the tables, because we had stopped them from doing *that.*

Then Chancellor Strong sent letters to four of us, saying that he was preparing to do anything to them that he wanted. ("The Committee's recommendation will be advisory to me.") So we responded by doing our best to stop Chancellor Strong.

Governor Brown has called us Anarchists. Nonsense. We have acted, and will continue to act, in accordance with the basic law of our country, the law which Governor Brown applied to us when we were in the hands of his deputies in the Alameda County Prison Farm at Santa Rita.

## FREEDOM IS A BIG DEAL—Barbara Garson

It seems very likely now that the University will liberalize its regulations on free speech and political activity. No doubt, hidden restrictions will be wrapped in the new rules.

The administration, of course, will deny that it yielded to direct pressure but we can take great pride in having for once, reversed the world-wide drift from freedom. We did not teach Clark Kerr the moral error of his ways; we simply showed him that in this case, blatantly repressing us was more trouble than it was worth.

But must we always make this massive effort in order to effect a minor change? The answer is yes. Yes, because power still lies with the administration. Our lives at school are still ruled and regulated by officials who are not responsible to us. Our recent rebellion did not attempt to change this. Indeed this change can not be made on one campus.

Yet I dream of someday living in a democracy. On campus, committees of students and faculty will make the minimum regulations needed to administer (not rule) our. academic community. I hope to see democracy extended to the offices and factories, so that everyone may have the satisfaction of making the decisions about the use of his productive energies.

I look past government by the grunted consent of the governed. Someday we will participate actively in running our own lives in all spheres of work and leisure.

## HOW TO OBSERVE LAW AND ORDER—Hal Draper

"The law in its majesty equally forbids both rich and poor to sleep under bridges." With this famous thrust, Anatole France went to the heart of the question of Law and Order, that is, the relationship of law to the social order. It is also at the heart of the current struggle over free speech on campus.

This struggle, remember, was touched off by the Administration's ruling against the "mounting," on campus, of off campus political and social action. The Administration therefore forbids students to use tables at the Bancroft & Telegraph entrance to recruit for off-campus projects like civil rights actions, to solicit membership, or collect money on campus for causes.

Now this restriction on political activity has been rightly attacked on the fundamental ground that it is destructive of the student's civil liberties as a citizen, his academic freedom as a scholar, and his rounded development as a human being. Even if none of these strictures were justified, however, it would still be true that, on still other grounds, the Administration's ruling is a fraud. The following note is directed solely to this last consideration.

The ban is allegedly based on a general admonition in the State Constitution against political and sectarian influences on the University. It is therefore, presumably, not limited in its impact to the student body, but should apply impartially to all other parts of the University community. If the ruling is so conceived and framed as to apply only to *student* activities, then it is a fraudulent appeal to the principle envisioned by the Constitutional provision.

In fact, it can be argued that if any part of the University community should be enjoined from embroiling the name of the University in off-campus political issues, it should be the faculty and administration, not the students. For it is the former that are popularly regarded as responsible figures of the University, not the student groups.

Is it seriously claimed that an off-campus action by a student group "involves" the University more than off-campus action by eminent and honored professors and administrators? When Dr. Edward Teller agitates all over the nation for an adventurist and aggressive H-bomb-brandishing policy (as is his democratic right), does this "involve" the University more than when Tom, Dick, and Harriet agitate all over the Bay Area against discrimination by the Oakland *Tribune* or the Bank of America? We are opposed to *any* inhibitions on off-campus activities, including Dr. Teller's; but if the logic of the Administration's position is to be carried out, it leads to a conclusion even more monstrous than the present one.

But, it may be objected, Dr. Teller does not "mount" his off-campus activity through tables at Bancroft & Telegraph; and he does not collect quarters on campus to finance his campaign for bigger bomb tests. Of course not; neither does he sleep under bridges.

*He* doesn't have to collect quarters or rattle a coin box. *He* doesn't have to use the open street to solicit membership in the Armageddon Association. He has—well, other resources. We cannot begrudge him these resources; but then, why begrudge the student groups the only, puny, relatively miserable resource *they* have, namely, the opportunity to ask for small change? A few dollars can mean a great deal to a SNCC office in Mississippi which has to scrounge for mimeograph paper; but the Armageddon Association has no use for pennies.

Now the impact of the Administration's ruling is that it illegalizes the student groups' way of "mounting" political action, without interfering in the least with that type of campus-mounted political action for which we have used Dr. Teller as an example. The Administration, in its majestic evenhandedness, has forbidden even Dr. Kerr from setting up a table to collect pennies for propaganda in favor of Proposition 2. But Dr. Kerr doesn't have to sleep under bridges—we mean, he doesn't have to collect pennies for Proposition 2. He has the resources of the University at his disposal. His Administration simply makes a ruling (known as Law and Order) which puts University money to work to ask for a vote for Proposition 2, and at the same time—shall we say, it does *not* use its money to work against Proposition 14? More than that: it makes another ruling (Law and Order) which positively prohibits students from even collecting quarters for this purpose!

Or let us take another eminent representative of the University in another type of off-campus political action. In January, 1960, the Cobey Committee of the state Senate held a hearing in Fresno on the problem of farm labor in California. Now the problem of farm laborers in this great state of ours can be highlighted in a few words: they are forced to starve a part of the year, and live and work in wretchedness for another part of the year, by the wage- and working-conditions enforced by the growers in their greed for profits.

If a group of students had picketed the committee bearing with demands for human treatment of farm labor, and if this action had been "mounted" on campus, this would have been a violation of the Administration's present version of Law and Order. But in 1960 a passel of professors went to the hearing for another purpose. For example, the director of the University's Giannini Foundation, George Mehren, went there to testify, with all of his university-mounted authority, that "there is no compelling indication of exploitation of hired domestic agricultural labor anywhere in any agricultural industry for any protracted period."

Thus, this academic flunky of the corporate grower interests (who has now been suitably rewarded with the post of assistant secretary of agriculture in the Johnson administration) mounted this political and social action as a contribution to torpedoing the claims of farm labor for a decent life. It can hardly be denied that this off-campus action was mounted at the University!

"But this is different," we will be told. Of course it is. Dr. Mehren doesn't sleep under bridges either. The Cobey Committee *invited* him to do this unsavory job for the growers; they never invite pickets. It follows, as the night the day, that mounting off-campus action on behalf of the growers is Law and Order, whereas mounting a CORE picket line against the Bank of America is Anarchy.

Of course, it's "different." The ruling Power Structure al*ways* legalizes the activity of its own servitors. First the Administration draws the rules so that the discrimination is built into them; then it "evenhandedly" demands observance of its Law and Order.

Law and Order should be observed. (In fact, observed very closely.) But it is also the responsibility of the Lawmakers to make such laws as can be obeyed not only by men's bodies but also by their consciences. If they fail in this, the responsibility is theirs.

## • *The Byrne Report to the Board of Regents*

*This is probably the most important interpretive document that has come out of Berkeley. In December the Board of Regents had set up a subcommittee under William E. Forbes to conduct an inquiry into the causes of unrest at the university. The Forbes Committee gave this commission to Jerome C. Byrne, a Los Angeles lawyer, who assembled a professional staff of experts on education and management, and carried on a three-month investigation with a budget of $75,000. We cannot here do justice to all of its important sections, particularly its recommendations, the most important of which proposed a sweeping decentralization of the state-wide university into autonomous campuses united in a "commonwealth." The following excerpts bear particularly on problems discussed in this book.*

## *Berkeley: The Student Revolt*

[In addition to money] freedom, too, is needed to maintain a great university. Experience has shown that in order to attract the best students and faculty, they must be given a large measure of control, either direct or indirect, over their own affairs. This does not, of course, mean that universities should be, or can be, entirely self-governing. The electorate, speaking through the Constitution, the Governor and the Legislature, must have a long-run voice in the development of a public university. But history suggests that this voice should be indirect. There is hardly a single example, either in America or elsewhere, of a distinguished university which has been directly responsible to popular opinion. Among the public universities of America, three of the most eminent have jealously guarded their autonomy. Without a tradition of independence, whether constitutionally or legislatively sanctioned, the lot of public universities has been mediocrity... .

. . . The university is established by a wise society to be its continuing critic. But while in principle we all welcome criticism of our established habits, in practice most of us resent it. The task of a modern university is to open the eyes of its constituents, and indeed of the whole world, to new possibilities: cultural and intellectual, social and moral, scientific and technological. A university which wishes to do these things is bound to attract a significant number of students, faculty, and even administrators who are, as the cliche goes, "people who think otherwise." Not only will they think otherwise; often they will do otherwise as well.

There can be no neat division between professional and personal lives, nor between unconventional thoughts and unconventional actions. As a result, a great university must, if it is living up to its responsibilities, attract many faculty and students who will choose to pursue paths that the great majority of people regard as silly, dangerous, or both. Such 'a university is bound to strain the tolerance of parents, taxpayers, and their elected representatives. In many cases, outsiders will not understand the necessity for certain features of university life. In some cases, both the public and its chosen officials will be profoundly offended by the ways in which members of the academic community go about their business, or by the ways in which they conduct their nonacademic lives. Considerable restraint will be required to tolerate habits and values which seem profoundly alien to most residents of the state.

If this restraint is not forthcoming, if a state habitually imposes popular opinion on its university, the result is that the state acquires a reputation for being inhospitable to the life of the mind. The immediate result is that many students and faculty who care deeply about such things seek them elsewhere. This in turn means a second-class university.

Clearly, then, the events which have rocked the University of California in the past eight months are part of a continuing and inevitable conflict between the values of the academic community and those of the larger society. This conflict has always existed, and it will continue to exist for as long as the academic community continues to do its job... .

[The] criticisms are rooted in one fundamental truth: *something is* seriously amiss in a system of government which induces a substantial fraction of the governed to violate the law and risk their careers in order to dramatize their dissatisfaction. The critics are right, too, in feeling that ultimate responsibility for this situation lies where ultimate power lies: with the Regents. . . . If the remedies are inappropriate, as have been many of those employed in recent months, the result will be the demoralization of the academic community and the gradual dispersal of its finest minds, both young and old, to more hospitable institutions

• • • • • • • • • • • • • • • • • • • • • • •

The crisis at Berkeley last fall has become known as the free speech controversy. It was that, but more fundamentally it was a crisis in government, caused by the failure of the President and the Regents to develop a governmental structure at once acceptable to the governed and suited to the vastly increased complexity of the University... .

It took the free speech crisis to dramatize the fact that large and complex campuses require a form of government qualitatively different from that appropriate for new campuses.

• • • • • • • • • • • • • • • • • • • • • •

The relationship between the. campus administrations and the student governments has long been a source of conflict. It has never been entirely clear whether, or to what extent, Chancellors were legally or administratively responsible for the actions of the various student governments. There has long been confusion between the proprietary aspects of student "government" and its assistance in the policy-making role. The need to safeguard the assets administered by the students is confused with other aspects of student "government." In addition, some campus administrations only sporadically and infrequently consult with student government about University and campus regulations affecting the students. When the student governments are consulted, their counsel is not given serious consideration on all campuses. One result of this has been to create considerable contempt for student government among undergraduates, especially at Berkeley. Another result has been to discourage many talented students from seeking office in the student government. This has produced governments which represent only a small part of the total spectrum of student interests and opinions. This has been particularly true at Berkeley.

• • • • • • • • • • • • • • • • • • • • • •

Today's students differ from those of the 1950's in their accelerating drive to become active rather than passive members of the society they are about to enter.

For some students, as for many Americans, it is sufficient to accept the society as they find it, and to adapt to change as it takes place. For others, whose views are also shared by many of their elders, change often is threatening and to be resisted. For a few, the opportunity to act in behalf of change is the essence of life itself.

This generation of students acts from a dissatisfaction with the rate of change in American society and that dissatisfaction is pointed and intense.

At the point of entry to the adult society, many students are deeply concerned about the commitment they can make to it.

In the main, they ask not that the society be perfect but that they have the opportunity to help. make it so....

Student interest in civil rights was both a symptom and a cause of the students' increasing concern with a wide range of political issues. A growing number of students began to ask themselves, "What kind of society has the older generation created?" and, having asked that question, gave the answer, "Not a very good one." Such students then inevitably asked, "What can I do to make America the kind of country I want to live my adult life in?" More and more began to answer, "Take political action."

They were young and earnest, and their political formulas were frequently radical... .

For some students, the desire to be part of the civil rights movement stemmed from direct concern for the Negro; for others, there was predominantly a desire to protest—directly, dramatically, and effectively—against the hypocrisy of the larger society. The Negro's plight was to them only one important symbol of that hypocrisy. For many students, racial inequality is not the only evil in the world urgently in need of attention, and in their view civil disobedience need not necessarily be confined to activity on behalf of civil rights. They were often eager to take "direct action" in behalf of disarmament, withdrawal from Vietnam, or (as it turned out) "free speech." These students saw direct action and civil disobedience as instruments for affirming their own moral commitment to a more just society, and as an outlet for their impatience with the seemingly glacial pace of social progress under society's orthodox procedures....

The American people have never been noted for their veneration of established authority. From the Boston Tea Party to the march on Montgomery, Americans have shown themselves ready to defy officially established laws in order to follow their own private visions of "higher law." The civil rights movement, as it developed after the Southern sit-ins, was in this tradition. Convinced that normal lawful procedures for the redress of grievances provided little hope for remedy, the civil rights movement went outside the law to move men's consciences. Non-violent violations of certain laws were a device for appealing to "higher law."

Violations of established law in the name of non-violent protest shocked many Americans. There has been widespread fear that the logic of civil disobedience could be applied not just to civil rights but to a multitude of other grievances, and that the result would not be greater equality and justice, but anarchy. The students' enthusiasm for civil disobedience is related to the older generation's fear of it. Yet it should not be assumed that .these students want to undermine law and order completely. Most of them want to bring down laws or customs they regard as unjust. They argue that civil disobedience is only effective against laws or practices which are widely regarded as unjust. If there is a vision of "higher law" in the minds of the majority of men, and if the demonstrators can appeal to this vision, civil disobedience "works." If such a vision is not present, if society as a whole thinks the cause of the demonstrators unreasonable and unjust, the proponents of civil disobedience argue that it will be quickly abandoned. This analysis rests on the assumption that if society as a whole thinks the demonstrators' cause unjust, it will accept, and indeed demand, police action against them. If that action is taken, and if the public conscience is not aroused, the demonstrators will begin arguing their case in less dramatic fashion.

Proponents of civil disobedience maintain that dissident minorities and professional agitators cannot use civil disobedience to disrupt society, or at least not for long. Unless their protests have support in constitutional law, or in the moral sentiments of the majority of the population, they can be dealt with in precisely the same way as other violations of the law. It is only when those in authority are on weak ground, and thus dare not use the force at their disposal, that civil disobedience becomes a tactic of enormous power. .

• • • • • • • • • • • • • • • • • • • • • •

CONCLUSIONS AS TO THE BASIS OF THE STUDENT UNREST

1. *The Nature of the Protest of the Free Speech Movement.* We conclude that the basic cause of unrest on the Berkeley campus was the dissatisfaction of a large number of students with many features of the society they were about to enter. This dissatisfaction led them to political action, particularly civil rights action. The students involved in the Free Speech Movement were genuinely and deeply concerned about off campus political and social action and their "freedom" to use the University property as a base for the organization of their efforts in this direction. They resented deeply any action of the Administration which, in any way, hindered or interfered with their view of their constitutional right to engage in what they considered to be fundamental and morally required social reform.

2. *The Extent of Participation.* The Free Speech Movement enjoyed widespread support among students on the Berkeley campus. The large numbers participating in the various demonstrations establish this fact. A reliable survey of student opinion, which we have had reviewed by independent experts, concludes that, before the December sit-in, about two-thirds of the students said they supported the FSM's objectives and about a third supported its tactics. Subsequent surveys showed that support increased after the December sit-in.

3. *The Question of Communist Influence.* We found no evidence that the Free Speech Movement was organized by the Communist Party, the Progressive Labor Movement, or any other outside group. Despite a number of suggestive coincidences, the evidence which we accumulated left us with no doubt that the Free Speech Movement was a response to the September 14 change in rules regarding political activity at Bancroft & Telegraph, not a pre-planned effort to embarrass or destroy the University on whatever pretext arose...

A variety of individuals and groups of a revolutionary Marxist persuasion participated in the demonstrations and in the FSM leadership, but our evidence indicates that they did not succeed in gaining any kind of control of events, nor indeed, did anyone else.

We have consulted several reliable and well informed sources concerning Communist influence in the FSM. Our information indicates that a few of the FSM leaders (though not the most influential leaders) had close ties with the American Communist Party. We found no evidence that any important FSM figure was involved in the pro-Peking Progressive Labor Movement. We found that those FSM leaders who had been closest to the Communist Party while radical in their aims, tended to be more flexible than many other FSM leaders and to advocate comparatively cautious and "responsible" tactics. We found, also, that these students did not always vote the same way on key issues. We found that decisions were reached by majority vote in the Executive and Steering Committees of the FSM only after interminable debate.

4. *Non-Student Involvement.* We concluded that "nonstudents" were not a crucial element in the disturbances or in the FSM. Of those arrested in Sproul Hall for example, 87 per cent were enrolled as students. Some of the "non-students" were recent alumni living near the University, and in some cases employed by it. Some were students who had dropped out of the University to work, but had retained their friendships on the campus and planned to return to formal studies. Others were wives of students, particularly graduate students. All of these individuals were for all practical purposes part of the "University Community." There were also some arrestees who had no connection whatever with the University. A few of these were substantially older than most students. A few well-known Bay Area radicals were prominently visible on the campus during the disturbances, but none appeared to have had much influence with the FSM leadership. Indeed, we found no evidence that any FSM leader was subject to *any* sort of "adult" discipline. Even those who are close to the various revolutionary Marxist groups seem in most cases suspicious of the older generation of "party line" Communists.

• • • • • • • • • • • • • • • • • • • • • • • • • •

[The] insistent question remained: Why? Who or what had failed? .. .

*1. Leadership. A* litmus test of leadership is the capacity to secure the willingness of others to follow in meeting a challenge or a crisis. On this score, the students were far more skillful—and, in the short run, successful—than the University. Even though the student protestants represented a great diversity of views and persuasions, and against the fact that hours of debate preceded most of their decisions, the leadership was capable of decisive action rooted in genuine support from its constituency... .

The University, too, displayed a consistent tendency to disorder its own principles and values.

While dedicated to the maintenance of a house for ideas and thought, it proved selective in determining whose ideas would gain admittance. While upholding the value of a continuing discourse in the academic community, it refused to engage in simple conversation with the membership of that community. While positioned as the defender of man's right to reason, it acted out of fear that a volatile public would react against the University if exposed to the reasonings of students. While championing the value of the individual and his responsibility for his own actions, it had sought to prevent the individual from suffering the consequences of his own self-determined actions in society. While postured to avoid prejudgment of facts, it sought to determine before the fact the legality or illegality of actions students would plan to take in the surrounding community. While responsible to and for itself, the University assumed it would be charged with responsibility for others, and in fear that the assumption would prove valid, established rules prohibiting others from acting on their own responsibility.

• • • • • • • • • • • • • • • • • • • • • •

## • *Student Political Activities and the Civil Rights Revolution*

*(from "A Suggestion for Dismissal)*

From the outset of the Berkeley controversy, the Free Speech Movement made frequent use of the controlled, nonviolent techniques of the civil rights movement. The significance of these techniques and the nature of their highly controlled use have been described. in the letter written by Dr. Martin Luther King from a jail cell in Birmingham, Alabama.

> You may well ask, "Why direct action? Why sit-ins, marches, etc.? Isn't negotiation a better path?" *You are exactly right in your call for negotiation. Indeed, this is the purpose of direct action.* Non-violent direct action seeks to create such a crisis and establish such creative tension that a community that has constantly refused to negotiate is forced to confront the issue. It seeks so to dramatize the issue that it can no longer be ignored. We must see the need of having non-violent gadflies to create the kind of tension in society that will . . . help men to rise from the dark . . . depths of prejudice and racism to the majestic heights of understanding and brotherhood. *So the purpose of the direct action is to create a situation . . . so crisis packed that it will inevitably open the door to negotiation. We, therefore, concur with you in your call for negotiation. (The Progressive,* July, 1963. [emphasis added].)

According to Dr. King, the very purpose of non-violent techniques of direct action is to create the conditions under which negotiation becomes possible. The use of non-violence proceeds from the premise that negotiation is impossible where one side to a controversy has a monopoly of power and refuses to negotiate. The application of the non-violent techniques by the Free Speech Movement to achieve a condition of negotiation may be illustrated by reference to the events related in the Heyman Committee Report and the Graduate Students Study.

[A number of points are then cited dealing with the events leading up to October 1.1

The events cited here, which are repeated in a more complicated fashion in the events leading up to the sit-in demonstration for which the arrests occurred, demonstrate that direct and meaningful negotiation with the involved students and student organizations occurred only after a crisis was precipitated by the use of non-violent techniques. The techniques in large measure accomplished the ends sought, so that the conditions for meaningful negotiation on the campus have now been largely achieved. . . .

The sit-in demonstration has achieved a measure of support even by the state legislature of California. A round-the clock sit-in demonstration in the State Capitol building was permitted for over two weeks at the end of the 1963 regular session of the legislature during the lengthy battle over the passage of the Rumford fair housing bill. (See, for example, *The Sacramento Bee,* June 6, 1963, page A.6.) And the very trespass provision under which the students are being charged in this action (P.C. Section 602(d)) was amended during the height of the sit-in demonstrations to curtail drastically its scope and impliedly prohibit its application to the sit-in demonstrators.

Non-violence as a justifiable technique has indeed achieved international support and standing. The 1960 Nobel Peace Prize was awarded to Mr. (ex-chief) Albert John Luthuli of South Africa . . . The 1964 Nobel Peace Prize was awarded to Dr. Martin Luther King for his advocacy and use of nonviolent violent techniques... .

If a measure of acceptance has been accorded to the use of non-violent techniques in the cause of racial justice, the United States Supreme Court has tacitly recognized the justice of the sit-in techniques in refusing to uphold the sit-in convictions of those whose cases have reached the court. The rationale of the Court in overturning the convictions of sit-in demonstrators has varied from case to case... .

The Court by such constructions legalized non-violent sit-in demonstrations in public accommodations covered by the act. Moreover, in applying the Civil Rights Act to invalidate retroactively state trespass convictions occurring before passage of the act, the Court recognized the basic injustice of punishing persons for acts of racial conscience in pursuance of goals which the Civil Rights Act recognized as just. The Court said: "In short, now that Congress has exercised its constitutional power in enacting the Civil Rights Act of 1964 and declared that the public policy of our country is to prohibit discrimination in public accommodations as there defined, there is no public interest to be served in the further prosecution of the petitioners."

And earlier the Court had emphasized that, *"The peaceful conduct for which petitioners were prosecuted was on behalf of a principle since embodied in the law of the land."* Anthony Lewis, commenting in *The New York Times,* December 20, 1964, said in respect to the decision, "From a practical point of view, the decision was doubtless a healthy one. More than 3,000 sit-in cases are pending, and most will be wiped out as a result. This will remove a final irritant from a situation that Congress was trying to calm in the 1964 Act." The principle contained in the *Hamm* case should be applied to the cases at hand. The great principles for which the) students engaged in the demonstration, are near being achieved.) The Academic Senate of the Berkeley campus has adopted overwhelmingly a set of principles which reflect the entire set of just claims of the students...

.

## • *The Campus and the Constitution (Berkeley-Albany ACLU)*

*This essay by the American Civil Liberties Union (Berkeley Albany) was issued directly by the ACLU chapter, but copies were widely distributed and used by the FSM. The following is an extract from the original article.*

### 1. FREEDOM OF INQUIRY AND ACADEMIC FREEDOM

A fundamental principle of academic freedom is the basic necessity for freedom of inquiry. This freedom can be irreparably compromised at an institution of higher education if either students or faculty are inhibited from full expression on social or political questions, whether this expression takes

the form of opinion or participation in lawful activities designed to give effective form to opinions.

The following remarks, quoted from the ACLU's National Policy on Students' Rights, provide a useful framework:

> The college which wishes to set an example of open-minded inquiry in its classrooms will defeat its purpose if it denies the same right of inquiry to its students outside the classroom—or if it imposes rules which deny them the freedom to make their own choices, wise or unwise.

• • • • • • • • • • • • • • • • • • • • • •

> The student government, student organizations, and individual students should be free to discuss, pass resolutions, distribute leaflets, circulate petitions, and take other lawful action respecting any matter which directly or indirectly concerns or affects them.

### 2. THE POLITICAL NEUTRALITY OF THE UNIVERSITY

In order to merit public confidence and support, the University must be diligent in preserving its reputation for political neutrality. This is a point which has been emphasized repeatedly by the University administration. The following .passage by former President Lowell of Harvard University deals with the relation of a university administration to faculty, but his point is equally applicable to students:

> If a University or college censors what its professors may say, if it restrains them from uttering something that it does not approve, it thereby assumes responsibility for

> that which it permits them to say. This is logical and inevitable, but it is a responsibility which an institution of learning would be very unwise in assuming ... If the University is right in restraining its professors, it has the duty to do so, and it is responsible for whatever it permits. There is no middle ground. Either the University assumes full responsibility for permitting its professors to express their opinions in public, or it assumes no responsibility whatever, and leaves them to be dealt with like other citizens by the public authorities according to the laws of the land.

It would seem that there is only one path to insure the reputation for political neutrality so essential to the well-being of a University that does not infringe upon the necessary freedom of inquiry which is the essence of scholasticism. This is the path of non-regulation of all student or faculty utterances and activities in the area of political opinion. University policy states that the University assumes absolutely no responsibility for student political activities off-campus. An extension of this neutral position to on-campus activities would be in the best interests of the University.

### 3. APPLICATION OF THE FIRST AND FOURTEENTH AMENDMENTS TO UNIVERSITY REGULATIONS

A university established and supported by any state government or federal agency is limited by those same constitutional provisions which forbid any governmental interference or abridgment of the right of the people to assemble peacefully or to speak freely. The limitations on State regulation in the First and Fourteenth Amendments are fully applicable to the University of California as an agency of the State of California and to the Regents, officers, and employees of the University.

4. SUMMARY: CONSTITUTIONAL PRINCIPLES AND UNIVERSITY STUDENTS

The University's regulations should be drafted and applied in light of our constitutional experience as embodied in pertinent cases. These cases attach the highest importance to the opportunity to engage in and hear public speech and political activities, and not only require substantial justification for any burdens on those opportunities, but insist that such burdens be kept to the necessary minimum. We believe that regulation of the form of speech or political activity which effectively precludes the students from using the campus, and requires that they use only off-campus facilities for their public speech or political activity, would be unconstitutionally burdensome on their opportunity to engage in those activities in light of any justifying interests of the State and alternatives for protecting its interest. Solicitation of funds in support of views taken in public speech and political activity is often vital in effectuating such speech or activity. Thus, we believe such solicitation cannot be entirely prohibited on the campus if it meets appropriate requirements of honesty and bona fides. We further believe that the rights of University students to hear speakers who are not members of the University, or the rights of such speakers to speak to students, are co-extensive with the rights of students themselves to speak on campus. These activities cannot constitutionally be prohibited on campus.

## • *The Position of the FSM on Speech and Political Activity (FSM)*

*This is the fullest formal statement of its position put out by the FSM, issued toward the end of November. By this time a number of previous administration stands had been abandoned, and the statement concentrates in particular on the view embodied in the decision of the Regents' meeting of November 20, regarding advocacy "for unlawful off-campus action."*

*1. Regulation of Advocacy Under the First Amendment.*

Civil liberties and political freedoms which are constitutionally protected off campus must be equally protected on campus for all persons. Similarly, illegal speech or conduct should receive no greater protection on campus than off campus. The Administration, like any other agency of government, may not regulate the content of speech and political conduct. Regulations governing the time, place and manner of exercising constitutional rights are necessary for the maintenance and proper operation of University functions, but they must not interfere with the opportunity to speak or the content of speech.

In contrast, the University regulations adopted by the Regents on November 20, *1964,* and interpreted by the Chancellor, read as follows:

> The Regents adopt the policy . . . that certain campus facilities carefully selected and properly regulated, may be used by students and staff for planning, implementing, raising funds or recruiting participants for lawful off campus action, not for unlawful off-campus action.

By making the distinction between advocating "lawful" and "unlawful" action, the Regents propose to regulate the *content* of speech on campus. It is this distinction that is at the heart of FSM opposition to these regulations. The U.S. Supreme Court has made clear that advocacy of unlawful conduct cannot constitutionally be punished—even in the courts—so long as the advocacy will not clearly and presently cause some substantial evil that is itself illegal.

*2. Impropriety of Non judicial Forums for Punishing Political Activity.*

Under the November 20 regulations, if the Chancellor accuses a student of advocating an unlawful act, the student and his sponsoring organization are liable to punishment by the University. A student so accused may appear before the Faculty Committee on Student Conduct, whose members are appointed by the Chancellor, and whose opinions are only advisory to him.

The Free Speech Movement considers this to be unconstitutional and unwise for the following two reasons:

(a) Since such a procedure allows the Chancellor to assume the roles of prosecutor, judge and jury simultaneously, the students have no confidence that the final verdict will be fair. In fact, the history of the treatment of civil liberties cases by campus administration reveals an insensitivity to safeguarding such liberties.

Further, the fact that the Administration is peculiarly vulnerable to pressures originating outside the University should remove it from consideration as the proper authority for determining guilt or innocence in the extremely sensitive area of speech, assembly and protest within the First Amendment. It must be emphasized that the current crisis has not developed in a vacuum. These rules work a grave hardship on the civil rights movement in Northern California. Organizations in this movement rely heavily on negotiations, demonstrations, picketing and other legal tactics. It is true however that in order to focus attention on a serious injustice and to bring pressure to bear for its correction, civil rights workers sometimes employ tactics which result in violation of law. Without passing on the propriety of such acts, the Free Speech Movement insists that the question whether their *advocacy* is legal or illegal must be left to the courts, which are institutionally independent of the shifting pressures of the community. Moreover, the standard that the Chancellor is free to apply is only one of "responsibility" of the act of advocacy for the act advocated, which is far more inclusive and vague than the "clear and present danger" test. Hence, guilt is likely to be founded upon much less substantial and compelling grounds than would be necessary to obtain conviction for illegal advocacy in a court of law. Students are convinced that the regulations providing for such a hearing are the direct result of pressure generated by the civil rights movement in the surrounding community and enable the Administration to respond to such pressures by disciplining student civil rights workers.

(b) Even if complete mutual trust existed between the Administration and student body, and even if the University attempted to observe the requirements of due process, it would be impossible for it to provide all of the safeguards of our judicial system, or otherwise to fulfill the functions of a court. The points in controversy, relating to the degree of responsibility of an act of advocacy for an act advocated, are of such a delicate and complex nature that even the courts have not built up wholly adequate precedents. Certainly, then, a nonjudicial body should be considered incompetent in this I area.

On the other hand, the students' position that the courts alone have jurisdiction does not in any way imply the creation of a haven for illegal activity on the campus. On the contrary, it involves just the opposite of this—the *removal* of any special protection the University may now afford, as well as any extra-legal punishment. The student becomes subject to the same process of trial and punishment for illegal acts that all other citizens must accept.

*3. On-Campus Regulation of the Form of Free Expression.*

The Free Speech Movement recognizes the necessity for regulations insuring that political activity and speech do not interfere with the normal educational functions of the University. Rallies must not be held so as to disturb classes, block traffic, damage University property, conflict with other scheduled public meetings or rallies, etc. Such regulation is purely formal; no discretion to regulate the *content* of speech can constitutionally be permitted the controlling authority. Furthermore, the regulations must be carefully tailored to protect or promote these State interests without unduly burdening the opportunity to speak, hear, engage in political activity on the campus.

At the present time, University regulations governing the *form* of expression on the campus are promulgated by the Administration, while other segments of the University community are limited to a purely advisory capacity. It is the general position of the Free Speech Movement that those persons and organizations subject to regulations must have a part in their final enactment. It is especially important as a safeguard against abuse or factual error that students share the responsibility for promulgations over the form of speech. The Administration has demonstrated many times its propensity to plead the necessity to regulate form as an excuse for regulating content. For example the

Administration has, until recently, designated a place removed from the area of normal traffic as the sole "Hyde Park area," thus seriously hampering access to listeners. As the local ACLU has pointed out:

> A denial of certain avenues of such access (such as the open areas of the campus) with the claim that there are others,, which though perhaps not as desirable are nonetheless available, will not avoid violation of the First Amendment unless the government entity . . . can demonstrate that there are no available alternative means of achieving its purpose, and that the purposes in question are so necessary as to be, in the language of the Court, "compelling."

Students have thus regarded the designation of such an area as an unreasonable and unconstitutional restriction and refused to accede to it.

Because of such past experience, and because of the important principle of democratic self-government involved, the Free Speech Movement has taken the position that final regulation of the form of exercise of speech should be by a tripartite committee consisting of representatives chosen independently by the students, faculty, and administration.

# About Haymarket Books

Haymarket Books is a radical, independent, nonprofit book publisher based in Chicago.

Our mission is to publish books that contribute to struggles for social and economic justice. We strive to make our books a vibrant and organic part of social movements and the education and development of a critical, engaged, international left.

We take inspiration and courage from our namesakes, the Haymarket martyrs, who gave their lives fighting for a better world. Their 1886 struggle for the eight-hour day—which gave us May Day, the international workers' holiday—reminds workers around the world that ordinary people can organize and struggle for their own liberation. These struggles continue today across the globe—struggles against oppression, exploitation, poverty, and war.

Since our founding in 2001, Haymarket Books has published more than five hundred titles. Radically independent, we seek to drive a wedge into the risk-averse world of corporate book publishing. Our authors include Noam Chomsky, Arundhati Roy, Rebecca Solnit, Angela Y. Davis, Howard Zinn, Amy Goodman, Wallace Shawn, Mike Davis, Winona LaDuke, Ilan Pappé, Richard Wolff, Dave Zirin, Keeanga-Yamahtta Taylor, Nick Turse, Dahr Jamail, David Barsamian, Elizabeth Laird, Amira Hass, Mark Steel, Avi Lewis, Naomi Klein, and Neil Davidson. We are also the trade publishers of the acclaimed Historical Materialism Book Series and of Dispatch Books.

CPSIA information can be obtained
at www.ICGtesting.com
Printed in the USA
LVHW042331070420
652489LV00001B/1